On the Nature of Things

Lucretius

ON THE NATURE
OF THINGS

De rerum natura

Edited and translated by
Anthony M. Esolen

The Johns Hopkins University Press
Baltimore and London

© 1995 The Johns Hopkins University Press
All rights reserved. Published 1995
Printed in the United States of America on acid-free paper
04 03 02 01 00 99 98   5. 4 3 2

The Johns Hopkins University Press
2715 North Charles Street
Baltimore, Maryland 21218-4319
The Johns Hopkins Press Ltd., London

ISBN 0-8018-5054-1
ISBN 0-8018-5055-X (pbk.)

Library of Congress Cataloging-in-Publication Data
will be found at the end of this book.
A catalog record for this book is available from the British Library.

*For my wife, Debra, my greatest proof
of God's benevolence*

CONTENTS

Acknowledgments / ix

Introduction / 1

ON THE NATURE OF THINGS

Book 1 / 25

Book 2 / 57

Book 3 / 91

Book 4 / 122

Book 5 / 159

Book 6 / 200

Notes / 237

Works Cited / 287

Index / 289

ACKNOWLEDGMENTS

FIRST AMONG those who have helped make this translation possible is Professor Kenneth Reckford of the University of North Carolina. His enthusiasm for things classical and his subtle ear for the art of poetry opened my mind to the riches of Lucretius's poem. For his encouragement of this project I owe him many thanks. Professor William Wyatt of Brown University gave me much-needed advice on some of the roughest passages in the poem, and my colleague John Lawless at Providence College helped me to understand Lucretius's etymological figures. My research assistant at Furman University, Kieran Brown, did a good deal of slogging for me through medieval and Renaissance texts, looking for evidence of Lucretius's influence upon later writers. I would be remiss if I failed to express gratitude toward my colleagues in the English Department and in the Program in the Development of Western Civilization. Their moral and intellectual support has been steadfast. I am especially grateful for the encouragement given me by my fellow English professor and lover of the classics, Edward McCrorie, whose own translation of the *Aeneid* spurred me to undertake this work in earnest. Many thanks are also due to the wonderfully efficient and cheerful editors at the Johns Hopkins University Press, for whose honesty, courtesy, and professional conduct of business I have the highest regard.

The person to whom I owe the greatest thanks of all is my wife, Debra. She has helped me mend more lines and passages than even she is aware of, and has listened patiently to sudden recitals and revisions and alternative translations. Her stylistic sense is impeccable. But for her wisdom, her refusal to indulge my doubts and hesitations, and her love, this translation may never have made it to the shores of light.

On the Nature of Things

INTRODUCTION

Lucretius's Milieu

W E KNOW little about Titus Lucretius Carus. He was probably born in the early first century B.C., with 99 and 95 the limits of possibility. The year 55 is usually given for his death. Saint Jerome, following a lost work by the historian Suetonius, relates two tantalizing bits of gossip about Lucretius: that Cicero edited his great poem, and that he was poisoned by a madness-inducing aphrodisiac given him by his wife. As for the first assertion, scholars doubt that Cicero had more than a perfunctory role in assembling Lucretius's pages for publication, if he did even that much. And we have no evidence for the second.

Certain things about Lucretius's life we can infer from the decades he lived through. The Republic was tottering. Soldiers swore loyalty not to Rome but to generals and booty-dealers like Sulla, Pompey, and Caesar. Says William Leonard:

> It was an age when a Verres plundered the province which the Senate had sent him to govern, when a nobleman Clodius got himself adopted into a plebeian family for election to the Tribunate for sinister political ends, when a Catiline (if we may believe Cicero and Sallust) gathered the riffraff of Sulla's army and the reckless gamblers and libertines of old families in order to burn the city and cancel huge debts. An age of desperate and bloody self-seeking on the part of the few; while the populace in the city cried now for one leader and now for another, knowing only that it was hungry; and while the yeoman in the Italian fields was run down by disbanded soldiery or bewildered by ever-diminishing returns from his plowing and sowing a depleted soil which he had neither science nor means to restore. (6)

Cicero prided himself on saving the Republic at its eleventh hour, but he ignored a truth that he recognized elsewhere, namely, that a republican

I

government requires a republican spirit in the people. But for better and for worse, Roman culture had from the time of the younger Scipio become increasingly Greek: slaves from Athens and not Roman patriarchs taught upper-class children; eastern mystery cults promised salvation for initiates, while Hellenistic philosophy (including Epicureanism) cast doubt upon the nature of the gods. All this could only weaken Roman devotion to its religion of family and state. In Rome as elsewhere, affluence and military success accentuated the differences among social classes while removing any strong incentive for people to join in a common cause. Rome's politics grew individualistic and treacherous, her highlife wanton, her piety introspective and morbid.

Into this world Lucretius is thrust—erudite, aristocratic, old-fashioned in his admiration of stern Roman morality. In his way he is a patriot. He boasts about "our" Ennius, the first great poet of Italy, and he calls himself the first to turn Greek philosophy into "our" Latin. Yet he shows no interest in reforming Rome. Perhaps he gave it up for hopeless. Instead of an aggressive civic life, he offers retreat into a quiet community of wisdom and friendship. The key to this retreat is an understanding of the teachings of Epicurus (341–271) about the way the world works.

The Master

Epicurus was born to Athenian citizens on the island of Samos. Like Lucretius, Epicurus lived through troubled times: the Greek city-states were being swallowed up by the Macedonian king Philip II, whose son Alexander would succeed him and spread despotism from the Adriatic to the Indus River. Men were not citizens but subjects, ruled by bureaucrats who were in turn ruled by a distant monarch. In such a world it was natural that philosophers turned to the strain of thought in Plato and Aristotle which focused not upon political organization but upon the life of the individual.

Epicurus was a loyal son and an irritating student. Fiercely independent, he derided his teachers for their timidity and never acknowledged an intellectual debt. Still, we should note a few philosophical currents that helped form his beliefs. One was the skepticism of Pyrrho. This is surprising at first, since Epicurus based his epistemology upon firm trust in the senses. We can know things for certain, he says, because our senses are never deceived; all deception arises from the false interpretations of the mind. Pyrrho, by contrast, taught that nothing can be known for certain. He preached equanimity (*ataraxia*), insisting, as George Panichas says, that a wise man should keep aloof from the vain pursuits of others (20). Epicurus adopted Pyrrho's ideal of *ataraxia* while linking it to a materialist epistemology. Yet there are traces of the skeptic in Epicurus's indifferentism. It does not matter, he says, which of many explanations for the motion of the stars is true, so long as they all rule out the intervention of the gods. Epicurus was more moralist than scientist.

Another important influence on Epicurus was the broad Greek tradition of the care of the psyche, a tradition embodied in Socrates. Like most Greeks, Epicurus viewed philosophy as the road to a fully human life. He disagreed with Plato on what that life is—in Epicurus there is no room for the soaring visions of love found in *Symposium* and *Phaedrus*—but the good life was his object nonetheless, and like Plato he sees that "of all the things which wisdom acquires to produce the blessedness of the complete life, far the greatest is the possession of friendship" (*Prin. Doc.* 27).

Atomism, however, was to lend intellectual justification for Epicurus's moral teachings. Epicurus did not invent atomism: Leucippus (fl. 430) and his disciple Democritus (460?–357) have that honor. Democritus in particular was a brilliant polymath, well-versed in physics, mathematics, and aesthetics. (The specifics of atomism are discussed below; Epicurus's most salient contribution was his notorious atomic "swerve," a kind of physical exception which he believed would allow for free will.) From the atomists Epicurus learned that knowledge begins with sense impressions and that supernatural intervention is not needed to explain the phenomena of the world. Atomism confirmed his distrust of dialectic and mathematics; there could be no realm of eternal truth and goodness beyond this world of material objects impinging upon our senses.

With the foregoing in mind, it is easy to see the origin of Epicureanism. Epicurus believed, with the Socratics, that the care of the soul was the philosopher's all-important task. He agreed with Pyrrho that most men are slaves to superstition and custom. The atomists taught him that physical law (inferred from sense impressions) and not the gods ruled the world. Thus it makes sense that Epicurus used atomism to equate good and evil with pleasure and pain and that he valued the pleasures of the mind more than the pleasures of the body—although we must remember that for a materialist these pleasures are not strictly separable. Finally, Epicurus altered Aristotle's definition of man as a political animal. The wise man, reports Epicurus's biographer Diogenes Laertius, "will be fond of his country," but he will shun public life (*Life* 119–20). Neither recluse nor statesman, he is to spend his life in the company of friends.

By 311, Epicurus was ready to start teaching on his own. Driven out of

Mytilene for alleged impiety (Epicurus never got on with other philosophers), he moved from place to place, gathering lifelong friends along the
way. In 306 he settled in Athens, where he bought a house with a garden and set up a private school open to men and women. There he and
his followers lived in simplicity and peace. As Panichas puts it, "gentle-
ness, persuasion, sympathy, compassion, and complete honesty and firm-
ness" marked the discipline of the school, whereby teachers and students
alike were urged to help in the purification of each other. "Epicurean edu-
cation, in short, sought to bring about the moral perfection of the individual" (23). According to Diogenes, "[Epicurus's] country honored him
with bronze statues," and "his friends [were] so numerous that they could
not even be reckoned by entire cities" (*Life* 9). That his school survived for
centuries after his death testifies to his followers' love for their benevolent
teacher.

Epicurus wrote about three hundred treatises, almost all lost. Diogenes has preserved his letters to his disciples Herodotus, Menoeceus, and
Pythocles; these discuss the basics of Epicurean physics and morality. He
also gives us the forty *Principal Doctrines,* a collection of aphorisms which
form the Epicurean creed. There are also the so-called Vatican Collection
(eighty-one aphorisms similar to the *Doctrines*) and fragments preserved
in Cicero, Plutarch, Sextus Empiricus, Philodemus, Porphyry, and others.
Finally there is Lucretius's epic *De rerum natura,* our most spectacular cache
of Epicurean thought.

The Usefulness of Rational Inquiry

De rerum natura, then, could never be just a poem about the physical world.
Of course, in large part it *is* about that world. Although we cannot expect scientific method, Lucretius was usually a careful observer of nature.
His poetry is steeped with an innocent curiosity about how things are put
together. The sweep of his observations will still strike a modern reader
as remarkable. One thinks of his comparing water to a mound of poppy
seeds, evincing a kinetic imagination that a polymer chemist would recognize. Then there are the boys spinning around and making themselves so
dizzy they think the roofs are about to tumble upon them; snakeskins dangling from the briars; the yelp of a dog when she licks her puppies, and
the different yelp when she slinks away from a beating; the "applause" of
a rooster's wings; the shimmering blue and coral plumage that rings the
throat of a dove. Lucretius delights in such homely details of things in

plain sight. But one of the tenets of Epicureanism is that, in fact, things in plain sight give us a glimpse of what is too small or too far for our senses to observe. Thus for Lucretius it is a short mental step from the ordinary to the sublime, as when he asks us to look into a puddle in the street where we see, in silent reflection, a spangled universe as deep as the skies above.

His is a poem about the physical universe, and not a page goes by without some artful observation of a curious, usually common, phenomenon. Lucretius is no romantic. He does not allow the world to be absorbed into human symbols, to be posted when the terrain ahead is poetical. Nature, for Lucretius, is what it is—fascinating, purposeless, beautiful, deadly. It may evoke emotion, and Lucretius will, for instance, seize upon the delight of watching a sunrise. But our delight is not a part of that dawn. Epicureans contend that once we see what Nature is and how it works, we will free ourselves from the superstitious fears that it arouses in the ignorant. Lucretius's project, then, is neither to advance our technological dominion over Nature nor to see in Nature an extension of our existential concerns. The former is futile, since our lives inevitably end, as will the world itself. The latter is a pollution, for we must learn to live with Nature as she is: lovely and terrible, creative and destructive. Acting without design, she makes nectar for the bees and carrion for the buzzards. Our duty is to live with her in a way that will make us both as human and as godlike as we can be. Epicurean physics and morality converge. Lucretius's poem is about the universe and how human beings ought to live in it.

Lucretius thus writes under the pressure of a great directive outward: to explore what things are really like and to set forth his findings in irresistible argument and music. His zeal takes him out of the realm of self-reference and self-promotion and leads him to what he feels will be timelessly important for his readers. His motives are religious in the deepest sense. He thinks the tales of the gods are hogwash and denies the public utility of traditional religion; but for those very reasons he is devoted to converting his readers to a healthier way of life. He brings the gospel of Epicurus. There is nothing to hope for in death and nothing to fear, since the soul dies with the body. Atoms create the wheeling stars and the planets; no power above awaits the time to punish. Our miseries are largely self-inflicted; we can shun the trials of ambition, greed, and lust. Reason cannot make us perfect; we will never be sure why the sun and moon make their circuits. But reason can tell us enough about ourselves and the world that despite our flaws we too may, as Epicurus says, "live like a god among men" (*To Menoeceus* 135).

That gospel made big claims. But in the last years of republican Rome, marred by debauches of bloodshed, such lessons may have been like the trickle of a brook calling men away from the dust of the Forum. We must take Lucretius at his word: he really believes that in Epicureanism lies our best hope for happiness, and he very much wants to let us in on the secret, so that we may be as happy as is possible in a world imperfectly suited for our existence. The work is addressed to one Memmius, a young libertine in need of a teaching as severe and clean as Lucretius's. But the poet addresses a wider audience besides. He invites all his readers into the Epicurean universe, and into the Epicurean garden of friendship.

As for that Epicurean universe, it has unhappily been argued that Lucretius was a great poet with a topic ill-suited for great poetry. Such critics like to spot oases of pure poetry in deserts of argument. But this is a bad lapse in sensibility and in the understanding of Lucretius's project. For the argument *is* the poetry, and it has its own vigor. It informs whatever images Lucretius uses that are commonly called poetic, and it gives us lines of brutal simplicity and power and acuity, lines like

> Utter illogic they accept as proof

and

> I have good reason too for doing this

and

> These things, however ingeniously presented,
> True reason must emphatically reject.

Argument has its crescendos and codas, as Lucretius knew.

But beyond that, the charge that the Epicurean universe is unpoetic is absurd. The skeletal tenets of the system do not, at first glance, appear exciting. The universe is made of two things, atoms and empty space, the "void." Atoms are, literally, indivisibles. They are the basic indestructible stuff of all things. They are infinite in number, finite in kind; and the number of each kind of atom is infinite. They have a finite number of shapes; but other than shape, size, and weight, they have no qualities at all. They move constantly. Their natural tendency is to plummet—if "down" can mean anything in an infinite universe—but they also are prone to infinitesimal and unpredictable tilts in motion. Things are brought into being by the chance entangling of atoms. As for the void, it stretches boundless in all directions, untouching, untouchable. Gods there are, but they have no effect on anything that touches us. The soul too is material. Perception occurs when we are struck by a series of singly insensible "simulacra," hulls or films that sheer away from the surfaces of things. Imagination occurs when these simulacra are so tenuous that they can be perceived only by the soul, which lurks as a kind of organ in the body.

So presented, Epicurean physics and epistemology seem interesting for their dogged materialism and for such insights as the creativity of chance. But what is really exciting about atomism is its insight into a world inaccessible to the senses but accessible to reason. Imagine that beneath the appearances of this world there is another world, one of ceaseless, senseless activity. Streams of atoms flood in upon us from sun, stars, and moon, streaking at incomprehensible speeds, clashing against each other, ramming and ricocheting, hooking up and working their way free, jostling and realigning, never quite stable and yet for all that bound by the physical laws inherent in their constitutions. Endless space yawns round us like a gulf; the earth and sky will crumble to ruin; atoms in themselves invisible and impotent create earth, sun, rivers, pasture, sheep, woodlands, cities, children. True enough, the universe is made up of matter and void. But what glorious matter it is, which, when tossed into the right combinations,

> Became the origin of mighty things.

For Lucretius, possessed of an eye for detail and a relentless imagination, the atomic world becomes *our* world just as our world is, fundamentally, the atomic world. It is one thing to say that the universe consists of atoms and void. It is quite another to allow us to know these atoms intimately by presenting them as just like things we see—things that, after all, are made up of the very atoms of which they are the metaphorical vehicle. So we have squadrons of atoms skirmishing like motes in a sunbeam, and like, in fact, squadrons of human beings observed from a far overlook. Atoms are purposeless; yet Lucretius anthropomorphizes them to show us most vividly how they behave. The atoms meet in congress, swim, swerve, fight, wed, worm their way through tunnels, and elbow through a bottle-necked exit. They are like poppy seeds, or hooks, or thickets. Sometimes Lucretius exaggerates the pathetic fallacy to the point of burlesque, especially when he teaches us that the atoms are *unlike* anything human. For instance, the atoms

> do not hold council, assigning
> Order to each, or flexing their keen minds with
> Questions of place or rank or who goes where.

But they are the vital seeds of all we see, animate and inanimate. Like our subatomic quarks, they are worthy of our curiosity, and even manage to command what can only be called affection. And their simplicity and indivisibility lead to all kinds of riddles. Can we use the few tenets of atomism to explain why a ball of lead weighs more than a ball of wool? Why wood burns? Why honey is stickier than water? How we can see images of non-existent Centaurs and Chimeras, or even of the dead?

The danger of Lucretius's atomism was not that it was arid but that it could become so richly clandestine and phantasmagorical as to leave the world of phenomena far behind. Yet Lucretius always brings us back to the shores of light, to this world we can readily see and know. Other than that Lucretius was a great poet who knew what he was doing, there are, I think, two reasons for this faithful return.

First, Lucretius genuinely likes the world. He likes what those atoms produce and destroy. Renaissance scholars say that Petrarch was the first man to climb a mountain for the sake of climbing it, but Lucretius evidently made an enjoyable habit of mountain walks, and *he* did not then turn around and allegorize all the joy away. Lucretius loves animals—he even projects his imagination into their minds in order to give us perceptions from their points of view. Children, fields of glossy corn, the beauty of a landscape plotted and pieced, awnings flapping at the theater, dancers moving their supple arms, saplings shooting up, the rose of the morning sun—all point to Lucretius's fascination with the energetic world that these restless atoms produce. But of course, since the world is not obligingly made for our enjoyment, and since what the atoms ally to create they will secede to destroy, Lucretius's portrayal of this world is evenhanded. He examines both the ugly and the beautiful because they are both true. Thus he shows us flash floods, epileptics, sick dogs twitching in the streets, the wail of a funeral procession, the swarms of maggots seething like a tide in the guts of a corpse. Things are born and things die, and

> Round the short track all generations change
> Like racers passing on the torch of life.

At such moments the terrible beauty of death merges with Lucretius's ruthless honesty, and we have poetry that even Vergil could only imitate, never surpass.

But again, all this observation of Nature is carried on for a purpose: to convert the reader. The poem's didacticism does not ease. Lucretius cannot abandon himself to speculation about the behavior of atoms, because he has a job to do. Again and again he reminds us why we study the teachings of Epicurus: to free our minds from the crush of superstition. The Christian God of love and consolation was unavailable to Lucretius. Greek and

Roman gods were to be feared, propitiated. The Psalmist may behold the stars and wonder at the smallness of man and the unreasonable love of God, that He should not only give a passing thought to something so trivial but indeed should make man little less than an angel. Lucretius's men look at the stars and are overawed; they cringe and worry that all the power that whirls the stars may be aimed squarely at *them*. Thus, the first purpose of studying atoms is to train the mind to find explanations for what looms above. Any explanation, even the faulty, will do, so long as it shows that the universe can have come about by means of the random collisions of atoms. Before Epicurus, says Lucretius, religion thrust its monstrous head from the sky, grimacing upon us, menacing. Human life was abject. But Epicurus's discovery of rational laws has set our spirits free.

Related to this fear of the gods is fear of death. Religions may work more efficiently when they threaten eternal torment than when they promise eternal bliss; it seems more urgent to avoid the former than to obtain the latter. But if the gods

> Enjoy eternity in highest bliss,
> Withdrawn and far removed from our affairs,

then death cannot frighten us. It is a long sleep, or not even a sleep—it literally has nothing to do with us, since as long as we are, we are alive, but when we are dead, there ceases to be a "we" to care about it. One may complain that Lucretius turns his back on the mystery of death. But Lucretius does not just preach that death is

> nothing to us, no concern,

since he shows, unceasingly, that death is another name for the burgeoning life we now enjoy. Strictly speaking, death is not the end of life but one of the poles of our existence. Life is the tireless shuffling of atoms, like the turmoil-whipped motes in the sunbeam. Death is our means of life, for Nature can only create from atoms, and these atoms must be supplied by sunlight, water, earth, and other living creatures. Nature cannot allow

> a birth, without a corresponding death.

To fear death, then, is to mistake life. It is to fear our own cradles.

What would life be like, if men did not fear death? I suspect that we might give up our strenuous attempts to secure various sorts of surrogate immortality. We might no longer worry so much about devotion to such institutions as clans or nations or churches, which outlast the individual.

We might not pursue fame so doggedly, or the creation of monuments of intelligence and ingenuity. Fear of death can be a great motor for human activity, and without energetic activity there can be no bubbling up of civilization. Unfortunately, human activity has its own atomic randomness; it is seldom directed by any design for the common good. Fearing death, men make their lives lethal by grasping after wealth and power, those delusive stays against insecurity. Since men will not accept that there is a limit to their lives, they believe that their pleasures should be limitless too, and they die like ill-mannered banqueters who resent ever having to leave the table. Not that such lusts bring pleasure to the banqueter, who is so worried about what he thinks he needs that he cannot enjoy what he has.

Thus, for Lucretius, the beginning of folly is the fear of death. If that fear could be eased, men would not fight over territory or wealth. For along with accepting the fact of death, the Epicurean accepts limits to pleasure and pain. Epicurean *ataraxia* is negative: it is peace, the freedom from cares, desires, and fears. It does not offer men spasms of joy. It is calm, wise, benignant, and happy.

If men lived in this Epicurean state, they would enjoy the most Epicurean of delights, friendship. Lucretius contrasts the pomp of opulent clothing and glittering chandeliers and military drills with what we nowadays call a picnic:

> When friends in the long grass will lie at ease,
> In the shade of a tall tree at the riverside,
> Their bodies refreshed and gladdened, at no great cost,
> Most pleasantly when the weather smiles and the season
> Sprinkles the meadow with fresh and lusty flowers.

It seems the poet himself has enjoyed such outings. This is no primitivism or distrust of civilization. Lucretius's point is just that our needs are very few. If we understood this, we could live in friendship, provide for those needs, and still enjoy the horse races, the festivals in town, the "artful polish of sculpture," and

> The honey of music that the nimble fingers
> Fashion and bring to life on the guitar.

If the highest joy of life is friendship, then people must be thought capable of living pleasantly and harmoniously together. So they are, we find. Lucretius aims much invective at his own Roman world, rife with militaristic pomp, political huckstering, greed, and shameless lusts. Yet he never soured on the human race. If ever a man had reason, in experience and philosophy, for assuming that people are worthless, Lucretius had. When he discusses prepolitical men—a discussion that Hobbes was to adopt for his own pessimistic "state of nature"—he presents them as atoms of rapaciousness in a cruel struggle for survival:

> Every man, learned in staying strong, surviving,
> Kept for himself the spoils that Fortune offered.

And the species is propagated by means of lust, force, or bribery:

> Mutual desire might win a woman over,
> Or the man's violent strength and reckless lust,
> Or a present: wild strawberries, nuts, or the choicest pears.

But that last humorous detail—the object of romance refuses to settle for any old pears, since she's a savage with class—shows where Lucretius parts company with Hobbes. As Wormell suggests, it is not human nature so much as the material conditions of human life which make the savages behave as they do (59). They have not learned any better. Their life is brutish; yet without the discoveries of language and fire leading to the moral discoveries of villages and families, how else could they live? Moreover, for all the brutishness, their life has moments of charm, and the brutes themselves are admirable for their strength and tenacity. Unlike superstitious Romans, these savages are not afraid of ghosts or gods or other bogeymen of the intellectual night. What they fear at night is real: prowling beasts.

Human happiness, then, is ready to be grasped. Human nature does not bar the way, since even the savages are basically amiable. Two conditions must be met. We must have enough material comforts to satisfy our bodies. As Lucretius tells us time and again, that "enough" is little indeed. We must also be socially and spiritually prepared for Epicurean friendship. Again, Lucretius does not require much. On the positive side, we need language, community life, and the social contract not to harm each other. The negative requirements are just those to which Lucretius has dedicated his instructive poetry. We are to give up our fear of the gods, knowing that all events in the world come about by natural causes; we are to accept limits for both life itself and the pleasures of that life.

On that last point Lucretius is vulnerable. Like many of the Greeks, he accepts the notion that people never knowingly do evil. If we are mired in wickedness, it is because we have not scaled those philosophic heights,

> The temples of truth, the strongholds of the wise.

Unfortunately, history provides little evidence for the hope that people might have the sourness leached out of them by philosophy. Not ignorance but desire fuels our greed—as it fuels many other things too, like romantic love, patriotism, and technological and artistic progress. None of these things does Lucretius accept wholeheartedly, and in particular he is deeply suspicious of romantic love. All things in moderation. The trouble is, the traditional moderator has been religion itself, which in Lucretius's own words clamps its bit in our mouths and reins us in. But if religion does not bridle us, what will? Epicurus's answer is the prospect of a life of calm friendship and sunny confidence in the face of death. It does not matter that few will be wise enough to accept the offer. Epicureans do not presume to save society, just those sociable beings who replace the old fear of the gods with a sane desire to live in peace. Epicureans are optimistic about human nature, holding that all men can, without much effort or cost, live a life worthy of the gods. Such a life, too, is in the highest sense social—its great attraction is friendship. Yet there is a cost. Epicureans must turn away from the deepest desires of their fellow human beings, the most energetic motors of creativity and human power. We cannot live forever, they tell us forthrightly. We can enjoy no union with the gods. Our lives are part of no design. We cannot care about the distant past or the distant future. Our technological advances, after a point soon reached, bring misery. Our dreams of romance are diseases of the mind, to be cured by a cool promiscuity. Whoever is unwilling to give over these desires—several of which, one may note, beat at the heart of the *Divine Comedy* and other religious-romantic myths inaccessible to the Epicurean—is to be pitied and abandoned. Despite Lucretius's disclaimer, there is a smugness in his admission that the trials of others make our own safety more pleasant:

> How sweet, to watch from the shore the wind-whipped ocean
> Toss someone else's ship in a mighty struggle;
> Not that the man's distress is cause for mirth—
> Your freedom from those troubles is what's sweet.

Lucretius does nothing by halves. Although he is loyal to his land, he is really out to subvert some basic Roman ways. Take war, for instance. Roman heroes, other than an occasional Numa who instilled religion in an ignorant populace, were war heroes, and they earned special names to commemorate their feats: Torquatus, Coriolanus, Africanus. But war is the ultimate betrayal of Epicurean principles, as is even intimated by the Latin words for friendship and enmity: *amicitia* and *inimicitia*, literally "friendship" and "lack of friendship." Where war or its spirit reigns, there can be no Epicurean peace. Thus, in the general proem to *De rerum natura*, the grand hymn to Venus, Lucretius prays that Venus will subdue Mars with the "eternal wound of love." A modicum of peace is necessary if Lucretius is to write his pacifist poem at all. A peace brought by the bursting power of Nature herself, by Venus the legendary mother of Romans, would be a welcome change for the people of Lucretius's day, who surely had more of Mars than they knew what to do with. And it would bring them into accord with the gods themselves, who

> Enjoy eternity in highest peace,
> Withdrawn and far removed from our affairs.

Romans will not be apotheosized for carnage. But if they give up their craving for wealth and power, they may live divinely here and now.

And so Lucretius never mentions courage or heroism when discussing warfare. His war scenes are tableaus of grotesque slaughter: lopped limbs, animals gone mad, dying men dabbling in their own gore. What is surprising is just how often Lucretius turns to war when he needs a metaphor for unremitting, chaotic atomic activity. One senses how pervasive war and its accouterments were in Lucretius's Rome. But something happens to that warfare when Lucretius uses it to describe, for example, the motes in a sunbeam

> realigning their squadrons, never
> Stopping for breath, assailed by alliance, secession.

The maneuvering motes, of course, become all the more dramatic. But the implied soldiers in turn become no more than inoffensive specks of dust. Lucretius uses the similarity of physical behavior to rob war of nobility and purpose. The activity is interesting *as pure activity;* to make any greater claims for it would be pompous. Imagine, secessions of atoms! But isn't that as absurd as squadrons of men fighting for some scrap of land?

A further indignity for militarists, in the same passage, is Lucretius's use of a drill scene to show that despite appearances of stability, atomic turmoil underlies everything. The atoms are so small that, as it were, we observe their action at a great distance, and from that distance their random movements resolve into stasis. Lucretius begins by comparing the atoms to a flock of sheep on a pleasant hillside. They graze and move lazily about; the lambs "frisk in their merry play," yet from far off the flock appears to be but a white glow on the green countryside. To drive the point home with an example of what looks to be purposive, frenetic activity, Lucretius directs our gaze to the drill field, giving us an engaging synesthetic display of martial razzle-dazzle. But if you observe the men from a distant overlook (surely the overlook of Epicurean wisdom, which we are invited to climb),

> They stand still in the field, one steady glow.

Again, the use of military activity, so apparently grand and purposive, to illuminate atomic activity, so minuscule and purposeless, lends greater interest in the atom while it reduces the military to a case in point, a phenomenon as interesting as a flock of sheep browsing peacefully. As interesting, perhaps, but less instructive morally: for while the sheep feed and play and enjoy the morning sun, the men carry with them their own bad weather, flashing their lightning to the skies and pounding the earth with thunderous hooves. In vain, as Lucretius might say. Wisdom resolves all their action into the manifestation of a simple physical or moral law.

Thus, Lucretius assaults one of the most Roman of Roman values. If war is waged for inane luxuries, how can preparation for war instill virtue? It cannot, he says. Captains and foot soldiers never do give up their fear of death. Only reason, only the Epicurean way, can make a man fearless. It follows that the only true war hero is Epicurus, the man strong enough to conquer with words, not weapons. Epicurus is accorded praise worthy of the noblest Roman (not Greek!) of them all. In the proem to book 1 he leads a mental guerrilla expedition:

> His vigor of mind prevailed, and he strode far
> Beyond the fiery battlements of the world,
> Raiding the fields of the unmeasured All.

and brings back spoils more valuable than gold:

> Our victor returns with knowledge of what can arise,
> What cannot, what law grants each thing its own
> Deep-driven boundary stone and finite scope.

The result is more glorious than mere rule of the known world:

> Religion now lies trampled beneath our feet
> And we are made gods by the victory.

Storm trooper of pacifism, Epicurus is also the *paterfamilias,* the male head of the Roman household. This is important to Lucretius, but not just for selling Epicureanism to Romans. His consigning religion to irrelevance, as well as Epicureanism's attenuation of patriotism and of concern for the past and the future, might loose the ties between generations. The risk is anarchy. To mitigate this risk, Lucretius takes devotion to Roman traditions and transfers it to devotion to Epicurus, who is not just the founder of a philosophical school:

> You, father, are the founder of truth; you confirm us
> With a father's lessons, and from your pages, sir,
> As bees sip all in the brambles decked with flowers,
> So we partake of all your golden words,
> Golden, and worthy of eternal life.

Epicurus himself asked his followers to celebrate his birthday on the twentieth of each month (*Life,* 18); he became the object of their piety, not as a god, but as that one man who taught us how to live.

And so Epicurus is *pater,* as Nature is our *mater.* She does not voluntarily nurture or give birth. But because of the infinitude of atoms and their many shapes and ways, she bursts into production and destruction. The wedlock of father and mother here is the wedlock of Epicurean truth with *Natura rerum*—and its progeny are those who are content with little, who are not afraid of thunder or eclipses, and who recognize that birth and death are part of the ceaseless atomic activity which we know as the world.

Lucretius's Influence

It has been preached to millions of pupils that what Homer was by nature, Vergil was by art; that Vergil altered the Homeric ideal of heroism to suit the Roman ideal of *pietas;* that Aeneas is a pale copy of Odysseus and Achilles, but that Vergil makes up for it with his haunting music. Granted that in a Homeric epic with Homeric characters we ought to expect adaptations of Homeric verse; still, I would argue that the most important intellectual and poetic influence upon Vergil was neither Homer nor Homer's Roman admirer Ennius but Lucretius.

Perhaps influence is the wrong word, suggesting as it does the impact of some outside force, or the contribution of a stream to the broader river. For Vergil was steeped in Lucretius. One critic estimates that every twelfth line of Vergil's is indebted to the Epicurean; in the *Georgics* the ratio seems so high as to make estimation pointless. There are Vergil's overt tributes to Lucretius and his philosophy, as when he declares,

> felix qui potuit rerum cognoscere causas
>
> [Happy the man who knows the causes of things!]

And there are lines that adopt Lucretius's didactic stance and diction for the explaining of nature:

> continuo has leges aeternaque foedera certis
> imposuit natura locis
> [These laws and everlasting pacts has Nature
> Ever imposed on certain regions.]

And catchwords, mannerisms, brush strokes too numerous to mention, from the archaic imperative *contemplator enim,* to the lovely *luminis oras,* "the shores of light."

But the deepest poetic influence is intellectual, not aural. Lucretius excited and disturbed Vergil, as I think he did most of the poets of the early Empire and, much later, the poets of the Renaissance. By Vergil's day it had become impossible for a sophisticated person to believe all of the myths of the Greek and Roman gods; Ovid, for one, subjected them to gleeful burlesque. But Vergil longed for some divinity in things, some plan or fate that men had to obey and that would justify Rome's dominance in the world. Lucretius posed a serious problem for him. On the one hand, he understood both Lucretius's love of nature and his desire to reveal how the universe works. And for both poets this revelation had moral implications for human beings—hence, Vergil's meshing of agriculture and politics in his poems about Earth, the *Georgics.* The long, noble roll of the Lucretian hexameter was a perfect vehicle for the Epicurean's high argument, and Vergil made good use of his predecessor's example. On the other hand, there were strains in Lucretius which stirred Vergil to intellectual struggle: the emphasis on chance, the retreat from the political, the utter disdain for war, the meaninglessness of history.

A trace of this struggle shows when Palinurus, Aeneas's helmsman, asks him to take him along across the Styx, a crossing forbidden for one whose body has not had the due funeral rites. Aeneas's guide, the Sybil, reproaches Palinurus:

> Desine fata deum flecti sperare precando.
> [Stop trying to sway by prayers the gods' decrees.]

That the gods cannot be supplicated is an Epicurean tenet, and this is not the only instance in the *Aeneid* of divine unapproachability. A cynic might wonder what purpose Vergil's gods serve, and ask whether they are just literary ciphers used to slip the poem past a naive populace and to wipe out any residual religion among the literati. Such a reader might translate the line in this way:

> Don't hope to bend the course of fate by prayer,

where fate is the blind falling out of events. But *fata* is a form of the old verb *fare*, "to speak," and so fate may be literally what the gods have spoken. Perhaps, since it has been spoken, it cannot be retracted: it is *meant* to be, whether there is some anthropomorphic divinity behind it or no. Palinurus's prayer is ineffective, not because there is no fate, but because fate has been set, and for a purpose too:

> Cease praying that what must occur can change.

As usual, Vergil leaves us with an ambiguity, born of a powerful and ardent mind whose search for truth has led him to reject his epic master but has not allowed him to settle upon any certainty.

Prolific during the years when Octavian had not yet become Augustus but was still jockeying for power, Cicero is another writer whose debt to Lucretius is huge but underestimated. Cicero mentions Lucretius only once, in an odd postscript in a letter to his brother that Lucretius's poem is brightened by many moments of genius (or ingenuity?), and much art in spite of that (or to boot?). We cannot be sure what Cicero thought of Lucretius, but *that* he thought of him, deeply and with many reservations, is incontestable. During the latter part of his life, after Lucretius had died and *De rerum natura* had become well known in the great city, Cicero turned his talents toward philosophy, writing, among other works, the *De finibus* (On Moral Ends), *De amicitia* (On Friendship), *Academici* and *Lucullus* (epistemological treatises), *De divinatione* (On Prophecy), *De natura deorum* (On the Nature of the Gods), and *Tusculanarum disputationum* (The Tusculan Disputations, on death and immortality). Over and over we find Cicero wrestling with the questions for which Lucretius provided his sect's answers, yet rejecting the notion that the senses are always to be trusted, that chance can have created so orderly a world, that friendship is based on mutual advantage, that the gods are corporeal, that the soul dies with the body.

Often Cicero's rejection of Epicureanism is abrupt and scornful, as in the Tusculans when he wishes to examine the nature of the soul: "We will not bother to discuss Democritus, a great man surely, but one who made the soul out of light and roly-poly little particles by means of some accidental collision or other" (1.22). But behind that quick dismissal is a mind that takes questions seriously and faults the Epicureans rather for their glibness than for the certain falsity of what they say. Like Vergil, Cicero wished to see divine purpose in the world, and this wish grew all the stronger as he advanced in years, witnessing the waning of republican ideals and suffering the death of his beloved young daughter. Thus, in the Tusculans he argues, as did the Socrates of the *Phaedo,* that death is not to be regarded as an evil, since either it is nothing at all, as the Epicureans say, or it is a chance to be with the likes of Scipio and Fabricius and the Decii, Roman heroes on earth, now immortals in the heavens. The Tusculans are heavily indebted to Lucretius's discussion of the soul, sometimes using Lucretius's own arguments as means to a different end. Lucretius says that the soul's quickness shows that it is made of the subtlest atoms; Cicero counters that atoms so subtle might very well remain intact and rise beyond the atmosphere (1.43). But ultimately Cicero's heart lay with Rome, not with a personal hope for salvation or with a clique of friends retiring from public life. The soul must live, he says, because "without great hope for immortality no one would ever give his life for his country" (1.32).

As for other important writers, Lucretius was admired by most, thought old-fashioned by some, and studied by all. Ovid loved his materialism and his spoofing the gods, and nobly wrote that the song of Lucretius would die only with the dissolution of the world. Horace took a cue from Lucretius's satirical set pieces, and though he could never be magniloquent without smiling at himself, he sometimes reverted to the massive, rough-hewn rhythms of the older poet. Petronius became a kind of black-humored renegade from the Lucretian flock. He took the earnestness out of Epicureanism and celebrated the very debauchery he mocked, yet showed that underneath the festivities all friendships were hollow and the fear of death still gnawed away at men's hearts.

Lucretius continued to be read and quoted through the fall of the empire. For Christians like Lactantius he was the poet they loved to hate; they admired his artistry and ridiculed his ideas. Yet a few enthusiasts, like Arnobius, believed that Christianity could be reconciled with Lucretian atomism. In general, the Greek calm of the Epicurean gods could not appeal to Christian fervor, and Lucretius fell into oblivion for over a thousand years until the recovery of his poem in the fifteenth century. His influence was felt almost immediately. Often, as it was with Vergil and Cicero, that influence was a spur to reaction, or to adaptation and correction. Such influence is notable in Torquato Tasso, whose *Jerusalem Delivered* is a careful transformation of the materialist's chance into the Catholic's Providence; in Edmund Spenser's *Faerie Queene,* where the great hymn to Venus is translated entire but with an emphasis on creation, action, and ardent Christian sexuality; and in Salluste du Bartas's *Divine Weeks,* where discussions of celestial phenomena are lifted wholesale from Lucretius's book 6, while Epicureans are attacked for their pernicious atheism. For a subsequent generation of writers, however, Lucretius was the great poet who may have actually found out the truth about the cosmos. These philosophers, scientists, and political thinkers saw in Lucretius what they saw in themselves, a fearless opponent of superstition. Bacon, Montaigne, Gassendi, Hobbes, and Newton come to mind in particular; centuries later, Shelley would continue the fight. Finally, there were writers who responded to the satirical in Lucretius and used him to show the folly of man while reserving theological decisions to themselves; of these we may number Molière, Swift, Dryden, and Byron. And that does not even touch upon Milton, who made his devils materialists, or Tennyson, whose great monologue "Lucretius" is but one more entry in the list of works for which Lucretius is both foe and inspiration.

Note on the Translation

Lucretius's meter is dactylic hexameter, the meter of classical epic. In English, only the blank verse of a Milton captures its inexorable forward roll. The hexameter line includes six feet, each a dactyl (long-short-short, like our word INdigo) or a spondee (long-long, like our STRAIGHT FLUSH). The fifth foot is very rarely spondaic, and the sixth foot contains only two syllables, the second of which may be either long or short. Classical meter is quantitative, not accentual. The "length" of a syllable depends not upon pitch or stress, as in English, but upon how long it takes to be uttered. With some exceptions, a long syllable contains a long vowel or a diphthong, or a short vowel followed by two consonants. Hexameters alternate combinations of spondees and dactyls to produce great rhythmic variety. A line may sweep along with dactyls:

NAM fierENT iuuenES subit' EX INFANtibu' PARVIS (1.186)
[A little baby is—presto! a young man]

or pound away with spondees:

PAULATIM CRESCUNT, UT PAR EST, SEmine CERTO (1.189)
[little by little
Things grow, as is proper, from a certain seed]

That is only a hint of the metrical complexity afforded the epic poet. Unfortunately, not even Milton's verse can replicate all of its main features. Hexameters keep regular time while varying the number of syllables; blank verse keeps regular numbers of syllables while varying the speed of the line. In hexameter, a syllable's length may clash or coincide with the accent of the word; in English, an accent is an accent and there is little a poet can do about it. Yet the English poet has great leeway for placing his accented syllables, while the Latin poet must follow a long with a long or with two shorts, and then repeat the process. Just about any word may somehow be shoehorned into blank verse, while there are thousands of words which cannot fit into hexameter—for instance, any word with syllables long-short-long.

And so a translator makes choices, hoping that a gain here will offset a loss there, that if he cannot attain perfect accuracy, rhythm, tone, freshness of imagery, and power, he can at least choose what he wishes to convey at all costs, what he will work hard to convey, what he will convey with fair reliability, and what he will accept as a gift from a sporadic Muse. I have tried to be scrupulously literal in rendering Lucretius's metaphors and puns. If *suppeditat* means "supports, as of a building's foundation," then I translate to preserve that building: "props up." I retain the rhythm of Lucretius's paragraphs, usually translating phrase by phrase and clause by clause, using enjambment and punctuation and odd syntax to stress in my English lines what Lucretius used other methods to stress in his Latin ones. My paragraphs are end-stopped, like Lucretius's; his one-line aphorisms are one-liners for me too; his capping a point with some tersely regular line is for me a return to strict iambic pentameter. My meter is accentual pentameter, with five strong beats and a variable number of short beats (but never three short beats in a row). The normative line, occurring about two-fifths of the time, is iambic pentameter.

I am deeply indebted to the thorough and sensitive notes in the edition by William Ellery Leonard and Stanley Barney Smith, and to H. A. Munro, Rolfe Humphries, and F. A. Copley, my predecessors in translation; David West's *The Imagery and Poetry of Lucretius* has been a delightful source of inspiration. I have always thought that one should gather from a translation as little of the translator as possible. He should be like Lucretius's "oil of the odorless olive," a base for distilling another's perfume. The best a translator can hope for is that he will be read with enjoyment and impatience, after which sales of the original will, here and there, be a little brisker.

LUCRETIUS

On the Nature of Things

De rerum natura

BOOK ONE

—◆—

Mother of Romans, delight of gods and men,
Sweet Venus, who under the wheeling signs of heaven
Rouse the ship-shouldering sea and the fruitful earth
And make them teem—for through you all that breathe
Are begotten, and rise to see the light of the sun;
From you, goddess, the winds flee, from you and your coming
Flee the storms of heaven; for you the artful earth
Sends up sweet flowers, for you the ocean laughs
And the calm skies shimmer in a bath of light.
And now, when the gates are wide for spring and its splendor   10
And the west wind, fostering life, blows strong and free,
Pricked in their hearts by your power, the birds of the air
Give the first sign, goddess, of you and your entering;
Then through the fertile fields the love-wild beasts
Frolic, and swim the rapids (so seized with your charm
They eagerly follow wherever you may lead);
Yes, across seas and mountains and hungering rivers
And the leaf-springing homes of the birds and the greening fields,
Into all hearts you strike your lure of love
That by desire they propagate their kinds.   20
And since it is you alone who govern the birth
And growth of things, since nothing without you
Can be glad or lovely or rise to the shores of light,
I ask you to befriend me as I try
To pen these verses *On the Nature of Things*
For my friend Memmius, whom you, goddess, have ever
Caused to excel, accomplished in all things.
All the more, goddess, grant them lasting grace!

In the meantime let the savage works of war
30   Rest easy, slumbering over land and sea.
For you alone can bless us mortal men
With quiet peace; Mars, potent of arms, holds sway
In battle, but surrenders at your bosom,
Vanquished by the eternal wound of love.
There, his chiseled neck thrown back, he gapes at you,
Goddess, and feeds his greedy eyes with love;
He reclines; his spirit lingers upon your lips.
Melting about him, goddess, as he rests
On your holy body, pour from your lips sweet nothings,
40   Seeking, renowned one, quiet peace for Rome.
For I cannot work with a clear mind while my country
Suffers, nor can the illustrious scion of
The Memmian house neglect the common good.

For by necessity the gods above
Enjoy eternity in highest peace,
Withdrawn and far removed from our affairs.
Free of all sorrow, free of peril, the gods
Thrive in their own works and need nothing from us,
Not won with virtuous deeds nor touched by rage.

50   Then withdraw from cares and apply your cunning mind
To hear the truth of reasoned theory,
That the verses I give you, arranged with diligent love,
You will not scorn before you understand.
I open for you by discussing the ultimate law
Of the gods and sky; I reveal the atoms, whence
Nature creates and feeds and grows all things
And into which she resolves them when they are spent;
"Matter," "engendering bodies," "the seeds of things"
Are other terms for atoms which I use
60   In setting forth their laws; and "first beginnings"—
For from these elements all the world is formed.

When before our eyes man's life lay groveling, prostrate,
Crushed to the dust under the burden of Religion

(Which thrust its head from heaven, its horrible face
Glowering over mankind born to die),
One man, a Greek, was the first mortal who dared
Oppose his eyes, the first to stand firm in defiance.
Not the fables of gods, nor lightning, nor the menacing
Rumble of heaven could daunt him, but all the more
They whetted his keen mind with longing to be   70
First to smash open the tight-barred gates of Nature.
His vigor of mind prevailed, and he strode far
Beyond the fiery battlements of the world,
Raiding the fields of the unmeasured All.
Our victor returns with knowledge of what can arise,
What cannot, what law grants each thing its own
Deep-driven boundary stone and finite scope.
Religion now lies trampled beneath our feet,
And we are made gods by the victory.

You hear these things, and I fear you'll think yourself   80
On the road to evil, learning the fundamentals
Of blasphemy. Not so! Too often Religion
Herself gives birth to evil and blasphemous deeds.
At Aulis, for instance: the pride of the Greek people,
The chosen peers, defiled Diana's altar
With the shameful blood of the virgin Iphigenia.
As soon as they tressed her hair with the ritual fillet,
The tassels spilling neatly upon each cheek,
And she sensed her grieving father beside the altar
With the acolytes nearby, hiding the knife,   90
And countrymen weeping to look upon her—mute
With fear, she fell to her knees, she groped for the earth.
Poor girl, what good did it do her then, that she
Was the first to give the king the name of "father"?
Up to the altar the men escorted her, trembling;
Not so that when her solemn rites were finished
She might be cheered in the ringing wedding-hymn,
But filthily, at the marrying age, unblemished
Victim, she fell by her father's slaughter-stroke

100 To shove his fleet off on a *bon voyage!*
Such wickedness Religion can incite!

You too, someday, will try to turn deserter,
Taken by so-called prophets and their ravings.
That's no surprise. What dreams they'll engineer
To overthrow your reasoned way of life
And stir up fear and trouble all your fortune!
They know their trade—for if men could see that hardships
Have their sure end, made strong by reason, they
Might then withstand those superstitious threats.
110 But now no reason, no force can stand and fight:
We fear perpetual torments after death.
Men don't know what the soul is, don't know whether
It's born or it slips into the child being born,
Whether torn apart by death it perishes with us,
Or views the gloom of Hell and the vast gulfs,
Or slips by miracle into other beasts
As our Ennius sang, the first Latin to seize
The evergreen laurel-crown from the lovely heights
Of Helicon; through our land his fame shines clear.
120 Yet though his verse is deathless Ennius still
Proclaims that regions of the dead exist,
Where neither the body nor the soul endures
But a sort of shadow or image, strange and pale.
From there, as he tells it, the specter of ever-thriving
Homer arose before him and wept salt tears,
Revealing to him in words the nature of things.
Well then, though we'll need a reasoned way to explain
What happens in the sky, the wandering tracks
Of the sun and moon, and what steers events on earth,
130 Our reasoning must be keen of scent indeed
To observe the nature of the mind and soul,
To tell us what those visions are which strike
When we're awake and ill, or tombed in sleep,
Terrible visions, as we hear and see
Near us the dead whose bones the earth has clasped.

It does not slip my mind that the Greeks' dark findings
Are hard to illustrate in Latin verse,
Above all when our language lacks the words
And new terms must be found to treat new subjects.
And yet your virtue and the hoped-for pleasure   140
Of a delightful friendship urge me to
Persevere in my work, to watch through the calm nights,
Seeking choice words, the song by which at last
I can open to your mind such dazzling light
That you may see deep into hidden things.

And so this darkness and terror of the mind
Shall not by the sun's rays, by the bright lances of daylight
Be scattered, but by Nature and her law.
Whose fundamental axiom is this:
Nothing comes supernaturally from nothing.   150
Fear grips all mortal men precisely because
They see so many events on the earth, in the sky,
Whose rational causes they cannot discern—
So they suppose it's all the will of the gods.
But once we've seen that nothing is made from nothing
We'll find our path and see straight through to what
We search for: we shall know that things can come
To be—and in what manner—without gods.

For if something could spring from nothing, then anything
Could be born from anything, would require no seed.   160
Men could leap out of the sea, from the earth could arise
The scaly snakes, and birds could hatch from the sky;
Cattle, sheep, horses—wild beasts too—would give
Birth to whatever, dwelling on farms, in forests;
And fruits would not stay faithful to their trees
But they would change: all things would bear all things.
Each thing, then, has its own engendering matter.
If not, how could the *mother* stay the same?
But since all creatures rise from their own seeds
They need a place stocked with their stuff, their atoms,   170

Whence they are born and emerge to the shores of light.
Everything can't just spring from anything;
Inner capacities make things what they are.
Why, too, does the rose bloom in spring, grain ripen in summer,
The vine pour forth its fruit at the urging of autumn,
Unless the seeds specific to each thing
Join at the right time to reveal the creature,
Which the mild weather and quickening earth will bear
Safely—so tender it is—to the shores of light?
180   But if they could come from nothing, at once they'd spring
Up out of season, gestations all haphazard,
For there would be no atoms to be blocked
From a birth-giving union at bad times.
Also, whatever grows would need no time
For the coming-together of seeds, if it rose from nothing.
A little baby is—presto! a young man,
And seedlings leap through the earth as full-grown trees.
None of this happens, we know—for little by little
Things grow, as is proper, from a certain seed,
190   And in their growing they preserve their kinds.
You see, then, that things grow tall and are nourished by
    matter
Suitable to themselves. And the earth could never
Send up its lusty offspring without certain
Seasonal rains; deprived of food, no animal
Can reproduce or stay alive. Believe, then,
As all words share one alphabet, so too
Many things may be made from the same atoms—
And not that things exist with none at all!
Besides, why is it that Nature cannot fashion
200   Giants to ford the sea in a few strides
And shear away great mountains with bare hands
And outlive many generations? Surely
A certain matter is given each thing for growth
And birth, determining what can arise.
Nothing from nothing—that must be admitted,
Since things need the right seeds, their first-beginnings,

To be brought forth into the gentle breeze.
Last, since we see that a tilled field repays
Our hands with finer crops, there must of course
Be atoms down in the earth, and when we plow   210
The rich clumps, turning them over, working the soil
Till it's loose and soft, we stir these seeds to life.
If there were none, then with no sweat we'd have
Those finer crops spring up spontaneously.

There's more: Nature dissolves all things into
Their atoms; things can't die back down to nothing.
For if things could die, atoms and all, then death
Would snatch them away before our very eyes.
No need then for a force to split them apart
Or to unravel the knitting-together of atoms.   220
But since all is made of everlasting seeds,
Until some force meets a thing head-on and shatters it,
Or penetrates the spaces between the atoms
And loosens their ties, Nature allows no death.
Besides, whatever old age clears away,
Were time to consume its matter and kill it completely,
How could Venus lead the animals, kind by kind,
To the light of life, or how could the artful earth
Feed them with food for their kinds and cause them to grow?
Out of what would the inner springs and the distant rivers   230
Sustain the sea? Or the heavens pasture the stars?
Anything made out of destructible matter
Infinite time would have devoured before.
But if the atoms that make and replenish the world
Have endured through the immense span of the past
Their natures are immortal—that is clear.
Never can things revert to nothingness!

Further, the same force, the same cause would crush
Anything at all, unless indestructible matter
Held fast the knots more or less tightly knit.   240
A touch would kill at once, unless there were

Indestructible atoms whose intertwinings
Some force would have to sever. Now, because
The weaves these atoms fashion are all unlike,
And matter itself is indestructible,
Things must remain intact, till a force comes
Sharp enough to destroy their inner structure.
Nothing returns to nothing; when things shatter
They all return to their constituent atoms.
250   Yes, the rain passes away, when Father Sky
Pours it down into the lap of Mother Earth.
But the glossy corn swells forth and the branches sprout
Green leaves and trees grow tall and heavy with fruit.
From these we and the beasts are nourished; from these
Come bustling cities that blossom out with children,
And leaf-springing woods that sing with young birds' song;
Cattle, weary, lie down in their fields, having fed
Of the fat of the land; glistening dew of milk
Drips from the swollen teat; the younglings caper
260   On their unsteady limbs through the tender grass,
Their little heads made tipsy by milk drunk straight!
Nothing can dwindle to nothing, as Nature restores
One thing from the stuff of another, nor does she allow
A birth, without a corresponding death.

Now since I've shown that nothing is made from nothing,
And that things once born can't be reduced to nothing,
Lest you begin to lose faith in my words
(After all, atoms are invisible),
Hear now of other particles whose existence
270   You must concede, though they cannot be seen.
First: the wind lashes and whips the ocean waves,
Scuttling huge ships and hurling the clouds along,
Then in a whirl it scours across the fields,
Felling tall trees and battering mountaintops
With forest-splintering blasts. Thus in its bitter
Roaring it rages—or seethes with a menacing whisper.
Rest assured, the winds are made of invisible atoms,

Which ruffle the sea and the lands and the clouds, which toss them
And turn them and sweep them away in a sudden whirl;
They flow and spread their destruction just the same   280
As does the gentle water when in a flash
The river spills its banks—when heavy rain
Swells the swift fall of mountain streams—it scrambles
Forest wreckage in heaps, whole trees it snaps,
Nor can the best-built bridge withstand the instant
Onslaught of water. Swirling and dark, the river
Rams against barriers with its furious might
And smashes them with a roar and plunges beneath it
Huge stones; it overwhelms all obstacles.
In such a way the high winds also ride,   290
For when like a surging river they roll forth
In any direction, all things in their path they pummel
And plow before them; racing and twisting, spinning,
They snatch them up and whirl them and whisk them away.
So the wind, I insist, is made of invisible atoms,
Since in behavior and results it clearly
Rivals large streams, whose matter can be seen.

Then too we sense the various smells of things
But never see them as they near our nostrils.
We can't make out the sweltering heat, or observe   300
Cold, or catch sight of voices passing by.
Yet all these things must of necessity
Be physical, to impinge upon the senses.
Matter alone can touch or can be touched.

Also, clothes hung above a surf-swept shore
Grow damp; spread in the sun they dry again.
Yet it is not apparent to us how
The moisture clings to the cloth, or flees the heat.
Water, then, is dispersed in particles,
Atoms too small to be observable.   310
And with the returning suns of many years
A ring will wear away on the inside,

Waterdrops gouge out stone; the hooked plowshare,
Iron though it is, when worked in the fields, will secretly
Grow thin; we see stone pavement trodden and worn
By the trample of crowds; bronze guardians of the gates
Show right hands thinned away under the touch
Of people greeting them as they stroll by.
And so we see long-handled things diminish,
320   But if we ask which atoms fall and when,
Envious Nature shuts the door on us.
And all the matter which time and Nature grant us
Little by little, leading to gradual growth,
Must escape the most concentrated sight,
As what is lost in the wasting away of age;
Nor can you watch the weathering of the rocks
That hang over the salt and gnawing sea.
In unseen atoms Nature governs all.

But things aren't crammed together everywhere
330   With matter: empty space also exists.
This knowledge settles many questions, holds you
To the sure path, lest you should puzzle forever
Over the world and lose faith in our teachings.

So empty space exists, untouched and void.
If it did not, motion would cease to be.
For that which is the function of matter, to
Impede and block, would operate at all times
In everything. Then nothing could advance,
For nothing would in turn begin to yield.
340   But through the seas and lands and the heights of the sky,
Before our eyes, things move in many ways
And by various means; so if there were no void
Not only would they lack this itching for motion
But they could never have been formed at all,
For bodies, crammed up everywhere, would rest.
Further, no matter how solid a thing may seem,
This shows you that its structure still has gaps:

Water will trickle and seep through rocks and caves
And the walls within weep plenty of big drops;
Food spreads to every part of an animal's body;   350
Trees grow and in due season pour forth fruit,
As up from the lowest roots through the trunk and branches
Nourishment rises and pours into the whole;
Sounds pass through walls, flutter and fly right into
A shut-up house; cold stiffens to the bone.
But without void for the atoms to pass through,
By no means would you see such things occur.
Then, how can one thing weigh more than another
Although their sizes are identical?
If there's no more matter in a ball of wool   360
Than in a ball of lead, they should weigh the same,
Since it's the function of bodies to press down
While empty space persists in weightlessness.
So take two things of equal size: the lighter
Proclaims its greater share of void inside,
While the heavier shows for certain that it's got
More matter within, and much less emptiness.
Thus what our keen-scented reason has sought to trace
Exists: the void, mixed into everything.

Here I must hurry to thwart objections, lest   370
What some pretend should lead you from the truth.
Water, they tell you, will yield to the push of fins,
Opening liquid ways, for the fish relinquish
A space where the yielding waves flow back again;
Likewise, they say, things move among themselves
And change place, though the world is filled with matter.
Utter illogic they accept as proof.
For where are their fish supposed to swim, unless
The water will give them room? And how should the waves
Give way, where will they go, if the fish can't move?   380
Then either bodies must be stripped of motion
Or we conclude that space is mixed in things,
And from this space things seize the chance to move.

Moreover, if two bodies brought into contact
Rebound from each other, the air must certainly
Take over all the empty space between them.
And though this air can flow together in currents
As swift as you like, it could hardly fill the space
In a single instant—first it must occupy
390   Each part of the space in turn, then take it all.
Now whoever should suppose, when objects bounce,
That the making-dense of the air allows it to happen,
Goes wrong. He'd empty what was full before
And fill up what had been an emptiness.
Not by such means, then, can the air grow dense—
Or if it could, it would need space, I think,
To draw itself in and contract its parts in one.

And so, though like a lawyer you delay,
You must admit that space exists in things.
400   Besides, I can present a host of proofs
To scrape up a little faith in what we say.
Though the traces are faint, for the keen of mind they will
    surely
Suffice, that you yourself may grasp the rest.
As hounds on the chase for beasts that roam the mountains
Sniff out and find their quiet leaf-thatched dens
Soon as they pick up the trail and the sure scent,
So in these matters you will see one hint
Lead to another till you yourself can burrow
Into the coverts and drag out the truth.
410   But if you lag or shy away a little,
This I can guarantee you, Memmius:
I shall pour out the treasure of my heart,
Deep draughts from springs so mighty, with song so sweet,
That I fear old age will creep its sluggish way
Into our limbs, and unbar the gates of life,
Before I can in verse regale you with
The wealth of proofs for any point you like.

Let me resume to weave my poetry.
The universe is made up of two things
Which exist in themselves: atoms, and void   420
Where the atoms take position and move and scatter.
That matter exists, the senses we all share
Make clear. And without strong trust first founded on these
We have no grounds, searching for hidden truths,
To affirm the results of inquiry.
Then as for place or space, which we call "void,"
If there weren't any, bodies would have nowhere
Simply to be, or to go their wandering ways—
As I have just now demonstrated to you.

And more: nothing exists which you can call   430
Free of all matter or sheltered from the void,
As if some third thing helped compose the world.
This Whatever would have to be *something,* after all.
Now if you could touch it no matter how slightly or softly,
You then could add to it greatly or even a little,
So it would have to be counted a bodily thing.
But if it could never be touched, if from any direction
It could not bar a thing from floating through,
Then it must be what we call space or void.
Also, whatever it is would have to act   440
Or itself be acted on by other things,
Or be the medium for being and action.
But nothing can act or be acted on which lacks
Matter; and only the void provides location.
So no third element can be admitted,
Nothing besides the atoms and the void,
Nothing which falls to the purview of our senses
Or which we grasp from reasoned argument.

Pick anything you like! Of matter and space
It's either a "property" or an "accident."   450
The first is so conjoint it can never be div-

ided from things without destroying them—
Rocks must be heavy, fire hot, water fluid; all bodies
Touchable, while the void remains untouched.
But slavery, riches, poverty, war and peace,
Freedom, and other such, whose chance arrival
Or chance departure leaves the nature of things
Intact—these we call, justly, accidents.
Even time is accidental; from things themselves
460   Our sense derives its notion of past action,
Of what is happening now and what will follow.
No one can say he senses time as such,
Apart from the motion or quiet rest of things.
For if they say, "Helen is kidnapped, the Trojan
People are plunged into war," we had better watch out
Lest they make us confess these really *are,*
When the people affected by these accidents
Irrevocable time has swept away.
For whatever happened was an accident
470   Either of the people or of the place itself.
And if there had been no matter to form things with,
No place or void for things to happen in,
The flame of love, which the beauty of Helen had kindled
And fanned high in the breast of Phrygian Paris,
Would never have set ablaze that savage war,
Nor the wooden horse given birth in the dead of night
To Greeks who burnt the city to the ground—
So you can see that past events do not
Exist all by themselves, as matter does,
480   Nor likewise can they constitute the void,
But rather you should call them accidents
Of matter and space, in which all things occur.

Now physical things are either first-beginnings
Or what their congresses unite to make.
As for the first-beginnings, the atoms, no force
Can quell them; their tough walls outlast all blows;
Though at first it seems doubtful that in objects

The fundamentally solid can be found.
For the lightning from heaven can fork through the walls of houses,
As can shouting, or talk; iron glows white in the fire,   490
Scalding liquid will often shatter rock;
Hard gold is rendered limp and soft with heat,
And flames in triumph melt the ice of bronze;
Warmth seeps through silver, as does searching cold:
Soon as we clasp the ceremonial cup
We sense the water poured in from above.
So far it seems there's nothing solid in objects.
But since true reason and the nature of things
Insist, now listen as I unfold in verse
What does exist that is solid, everlasting: 500
The seeds, the first-beginnings, the atoms we teach of,
Which constitute this whole created world.

First of all, since we've found that nature is twofold,
Made of two far dissimilar things, that is,
Matter and space, in which all things occur,
Each must exist in pure form, by itself.
For wherever space—which we call "void"—lies vacant,
There is no body; wherever body in turn
Holds its place, void cannot exist at all.
So the atoms, "first bodies," exist—solid, no void.   510
Also, since void is a part of all things born,
Solid must close around it—that is certain.
Nor logically can anything be shown
To hold and hide the void within its mass,
Unless you grant some solid to lock it in.
This solid can be no other than the congress
Of atoms, which can lock the void inside.
Thus matter, made of solid atoms, lasts
Forever; things themselves disintegrate.
Again: if there were nothing to call void,   520
All would be solid; but if there were no atoms
To fill whatever space they occupy,
All the world would be void and emptiness.

Matter and void are marked off from each other,
That's clear; for the world is neither wholly full
Nor empty. Then those bodies must exist
To mark their fullness off from empty space.

These atoms can't be buffeted to destruction
Nor can they shred or fray, attacked from within,
530   Nor collapse under any influence—
As I have just now demonstrated to you.
For without space it's clear that nothing can be
Battered or broken or cut clean in two,
Nor can water get in, or the creeping chill, or fire
That burns to the marrow—the things which ruin all.
And the more empty space a thing contains,
The sooner it totters from their deep attacks.
So if, as I have taught, atoms exist—
Solid, no void—they must be everlasting.
540   Besides, if matter were not everlasting,
By now this world would have returned to nothing
And all we see from nothing again been born.
But since, as I say, nothing can come from nothing,
And nothing formed can die back down to nothing,
There must be atoms, everlasting bodies
Into which things dissolve when they pass on,
Providing matter to restore the world.
Atoms exist then, solid, single-natured;
Only as such can they preserve themselves
550   And recreate things for eternity.

Now then, if Nature had not set a limit
To the splitting of things, by now time's ravages
Would have reduced the atoms to such fineness
That from them nothing could at the right moment
Be conceived, and attain maturity.
For things can be shattered more easily—as we see—
Than they can be restored. So what the long
Infinite march of ages previous
Has broken, scrambling its structure, disturbing, undoing,

Would have too little time to be repaired.   560
Therefore a limit to the splitting of things
Is set: we see that all things are restored,
That they are each endowed with finite seasons
For growth, in which they flower and mature.

Furthermore, though the atoms are perfectly solid,
They can explain the existence of soft things too,
Air, water, earth, and heat; how these come to be
And by what power they function and persist;
Since void, with matter, is mixed in everything.
But if the first-beginnings were soft and pliant,   570
By no means could they ever form iron, or blocks
Of durable basalt. For Nature would utterly lack
Foundation for a first solidity.
Atoms exist, then, thriving in hardness, in
Simplicity; packed in denser structure, they
Enable tight-knit things to show their strength.

Suppose there were no end to the splitting of bodies.
Nevertheless, through endless ages, something,
Some atoms needs must have survived in things,
Not yet assailed by any peril. But   580
If they were furnished with so frail a nature
It hardly follows that they could outlast
Long time, harassed by constant, countless blows.

Now then, since everything after its kind is granted
A limit for growth and holding to life; since, also,
It is established by the bonds of Nature
What each can do and what each cannot do,
Unalterably (for in fact things are so fixed
That generations of dappled birds will show
The typical marks of their breeds in the typical places),   590
Each must of course possess a basis of
Unchangeable matter. For if the first-beginnings
Could ever be beaten and changed by any means,
We could never know for sure what can arise,

What cannot, what law grants each thing its own
Deep-driven boundary stone and finite scope,
Nor could so many generations keep
The parents' nature, habits, diet, movement.

To proceed: since in all these atoms which
600   We can't perceive, there are points or vertices,
Each point is irreducible, remains
The minimal atomic part; it cannot
Ever be isolated; it was and is
The unitary base for something else.
These points in phalanx, one after the other,
In crowded order, constitute the atom.
Since they can never exist alone, they must
Cling where no force can ever pry them free.
Atoms exist, then, solid, single-natured,
610   Cohering, by means of their tight-packed least parts;
Not brought into being by *their* coincidence, but
Potent in everlasting singleness.
Nature forbids that atoms be stripped or diminished
Of any part: she saves these seeds for things.
Now unless there were a smallest part, the tiniest
Object you could imagine would consist
Of infinitely many tiny parts
Divisible into tiny parts—no end!
Between the least and greatest, then, what distance?
620   None—for although the world is infinite, still
The tiniest specks would be composed the same
Of infinitely many tiny parts.
True reason calls us to our right minds, vetoes
Belief in such a thing; therefore you must
Concede, these unitary points exist;
Nothing is smaller; if so, then you must grant
That atoms too are solid, everlasting.
For if into smallest parts Creating Nature
Habitually made all things be resolved,
630   She'd never be able to form new things from them.
Besides, whatever is not equipped with parts

Can't have the traits creative matter needs
To make things: all the tangles and weights and punches,
Clashes and motions—through which all things take place.

So whoever thinks the universe is made
Of fire alone, all matter summed in fire,
Has clearly fallen far from truth and reason.
Enter the vanguard Heraclitus, famous
Among the silly for his cryptic style—
Not among serious Greeks who seek the truth.   640
Stoical stoneheads gape the more at what
Lurks under twisted words, and fall in love,
Taking for truth what can tickle their ears, or what
Primps itself with the rouge of pretty sound.
For how can various things exist, I ask you,
Created all from fire alone, pure fire?
It wouldn't help you to rarefy or condense
Bright fire, since all the parts of the fire possess
The qualities of the fire which they compose.
Force the fire parts together—fiercer heat;   650
Scatter or split them, and it languishes.
No further effects imaginable can follow
From these two causes, the thinning or packing of fire,
Let alone the world in all variety.
This too: if they'd grant that void is mixed in things,
Then fire could be condensed or rarefied.
Their Muses see so many obstacles
But are too shy to allow pure space in things;
So fearing the steep hard way, they lose the true.
Nor do they notice, if things were free of void,   660
Their world would stay packed tight, all would make up
One body, which could shoot forth nothing—as
The fire ablaze slings light and smoke; you see
It cannot be composed of crammed-up parts.
But if they think fire parts can be compounded
Somehow, and snuffed to change their substance—if
They must insist on no concession—then
All the blaze must of course die down to nothing,

And out of nothing will the new thing rise.
670   For change which leads a thing beyond its limits
Is instant death to the original.
So something must outlast whatever dies,
Intact, lest the whole world return to nothing,
And from nothing again this plenty be born and thrive.
But since these particles indisputably
Exist, which keep their states and natures constant,
Whose comings and goings and shuffled arrangement alter
The nature of things, and turn them into each other,
We can be sure these atoms are not fire.
680   Nor will it help to say some fire can vanish,
Recede, or be added, or somehow change its arrangement;
So long as all the particles are fire
Fire will in every way be what they make.
This is the truth: atoms exist, whose motion,
Order, position, shape and combination
Cause fire; alter their order and they alter
Whatever they make; they don't resemble fire
Or anything else that casts its particles
Against our sense to touch and to be touched.

690   Then to say, "All things consist of fire, no other
Substance but fire counts in reality,"
As *he* says, is to be stark raving mad.
For he battles the senses from the vantage of sense,
Shaking the bedrock on which all we know
Relies—the power that lets him know his "fire"!
Senses, he thinks, can learn the truth of fire
But not of other objects just as clear!
Foolish and crazy that all seems to me.
Where shall we turn? What is more worthy of trust
700   Than our senses, by which we mark the true and the false?
And if he wants to cross out everything,
Why leave the flame for the only element?
Why not some other—and deny the existence of fire?
The tenets share the same insanity.

Therefore whoever thinks the universe
Is made of fire, the only element,
Or those who hold that in creative matter
Air is the prime constituent; those who dream
That water alone is the maker, or that earth
Creates the world, converts into all things— 710
They have all wandered very far from truth.
And throw in too those who double the elements,
Harnessing air with fire or the earth with water,
And those who think the universe can grow
Out of all four: fire, earth, and air, and water.

Empedocles of Agrigentum is
First among these; the three-coast island bore him,
Round which the wide-whorled Ionian splashes and sprays
The brine of its green waves; the swift sea funnels
Into a strait and divides with its waves the limits 720
Of Sicily from the Italian shore.
Here is the gaping Charybdis; here the grumbling of Aetna
Warns that once more its fiery wrath will mount
And spew from its jaws the bursting and violent flames,
Flashing its lightning to the sky once more.
Many and various wonders does this place
Offer, they say, for people to visit and see;
A fruitful land, well fortified with men;
Yet this man is its greatest excellence—
Most wondrous, holiest, worthiest to be loved. 730
For out of his godlike heart he brought forth song,
Revealing in verse such brilliant findings that
It seemed he was not born of human stock.

Yet he, along with those small minds we've mentioned,
In many ways inferior far to him—
Though out of their hearts' oracles they give us
Miracles of discovery for our questions,
Holier, founded on far surer reason
Than what the laurel-toking Priestess utters,

740 Still, in their first-beginnings they fall to ruin
And their merits, though great, come crashing in that fall.
First, they allow for motion without void,
Admitting soft and penetrable things
(Air, water, earth, fire, plants, and animals)
Without a mix of void into those bodies;
They err, too, when they fix no limit for
The splitting of matter, no end to disintegration,
No tiniest irreducible point in things.
(We can observe in objects around us points
750 Utterly small, as far as our senses discern,
So we infer, in what we cannot see,
A liminal point, a minimum of size.)
Also, they make the first-beginnings soft,
And as we know soft atoms would be born
And die, would be mortal to the core, so that
This universe would turn again to nothing
And from nothing again this plenty be born and thrive.
(Neither of which, you have seen, is close to the truth.)
Last, they go wrong by making the elements mutually
760 Poisonous, hostile—they'd perish if brought together
Or scatter and fly, as in the gathering storm
We see the lightnings fly and the wind and the rain.
Then if four elements create the world,
And into those again all things dissolve,
Why should we call the four the first-beginnings
And not instead the things whose dissolution
Lends them their matter? For from other things
They are born and change their color and their whole nature
Continually. And if you think that fire,
770 Earth, water, and air can mix so perfectly
That none of them will change in the conjunction,
Then you'll prevent the making of new things—
No animal life, or inanimate, like the trees.
But in that jumbled heap each element
Will show its nature: air, mixed with earth, will appear
As air, and in water fire will just stay fire.

But atoms, in begetting things, should keep
Their power hidden, unobservable,
And let no quality obtrude which fights
Against the proper being of what they make.   780

Worse yet, they start with fires from the sky, supposing
That fire converts itself first into air,
From the air the waters are born, and the earth from water,
And turning in reverse from earth again
The others arise, first water, then air, then fire;
Nor do these shirk from alteration, wandering
From heaven to earth, from earth to the stars in the sky;
Which atoms could not do by any means.
Something immutable must needs survive
Lest the world be reduced to nothingness.   790
For change which leads a thing beyond its limits
Is instant death to the original.
So, as I said a little while ago,
Things change continually, but from them something
Has to survive which cannot be converted,
Lest all the world return to nothingness.
Why not assume that there are atoms of
Unchanging nature; that, if they create
Fire, the same atoms (give a few, take a few,
Shuffle the order and motion) can make air—   800
So that all things change into other things?

"But," you argue, "look at the plain facts! Things are all nourished
By the earth, and sprout up into the air, and unless
The season indulges them with timely showers,
Soaking the groves with cloud-melt and making them tremble,
And unless the sun broods over them, lending its heat,
No grain or trees or animals can grow."
Sure: and if solid food and juice did not
Aid us, all life too from our wizened bodies
Would slip the manacles of bone and muscle.   810
But we are so aided, it's clear, and nourished by

Our particular foods; things nourish other things.
That's only natural. Mixed into things there are
Atoms common to many, and in many ways,
And the mix determines for each its special food.
But much depends on how the atoms are
Arranged to hold together, and with what others,
And how they can move each other or be moved.
For the same atoms make the sea and sky,
820   Sun, earth, and streams, grain, trees, all things that breathe,
Mingling and moving differently in each.
Why, notice that scattered throughout these very verses
Are many letters common to many words,
But still you must admit, these words and verses
Diverge from each other in meaning and in sound;
So many things the alphabet creates
From a simple shuffle of order! But atoms allow
More shufflings—therefore more variety.

Now let's delve into Anaxagoras'
830   "Homoeomeria," as they say in Greek,
For which spare Latin lends us no translation,
Yet the thing itself is easy to explain.
First, for that trait he calls "homoeomeria":
Bones are made up, you see, of teeny-tiny
Bones, so he says, and flesh from teeny-tiny
Gobbets of flesh is born, and blood is created
From many dribbles of blood that gather and join;
Gold, he believes, consists of gold flakes, earth
Clumps together from little clods of earth;
840   So fire from fires, and water from drops of water.
Similar stuff he dreams up and believes.
Nor does he allow to void a part in things,
Or limit a thing's divisibility.
So on both grounds I think he goes astray—
Like those whom I've alluded to above.
Still worse, he makes his atoms flimsy (if
"Atom" 's the proper word, since they're just like—

Never mind, *are* the things themselves, and toil
And perish; nothing reins them back from death).
For what could flee destruction or survive   850
The mighty crushing in the teeth of Death?
Fire, water, air—what of them will last? Blood, bones?
Nothing! For to the core all things will be
As prone to death as what before our eyes
Is laid low by some force and perishes.
But matter cannot fall back to nothingness
Or grow from nothing—witness my proofs above.

And since food swells the body and nurtures it,
It stands to reason our veins and blood and bones . . .

If they say all food's a mixture and contains   860
The little atoms of muscle hidden inside,
Little bones too, and vein scraps, and drops of blood,
It follows that all food, dry and liquid, he
Thinks is made up of foreign and disparate parts,
Of bone and muscle mingled with lymph and blood.
Now then, consider a thing that grows from earth.
If it's hidden in earth bits, then the earth must also
Be made of the disparate things that rise from earth.
This reasoning holds for other elements too.
If, in wood, flame and smoke and ashes are hiding,   870
Wood then must be made up of disparate things,
Of foreign things that rise out of that wood.

This theory leaves a little shuffling room
Which Anaxagoras puts to use: for he says
Everything's mixed and hidden in everything else,
But only the main ingredient appears,
What's ready to sense or placed toward the top—a notion
True reason must emphatically reject.
For if he were right, then grain should yield a sign,
When it is cracked under the rumbling millstone,   880
Of blood, or of something which our bodies need.

So too it would be proper for grass when pounded
With mortar and pestle to seep a little blood,
And water should yield sweet drops that savor of
Milk from the udder of the woolly ewe;
Never mind! Clods of earth when rubbed and crumbled
Should reveal, hidden inside, in tiny portions,
All sorts of scattered grass and grains and leaves;
And in wood snapped in two we should see cinders
890   Hiding away, and smoke, and tiny flames. ·
Since the facts clearly show this to be false,
There can't be bits of objects mixed in things;
Rather, the atom-seeds are hidden, mingled
In many ways, and shared by many things.

"But often," you argue, "high on the mountainsides
The tops of towering trees may rub together
In the mighty force of the east wind, until
The trees flash out in an open flower of flame."
Yes—but that doesn't mean that wood is laced with fire;
900   The truth is, there are many seeds of heat
Which converge in the rubbing and set the forest blazing.
But if ready-made flames were hidden deep in the wood,
The fires could never hide for very long.
They would level woods far and wide and reduce them to ashes.
Now do you understand what I've been saying,
That much depends on how the atoms are
Arranged to hold together, and with what others,
And how they can move each other or be moved,
So that the same atoms, shifted a little, create
910   Both fire and wood? Just as these very words
Are made with little changes in the spelling—
As we call "flame" and "elm" by distinct names.
Well, if you can't believe that what you see
Before your eyes can exist, unless you invent
Atoms endowed with the natures of visible objects,
This reasoning puts your elements to death.
Could be, they're struck by something funny, and shake
In a fit of laughter and wet their cheeks with tears!

Now know and hear more clearly what remains.
I admit these are dark and difficult matters, but   920
A prophet's great hope for praise lashes my heart,
Stinging my breast with the sweet love of the Muses.
Charged with this love, robust of mind, I explore
The trackless haunts of the Pierides,
Untrodden by man. What joy it is to drink
Deep from those pristine fountains! What joy to pluck
New flowers, to weave a garland for my temples
Which the Muses have never veiled anyone with before!
Let the fame be mine, for I teach great things, stride forth
To free the soul from the stranglehold of religion;   930
Also, I sing dark matters into the light,
Spicing all with the grace of poetry.
I have good reason too for doing this:
When doctors try to coax children to take
Foul wormwood, first they brush the rim of the cups
All around with the sweet and golden juice of honey,
To fool their short-sighted years, fool them all the way
Past the lips, so they drink down those bitter drops
Of wormwood and are tricked but not betrayed,
For all the sooner is their health restored.   940
So I too, since this doctrine seems so harsh
To many who have never sampled it,
Since the mob shrinks back in horror—I have desired
To reveal our doctrine in sweet-throated song,
Touching it with the honey of the Muses,
That I might hold your mind by this device
To attend to my verse, until you grasp the entire
Nature of things—the structure of the world.

But since I have taught that the atoms, impermeable,
Fly never-vanquished through eternity,   950
Now is the time to unroll the question of whether
Their number is finite; so too with the void we've found—
The site or space in which all things occur—
Let's now observe whether emptiness too is bounded
Or whether it stretches vast and deep and endless.

Well, whatever road you take through the universe
You'll find no end; for it must then have some limit.
Now it's clear that nothing can be limited
Without something beyond for boundary, some
960   Point beyond which our sense can't follow it.
But you must admit that nothing exists beyond
This All; therefore it has no limit, no end.
Nor does it matter in what place you stand:
Take any point you like—you leave the whole
Unbounded in all regions equally.
Suppose, though, that this all-encompassing space
Were bounded; then if someone should race to the shore,
To the utter edge of the world, and fling a spear,
Would you say that the spear should spin from his strong arm
970   And fly far in the direction it was sent,
Or that something could prevent it and block its flight?
Confess: one or the other you must say.
Either one cuts off your retreat: you must
Concede, the world's extent is free and endless.
For if something or other should block the spear, prevent
Its flight to the target, something at the end
Or even beyond, that means we hadn't begun
From the true edge. I'll follow you then; wherever
You place the shores, I ask, "What of the spear?
980   Where does it fly?" No end can be established;
Immensity prolongs the flight forever.

Besides, if all the space of this whole world
Were finite, like a harbor huddled between
Specific shores, by now its plenty of matter
Would have sunk to the basin—nothing could happen beneath
Heaven's roof, if sky and sunlight could even exist,
For matter, all heaped up and clogged, would lie,
Settled in heaviness, age upon endless age.
But as it is, no quiet is granted the atoms,
990   The first-beginnings; there is no bottom to
The world, where they might flow and take their rest.

In tireless motion all things everywhere
Exist, and are propped and supplied from below by a wealth
Of matter speeding out of endless space.

Look around you. All things limit something else:
Hills divide air, air hedges one hill from another,
Land limits sea, sea limits all land, but nothing
Exists beyond this All to close it in.
Space—where things are—is so deep, that bright lightning
In all its speed cannot strike through to the end   1000
Even if granted perpetuity,
Or make the remaining journey any the shorter;
So plentifully does space extend around
All things—this way or that, space has no end.

In fact, Nature herself constrains the world
From granting itself a limit. She forces the atoms
To be bounded by void, and to bound the void in turn;
By alternating these she gives the world
Endlessness. If they did not bound each other
One of them in pure form would stretch forever . . .   1010

Neither sea nor earth nor the brilliant fields of the sky,
Nor mortal man nor the gods' most holy bodies
Could hold together for the tiniest moment.
Wrenched apart and set free from their alliance,
The atoms would drift along through the great void—
And who knows, perhaps they could never have clung together
To create a thing, too scattered to combine.
For surely the atoms did not hold council, assigning
Order to each, flexing their keen minds with
Questions of place and motion and who goes where.   1020
But shuffled and jumbled in many ways, in the course
Of endless time they are buffeted, driven along,
Chancing upon all motions, combinations.
At last they fall into such an arrangement
As would create this universe, preserve it

Through the Great Years, so many and long, as soon
As its atoms should toss together in suitable motions—
Then at once the rivers brim, and spill their riches
To refresh the sea, and the earth, sun-cherished, warm,
1030   Brings forth new brood; meek cattle brought to mate
Bloom, and the wheeling sky-flames come to life.
These things could never chance to be, without
An infinite supply of matter whence
They could repair their losses in due season.
For as an animal deprived of food
Loses his matter, trickles away, so at once
All things dissolve when matter is somehow turned
Out of their path and fails to shore them up.
As for the atoms beyond what's joined together,
1040   The ones still free—they can't preserve the world.
They can hammer away for a while and win some time
Till other atoms arrive to supply the whole.
But sometimes they'll be forced to ricochet,
And so lend ample space and time for the atoms
To fly and free themselves from their assemblies.
So a multitude of atoms must come forth—
Even to keep those outside blows fresh-stocked
We will need countless atoms everywhere.

Memmius, fly far away from this belief:
1050   That (so they say) all things in the universe press
To the center, that the world can't be unraveled
From any side, and stands without external
Support, since top and bottom push to the middle
(As if anything could rest upon itself!);
That bodies down under should also rise and strive
To rest on the earth's surface upside down;
That, just so, topsy-turvy animals roam
Like the reflections we see in a pool of water;
They argue that those below us can no more fall
1060   Into the sky than our own bodies can
Spontaneously fly up to the fields of heaven;
That whenever the sun shines there, we see the stars;

That, below, they divide the seasons of heaven with us,
Passing through nights that parallel our days.
One fatuous error spawns this stuff: the stoneheads
Grapple the problem with skewed reasoning.
How can there be a center when the world
Is endlessly deep? And what if there *were* a center—
No reason why a thing should plant itself
There, and not rather somehow be repelled.   1070
All place or space (which we have called the "void"),
In the middle or not in the middle, must yield alike
To the weight of the atoms, wherever their motions drive them.
No place exists where atoms can arrive
And give up their gravity and stand in the void,
Nor can the emptiness provide support
Since, as its nature calls for, it must yield.
And so things can't be held assembled by
Some overpowering lust to reach the center.

Besides, they make believe that not all bodies   1080
Press to the center, but only earth and water—
The waves of the sea and the rivers that rush from the mountains
And anything made of so-called earthly stuff.
But they explain that the light air is whisked
Away from the center, along with the bright hot fire.
So the signs of heaven tremble in the dome
And the sun's flame feeds on the deep blue meadows above;
For, flown from the center, all heat's collected there,
And the topmost limbs of trees could never bud
Unless they slowly drew food from the earth . . .   1090

Lest like swift-flying flame the walls of the world
Loosen and scatter at once through the great void,
And other disasters follow for like reason:
The thunderous temples of heaven fall from on high,
Earth snatches itself from under our feet and flees
Into the emptiness profound, among
Flotsam of objects, ruins of the sky,
All atom-fabric fraying—instantly, nothing

Is left but the wastes of space and the blind atoms.
1100   For wherever you first allow the atoms to
Escape, annihilation's door is there,
There will all matter crowd and rush away.

A little work will guide you—you shall know.
One point illuminates the next, nor will
The blind night steal your path, till you have read
Nature's last truths. Knowledge: a torch for knowledge!

BOOK TWO

How sweet, to watch from the shore the wind-whipped ocean
Toss someone else's ship in a mighty struggle;
Not that the man's distress is cause for mirth—
Your freedom from those troubles is what's sweet;
And sweet, to see great lines of soldiers marshaled
In the plains of war, when you are free from peril;
But nothing is sweeter than to dwell in the calm
Temples of truth, the strongholds of the wise.
You can, from there, look down upon others wandering
Randomly, straying, seeking the path of life,   10
Warring with all their talent, wrestling for rank,
Night and day straining with the utmost toil
To fight their way to the heights of wealth and power.

O heart of man, how pitiful and blind!
In what benightedness with all its perils
Our time, so short, is squandered! And not to see
That our nature yelps after this alone: that the body
Be free of pain, the mind enjoy the sense
Of pleasure, far removed from care or fear!
And so we see what little our bodies need,   20
Only such things as soothe the pain away.
This little too will spread the table and make
Many delights more welcome—though Nature doesn't
Demand that golden statues of young men
Grasping the fiery torches in their hands
Light up your midnight palace bacchanals,
Or your halls blaze with silver or gleam with gold,

Or the lute resound from gilded tile and timber—
Rather, when friends in the soft grass lie at ease,
30   In the shade of a tall tree by the riverside,
Their bodies refreshed and gladdened, at no great cost,
Most pleasantly when the weather smiles and the season
Sprinkles the grassy meadow with new flowers.
But the flush of fever will not subside the sooner
For your floral quilts, your tossing and turning in purple,
Than if you slept in homely coverlets.
Since luxury, then, is useless for our bodies,
Nor can rank or rule do us the slightest good,
It stands to reason they cannot aid the mind—
40   Unless, perhaps, as you watch your troops in the drill field
Seething and swarming and spurring their shadow-battles,
Shored up with vast reserves and cavalry,
Each side adorned with equal arms and courage,
Or you see your fleet churn up the far-flung sea,
At the sight of these religion panics, flies
Quaking with fright from your soul; the fear of death
Will leave your heart then, light and free of care.
But this is silly pomp and circumstance.
In fact, the fears of men, their dogged cares
50   Never fly the clashing of steel or the fierce spears,
But among kings and potentates yet strut
With bold contempt—won't bow to the flash of gold
Or the bright splendor of a purple robe.
Why doubt, the power belongs instead to reason,
Seeing that all life struggles in such darkness?
For as little boys tremble and fear whatever's lurking
In the blind dark, so we in the light of day
Tremble at what is no more terrible than
What little boys dream in the dark and fear will come.
60   And so this darkness and terror of the mind
Shall not by the sun's rays, by the bright lances of daylight
Be scattered, but by Nature and her law.

Listen: what motion of the engendering bodies
Brings various things to birth, then slips their knots,

What force makes atoms act this way, what great
Restlessness whirls them along through the depths of space,
I shall make plain. You mind now what I say.

Certainly matter isn't crammed tight, gummed
Together: for we see all things diminish,
Watch all flow, as it were, down the long ages,   70
Antiquity snatching them from under our eyes,
While whole and safe the universe persists.
For when atoms fall away, they leave the thing
Diminished; where they come they lend increase;
That withers with age, but this they cause to blossom,
Nor do they dally long. So the Whole is ever
Renewed, while mortal things exchange their lives:
One clan grows greater, one diminishes,
Round the short track all generations change
Like racers passing on the torch of life.   80

Now if you think that atoms can stand still,
Begetting in things new motion by this stoppage,
Far from the path of reason you have erred.
Since they go erring through the void, the atoms
Have to be driven along by their own weight
Or perchance by an outside stroke. See, often in traffic
They dash together and in an instant bounce
Every which way—no wonder, so tough they are
And solid of bulk, with nothing to block them behind.

That you may see the sooner how all atoms   90
Are tossed and tumbled, remember that there's no
Bottom to the universe where the atoms
Might stand tight, since the limitless span of space
Stretches unmeasured forever in all directions,
As I have shown and with sure reason proved.
That being the case, no wonder that rest is never
Granted the atoms that spin in the depths of space,
But harried by tireless motion this way, that way,
Some crash head-on and rebound over vast chasms,

100 While some veer slightly apart from a close-dealt blow.
And atoms that jar and rebound over tiny spaces,
So tightly wedged in their assembly, tangled
Up in their snagged shapes, inter-twined and -locked,
These constitute the strong rock-roots, the rugged
Structure of iron and all things of like strength.
But the rest, the few that wander the great void,
Ricochet far and round from afar vast chasms
In speedy return; these atoms furnish for us
The thin air and the sunlight in all splendor.
110 Many there are too, wandering through the void,
Repulsed from every assembly, forever unable
To join their motions to some common end.

Of this, as I describe it, a shadow or semblance
Hovers before our eyes, demands attention.
Consider the rays of the sun that are always stealing
Into the shade of a house to pour their light.
There in the void you'll notice many and sundry
Dust flecks that mingle among the rays themselves,
Stirring up in a sort of ceaseless strife
120 Skirmishes, wars, realigning their squadrons, never
Stopping for breath, assailed by alliance, secession;
From this you can project how atoms are
Constantly tossed along the gulf of space—
If small things can provide analogies
For greater, and set us on the trace for knowledge.
Those crowding motes you see in the rays of the sun
Should pique your interest all the more, for they
Suggest that just such turmoil underlies
Their matter, hidden and invisible.
130 You'll notice many, stung by the unseen lash,
Alter their course, routed and forced to retreat,
Scattering helter-skelter in every direction.
Know that in all things atoms cause this scatter:
Of themselves the atoms are the first to move,
Then things assembled of small atomic groups

(Things closest, if you will, to the force of the atoms)
Are driven and thrust by their invisible blows;
By these, things slightly larger are whipped in turn.
Motion arises thus from the atoms and reaches
Our senses little by little, till we can just   140
Make out those movements of the sunbeam flecks,
Yet by what blows they move does not appear.

With what velocity the atoms travel,
Judge, Memmius, from the few words following.
When the dawn first sprinkles the earth with her new light,
And dappled birds that flutter through untracked forests
Fill the land and the gentle air with liquid song,
Instantly at such time the risen sun
Pouring its robe of light over the world
Is here at hand for all and shining clear.   150
Yet the warmth which the sun sends and the peaceful light
Travel across no vacuum; they're forced to slow
As they strike and sweep aside the waves of air.
Not one by one do the tiny atoms of heat
Travel, but woven (and all rolled up) together.
Two causes slow them, then: without, they're hindered;
Amongst themselves, they're drags upon each other.
But the first-beginnings, solid, single-natured,
When they travel through empty space and nothing beyond
Delays—each atom one in all its parts,   160
One—when they're driven to the place they strive for,
Certainly their velocity excels
And ferries them faster by far than the light of the sun,
Racing across the same space multiplied
In the time the lightning-sun will fill the sky . . .

Nor can they follow the atoms one by one
To see the law that governs all events.

Now some (they just don't know what matter is)
Say that Nature needs the will of the gods to turn

170   The times of the year so very temperately
      For human purposes; create fruit, grain, all
      The rest that divine Pleasure, the queen of life,
      Our escort, urges mortals to enjoy,
      Who teases us with Venus to increase
      Our generations, lest man die. Man's welfare
      Is why the gods establish all—they dream;
      For they have fallen far from truth and reason.
      Say I knew nothing of atoms, of what they were,
      Still from the very ways of the heavens, from many
180   Other things I could name, I'd dare to assert
      And prove that not for us and not by gods
      Was this world made. There's too much wrong with it!
      Later I'll make these points clear, Memmius.
      Now to untangle the rest of the problems of motion.

      Here is the place, I think, to assert for you
      The following also: no corporeal thing
      Can of its own power rise and ride aloft—
      And in this matter don't be fooled by fire.
      For the flames are born arising and seize increase,
190   And the glossy corn and the trees arise and grow,
      Yet whatever weight they have presses them down.
      Nor should you think, when the housefire leaps to the roof
      And quick flames lick the tilework and the timber,
      It's doing so all by itself, not forced from below—
      Forced, as our blood when shot from the body flashes
      In a high fountain-leap and sprays its stream.
      Don't you see too how forcibly the water
      Will spit back tile and timber? The deeper we plunge them
      Straight down, many men pushing with all their might,
200   The more eagerly it chucks them up and sends them
      Leaping well over half into the air.
      Yet don't doubt that so far as they have weight
      These things are all brought back down through the void.
      In the same manner, squirted from below,

Flames can leap up into the air, although
What weight they have struggles to drag them down.
The torches of night that fly through the high heavens—
Don't you see them leading their long trails of fire
In the direction Nature gives them way?
Haven't you seen the stars fall to the earth?   210
Even the sun from the summit of heaven scatters
Warmth everywhere and sows the fields with light
(So the warmth of the sun will also bend toward earth),
And lightnings flash through stormclouds turned athwart them;
Now here, now there, you see the cloud-torn fires
Skirmish—and often enough they fall to earth.

Another fact I wish to have you know:
When the atoms are carried straight down through the void
By their own weight, at an utterly random time
And a random point in space they swerve a little,   220
Only enough to call it a tilt in motion.
For if atoms did not tend to lean, they would
Plummet like raindrops through the depts of space,
No first collisions born, no blows created,
So Nature never could have made a thing.

But whoever believes that heavier atoms, carried
All the more swiftly straight down through the void,
Can bump from above the lighter and so beget
Collisions that might give rise to the motions of life,
Falls far out of the way of truth and reason.   230
For whatever drops through water or the thin air
Hastens its falling by its weight—it must,
Since the water-matter and the light fabric of air
Can hardly stop a falling thing or slow it,
But, routed by the heavier, they give way.
Yet the emptiness of space can't ever stand
Firm against anything from any direction—
In fact, its nature calls on it to yield.

Therefore all things, no matter the weight, must be
240 Driven the same through quiet emptiness.
Impossible, that the lighter atoms are bumped
From above by the heavy, and of themselves engender
Collisions and motions for Creating Nature.
And so the atoms swerve a little—they must,
No more than the slightest, lest we seem to invent
Slant movement which the plain facts will refute.
For this is clear and ready to be grasped:
Insofar as a thing has weight, it cannot travel
Aslant as it drops from above—that, you can see.
250 But that nothing at all can lean from the vertical,
Who is there who can see and ascertain?

Then, if all motions are forever linked,
The new from the old arising in fixed order,
If the atoms never swerve to form the basis
For motion which would break the bonds of Fate,
Lest for eternity cause follow cause,
Where is that freedom for those that breathe on earth,
That will—where is it, I say!—we wrest from the fates,
By which we go wherever our pleasure leads,
260 Swerving our motions at no certain time
Or place, but where the mind itself has swept us?
Doubtless for such decisions the will first
Impels, then motion ripples through the limbs.
When in an instant the stalls at the races fly open,
See how the horses, so eager and powerful, can't
Break through as fast as the mind itself can yearn!
For all the body's multitude of atoms
Must be stirred up, spurred on in every limb,
Striving together to follow the mind's desire;
270 So you see motion first created in
The heart, proceeding from the mind and will,
Passing on through the limbs and the whole body.
Not so when we are thrust ahead by force,

By the great coercing strength of another man.
How patently clear that all our body's atoms
Are then dragged, kidnapped, going in spite of us,
Till through the limbs the will bridles them in.
So you see that although an outside force can push
Many men forward against their will, and drag them
Or pitch them headlong, still in our hearts there is   280
Something which can stand up to block it, fight it,
At whose decision the multitude of atoms
Are meanwhile spurred, in the joints and the limbs, to turn
And be reined in from the gallop and stand still.
Therefore this power in atoms must be granted:
Beyond collision and weight a cause of motion
Exists, whence we derive this inborn power,
Since we see nothing ever comes from nothing.
Now weight prevents collision—that invader—
From making any and every thing. So too   290
Inner necessity that would press the mind
To own defeat, to suffer and bear all things,
Is countermanded by the tiniest swerve
Of seeds, at random points in space and time.

The wealth of the world's matter has never been crammed
More tightly, nor spread thin at greater distance.
Nothing can add to the sum; no matter dies.
So whatever motion the first-beginnings now
Possess, in past times they possessed the same,
And will in the future likewise, ever and ever.   300
What was once conceived will under the same conditions
Be conceived and come to exist, grow strong and thrive,
As to each is granted by the pact of Nature.
No force can ever change the universe.
There's no escape for any sort of matter
To flee the whole, no source from which a new
Force might rise up and burst into the world
To turn all motion and alter the nature of things.

Here's something which should not astonish you:
310   Although the first-beginnings are in motion
Totality yet stands in total peace,
Save for the movement proper to each body.
For far beneath our senses lie the atoms;
Since we can never see them by themselves
Their motion, too, is filched from sight—no wonder,
When even the things we *can* see sometimes hide
Their motion, if some distance intervenes!
For often, cropping a hillside glad and lush
With grasses, the sheep will dawdle along to where
320   Leaves beckon them, bejeweled with morning dew,
And the lambs full-fed frisk in their merry play—
All of which, as we look from far off, melts
Into one still white glow on the green hill.
And great battalions swarming over the fields,
Filling them as they flourish their war maneuvers,
Flash lightning to the skies, and the earth around them
Is all a glittering bronze; the hearty men
Beat thunder beneath their feet; the battered mountains
Rebound the shouts and cries to the heavens above,
330   And cavalry dash and charge through the thick of the battle,
Shaking the earth with the pounding of galloping hooves.
Yet there will be an overlook from which
They stand still in the field, one steady gleam.

Listen and understand what atom-fabrics
Compose all things, what they are like, how far
They diverge in form, how many shapes they assume;
Not that only a few share similar form,
But all are not alike in all respects.
No wonder—for since there's such a wealth of atoms,
340   Beyond all sum and limit (as I've taught you),
It stands to reason that they won't all be
One size, or molded all in the same shape.
Besides, the human race, and the soundless shoals

That swish their scales in the sea, sleek cattle and beasts
And the dappled birds who brood in the wet rich lands
That ring the riverbanks or the springs and lakes,
Or who flutter across and fill the untracked forests—
Take any one breed you like, come! You will find
They vary in appearance anyway.
Otherwise how could the young know their mother   350
Or the mother her young? Which we see they can do
As well as men can recognize each other.
For at some holy incense-smoking altar
A calf will crumple under the slaughter stroke,
Breathing his last in a gush of warm heart's blood.
But his mother, alone in the world, will roam the green woods,
Searching the earth for tracks of the cloven hoof,
Everywhere looking and looking if she could only
Glimpse her lost baby; she pauses, fills with moaning
The leaf-springing woods; then back to the barn again,   360
Pierced to the heart with yearning for her calf.
Not the tender sallows or grass refreshed with dew,
Or those brooks that glide and wash their banks to the brim,
Can tease the trouble of her heart away;
No other shapes of calves in the glad pasture
Divert her thoughts and make her burden light:
So much she wants her own, the one she knows.
And the baby goats too, with the bleats that wobble,
Know their horned mothers; the rough-and-tumble lambs
Answer the baaing. Thus—as Nature orders—   370
Each scampers, as a rule, to his own milk-tap.
Take grains of any kind you wish: you won't
Find all of them identical—no, indeed,
Slight differences in shape will intervene.
With the same variety the conch shells litter
And paint the swell of the earth where the soft waves
Roll flat and slake the sands on the harbor shore.
Therefore I say the same rule holds for atoms,
Since they are bound by nature and not hand-tooled

380 For any one particular form: they must
   Hurtle together with somewhat different shapes.

   It's simple, too, to figure out why lightning
   Can pierce to the quick with such a sharper force
   Than can the fire we light in earthly torches.
   For you may say that the sky-born flame of lightning
   Is subtler, made of tinier atoms which
   Allow it to pass through tighter crannies than
   This fire of ours can, risen from torch or tinder.
   Again, light passes through thin horn, while water
390 Splashes against it. Why? Why else: light-atoms
   Are smaller than those of the clear life-giving water.
   And we see wine as readily as you like
   Slip through the strainer; but olive oil, thick, sluggish,
   Struggles; no wonder: its atoms are bigger, or
   More inter-hooked up with themselves and -twined.
   So much so, that the atoms can't be swiftly
   Sifted, to let each atom squeeze, seep
   Through the pores of the strainer, one by one.

   Here notice that a sip of milk or honey,
400 Rolled on the tongue, will lend a pleasant feeling,
   While sickening wormwood and harsh centaury
   Pucker the mouth with the twists of their foul taste.
   Easy for you to see that smooth and rolling
   Atoms compose what touches the sense with pleasure,
   While what seems harsh, bitter, these things are stitched
   And held together in more hooked connections,
   Which forces them to wedge and split their way
   Into our senses, slashing through the body.

   Finally, all that's good and bad to the touch
410 Battle each other, made of different shapes:
   So never think that the nerve-shredding shrill
   Rasp of a saw is made of the same smooth atoms
   As the honey of music which the nimble fingers

Fashion and bring to life on the guitar;
Nor think that similar atoms penetrate
The nostrils, when we cremate rotting corpses,
As when the stage is sprinkled anew with saffron
And the altar's all a breath of Orient spice.
Nor say that soothing colors which refresh
The hungry eyes are made of the same atoms   420
As those which stab at the eyes and wring out tears
Or those so ugly and frightful they repel.
For whatever can caress the senses must
Possess a smoothness in its first-foundations.
By contrast, things that offend or chafe or grate
Have in their stuff a certain crudity.
Then there are things which cannot rightly be
Considered smooth, or bent into barbed spikes,
But rather a little angular and projectile,
The sooner to tickle the senses than to bruise them: 430
For instance, pickling spice or the lees of wine.
Yes—and the fact that fire and the hard frost
Are toothed in different ways to nip the senses,
The touch of each will indicate to us.
For touch it is, by the holy powers! touch,
When we feel an object from outside the body
Work its way in, when an abscess aches, or when
The semen issues forth in the thrill of sex,
Or when from some collision the body's own
Seeds jumble among themselves and jar the senses,   440
As you yourself can test if you'll just strike
Any part of the body with your fist.
Therefore the shapes of atoms differ far—
They must, to give us various sensations.

And what feels hardened to us, tightly packed,
Must be more deeply interlocked with atoms
Hooked to each other, like a tangled thicket.
Now in the first rank of such substances
Stands adamant, long hardened in contempt

450 Of all blows, and tough flint, and stiff-trunked iron,
And brazen bars that screech shut in the locks.
But out of smooth and roly-poly atoms
Whatever flows like liquid must be made.
For a swallow of poppy seed's as easy as water
Since the rolling particles never glob together,
But splash and spill like water when you strike them.
Finally, things that fly away in a single
Moment—like smoke or clouds or flame—these must,
If not all formed from smooth and rolling atoms,
460 Be free of atom-snarls and blockages,
So they can slash through bodies and split stone,
Not clog together; thus you can easily see
That properties of prickly things arise
From atoms free of snarls and needle-sharp.

But, you say, there are liquids that taste bitter,
Like the salt sweat of the sea; no cause for wonder . . .

For since it's fluid, of smooth and rolling atoms
It's made, with crude rough atoms intermixed,
Harsh—yet not necessarily hooked together.
470 See, they are roundish even though rough and crude,
So that they can both roll and sting the senses.
This too will show you that the sea's bitterness
Comes from rough atoms mixed up with the smooth:
There is a way to filter them and see.
Strain saltwater through the earth next to a trench;
Sweeter and sweeter water will trickle through.
For it leaves above the seeds of the salt brine,
Rough atoms that would sooner catch in the earth.

To what I have shown I shall proceed to link
480 A corollary truth: the number of
The various atom-shapes is limited.
If not, again it would follow that some seeds
Would have to be unlimited in bulk.

For given the confines of one tiny thing,
Whatever it is, the shapes it can assume
Cannot be many. Suppose our atoms have
Three minimal parts, or even add a few:
Sure, shuffle all the parts of a single atom,
Bottom and top, switching the right with the left;
You will learn every permutation and   490
What shape each gives the atom as a whole,
And then, if you should happen to want new shapes,
You'd have to add more parts. The consequence:
The shufflings will require, by the same logic,
New parts, should you want even newer shapes.
Therefore a growth in bulk must follow upon
This novelty of forms. You cannot think, then,
The number of atomic shapes is endless—
You'd have to say that atoms of monstrous size
Exist, which I have proved impossible.   500
As for your Persian robes and the gleaming purple
Of Meliboea, crushed from Thessalian shells,
And golden peacocks dipped in the tint of delight,
They would lie, drab; new colors would win the field;
So too the odor of myrrh and the savor of honey,
Scorned; and the song of the swan and the artful lyre,
The Muse herself, defeated, would rest silent.
One excellence would spring up to pass the next.
Then too things would regress the other way,
Surrender to the worse, as to the better.   510
For things would sink in greater nastiness
Of smell or sound or sight or taste. But since
Such out-of-bounds do not exist, since limits
Cap the whole range of things, you must confess
Atomic shapes are also limited.
Why, from the summer's scorch to the frost of winter
The year is bounded, and measures the same road back.
All heat and cold and middling weather lie
Between both ends, and fill the range in sequence.
Thus they are made to stand apart so far,   520

No more; they're marshaled by two sharp points, here
Harassed by fire and there by the stiffening cold.

To what I have shown I shall proceed to link
A corollary truth: the number of
The first-beginnings made of one same shape
Is infinite. For since the number of shapes
Is finite, it follows, atoms of similar form
Are infinite—either that, or the sum of things
Is finite—which, I've proved, is not the case,
530 Showing in verse that tiny particles
Uphold the universe in endlessness,
Everywhere, ever, an oxen train of blows.
Now, sure, some animals may seem to you
Rarer than others, and less fertile also,
But in another land, in parts remote,
Thousands and thousands may fill out the number.
As especially among four-legged beasts we see
The snake-handed elephant, whose many thousands
Have palisaded India with their tusks
540 And made it proof against invasion—so
Vast are their herds, though here we see but few.
But anyhow, let me grant that there exists
Something unique, alone in its one birth,
Whose like cannot be found in all the world;
Still, if the store of matter were not endless,
It would lack the atoms to be begotten and born,
To be nourished and to grow: it could not be.
Assume that a finite number of gendering atoms
For one sole thing are hurtling through the All;
550 Whence, where, how, by what force can they unite
In such a swirling sea of foreign matter?
They'll have no means, I think, to form an alliance,
But as in the surge of big ship-splintering storms
The great sea smashes and scatters crossbeams, hulls,
Sailyard and prow, sails, oars well-slimmed for the water,

And on shores far and wide the woodwork trim,
Now flotsam, points its warning to us mortals
That we should shun the ocean's power and fraud
And never trust that traitor, no, not when
The water is calm and lures us with subtle laughter—   560
So if you go ahead and set your limit
To one kind of atom, the swirling crosscurrents of matter
Will scatter and spray them once and forever, so that
They'll never be able to hurl into alliance,
Keep their truce stable or add new atoms and grow.
Both of which happen, as facts at hand show plainly:
Things are begotten and born, then they increase.
Therefore the number of any sort of atom
Is clearly infinite, to supply all things.

So lethal collisions cannot prevail forever,   570
Shutting all life in a perpetual tomb,
Nor indeed can the birth- and increase-giving
Collisions keep the creature safe for good.
Thus battle lines of atoms drawn and deadlocked
Engage their war for all eternity.
Now here, now there, the forces of life prevail
Or are put to flight; the funeral song is mingled
With the cry of babies come to the shores of light.
No night has followed a day, no dawn a night,
Which has not heard, mingled with infants' cries,   580
Weeping that walks with funerals and death.

Along these lines you should seal up this truth
And keep it guarded well in memory:
Nothing exists, of those things in plain view,
Consisting of one single kind of atom;
Nothing which does not jumble various seeds.
And anything possessed of numerous
Strengths and capacities shows us that its atoms
Are the more various both in kind and shape.

590   For starters: in the earth lie the first-bodies
Whence the cold rollicking springs replenish forever
The measureless span of the sea; whence fire arises
(For in many spots earth's crust is fired from below,
And from deep flames the fury of Aetna rages);
Earth also has the seeds to raise for man
The glossy corn and the glad orchard, seeds
To offer, for the beasts that roam the mountains,
Rivers and leafy trees and the glad pastures.

So Earth alone is called "Great Mother of Gods"
600   And "Mother of Beasts" and "She Who Formed Our Flesh."
Of her the Greek poets, the old and learned, sang,
From her chariot-throne lashing her twin-teamed lions,
Thus teaching that this great world hangs in air—
Earth cannot stand upon another earth.
They yoked those beasts—for no matter how wild the children,
The parents' care must tame them to obey.
They bound her forehead with a crown of towers
For from her walled heights she makes cities strong;
So symboled, over the wide world, striking awe,
610   The idol of the Goddess Mother rides.
Various peoples keep her ancient rite,
Call upon "Mother Ida" and give her troops
Of Phrygian followers, for, they say, from Phrygia
The "phruited" fields first spread for all the world.
Capon-priests they assign her—they wish to show
That those who sully the Mother's Law, those found
Ungrateful to their parents, are unworthy
To bear their children live to the shores of light.
Palm-thunder on drums drawn taut—the crashing and clashing
620   Of cymbals about her—threats blared raw on the horn—
With the pipe and the Phrygian tempo they whip to a frenzy
And brandish the daggers, the signs of their fury and bloodshed,
That the crowd of sinners in their thankless hearts
Will quake with fear before her Majesty.

So when the Goddess is ushered through great cities,
Silently granting men her benediction,
They pave her path with generous contributions,
Copper and silver coins, and rose-flowers fall
Like snow, to shade the mother and her train.
Then men in arms take sport in a weapon dance,   630
Leaping in rhythm and glad and gleaming with blood,
Nodding their heads and shaking their horrible crests.
Greeks call these dancers "Phrygian Curetes,"
Recalling the Curetes of Mount Dicte
Who once in Crete, they say, drowned out Jove's wails,
Boys in a brisk dance round the baby boy,
Pounding their tempo on brazen shield and helm,
Lest Saturn should snatch him and send him down the gullet
And give his mother's heart a lasting wound.
So men in arms accompany the Great Mother;   640
Or else they symbolize her law, that all
Defend their fatherland with arms and manhood,
Prepared to be their parents' guard and pride.

These things, however ingeniously presented,
True reason must emphatically reject.

For by necessity the gods above
Enjoy eternity in highest peace,
Withdrawn and far removed from our affairs.
Free of all sorrow, free of peril, the gods
Thrive in their own works and need nothing from us,   650
Not won with virtuous deeds or touched by rage.

In fact the earth has never felt sensation,
But since it's stocked with a wealth of first-beginnings
It delivers all sorts of things to the light of the sun.
If a man insists on calling the sea "Neptune"
Or the grain "Ceres," and would sooner abuse
The name of Bacchus than to call wine what wine's called,

We'll give way, let him tell us and tell us the world's
The "Goddess Mother"—so long as in truth he still
660   Keeps his mind clean of the taint of vile religion.

And often, grazing the pastures in one plain,
The wool-backed sheep and the brood of war-loving horses
And the horned herds, under the one vault of heaven,
Setting their thirst to rest at a single stream,
Differ in feature, but preserve the parents'
Nature, and keep the habits of each kind:
There's such a smorgasbord of matter in
Any sort of grass you like, in any stream.
And any one of all these animals is
670   Built from the same stuff—bones, blood, veins, heat, water,
Muscle and guts—things far dissimilar,
Fashioned of atoms not alike in shape.
Furthermore, all things roasting in the fire,
If nothing else, must smuggle away in the body
Atoms that can sling fire or shoot out light,
Bring sparks to life and send the ashes flying.
Use the same logic, search through other fields:
You will find, hidden in the body, seeds
Of many things, all shaped in various ways.
680   Yes, you'll find many things endowed with color
Along with aroma and flavor—like altar gifts—
Which must consist of seeds of various shapes.
Smell penetrates where Color cannot go;
Color on its own, on its own Taste curls its way
Into the senses; hence they differ in shape.
Dissimilar forms, then, into one lumped-up mass
Combine; and things consist of mingled seeds.
Why, notice that scattered throughout these very verses
Are many letters common to many words,
690   But still you must confess, each word and verse
Has different letters for its elements;
It's not that only a few run common to all,
Or no two words are made from the same letters—

All words are not alike in all respects.
So, although various things possess a mix
Of atoms shared by many other things,
The constituted wholes may be unlike,
And it is right to say that different atoms
Make up mankind and grains and the glad orchards.

Don't suppose atoms link in every way.   700
You would meet freaks and monsters wherever you turned:
Races of half-beast men would spring up, tall
Branches might sometimes sprout from a living torso,
And land-dwelling members link with the life of the sea,
And Nature, mothering anything anywhere,
Would feed Chimeras snorting stench and flame.
None of this happens, we know, for everything
Is made of certain seeds, by certain parents,
And in their growing they preserve their kinds.
Of course they must; a fixed law makes it so.   710
For the atoms proper to each—from the right food—
Stream into the limbs and, linking, bring about
Suitable motions. By contrast, we see Nature
Shed to the earth the foreign stuff, and much
The body will expel with unseen blows,
Atoms that can't link up or replicate
The inner motions and the bonds of life.
Don't think these laws hold fast for animals only:
All things are bound by the same principle.
As every creature, taken as a whole,   720
Differs from every other, so each must be
Made up of atoms not alike in shape.
It's not that only a few share similar form,
But all are not alike in all respects.
And different seeds will have to result in different
Walls and ways and tangles and weights and punches,
Clashes and motions—which segregate not only
Animals, but divide the land and sea
And hold back all of heaven from the earth.

730   Listen, and heed my labor of love, these verses
      I search for: lest you happen to believe
      White atoms make white things that dazzle the eyes,
      Or that black things are born of black beginnings,
      Or that whatever is dyed in any color
      Wears just that color since, as you suppose,
      Its atoms are all tinted with the same.
      For atoms are completely colorless,
      Not colored like or unlike what they make.
      If it seems to you no cast of the mind can search
740   The truth of atoms, you go far astray.
      For as men born blind, who have never beheld the sunlight,
      Nevertheless, from their earliest years, by touch
      Recognize things they cannot join with color,
      Surely we can turn atoms in the mind,
      Unpainted though they are, and come to knowledge.
      And when we ourselves in the darkness feel for something
      Blindly, we do not sense a color in it.
      Now that I've won this point, I'll show you that . . .

      All colors turn completely into all—
750   Which atoms cannot do by any means.
      Something immutable must needs survive
      Lest the world be reduced to nothingness.
      For change which leads a thing beyond its limits
      Is instant death to the original.
      Be careful then, don't taint the seeds with color,
      Or all your world returns to nothingness!

      Furthermore, if by nature atoms are
      Colorless, but are stocked in various shapes,
      From which they bring to birth all sorts of color—
760   Since much depends on how the atoms are
      Arranged to hold together, and with what others,
      And how they'll move each other or be moved—
      It's trivial for you to give the reason
      Why things which looked black just a moment ago
      Can all of a sudden glow as white as marble,

As when high winds whip over the plains of water
And the sea turns into a spray of gleaming white.
For you can say that what we see as black,
When its atoms are scrambled and their order shuffled,
Or when some atoms are added or taken away,   770
Instantly looks as if it's white and glowing.
But what if the plain of the ocean were composed
Of deep blue atoms? It could never then turn white.
For however you jumble a sea of deep blue things,
They never will stray into marble-white.
And if there are atoms tinted this or that
Which cause the one pure shining of the sea
(As sometimes out of various shapes and forms
One thing all square and uniform is made),
It would be natural (as inside that square   780
We can find various shapes) to find on the sea
Or in anything else of one pure brilliant hue,
Various colors, far dissimilar.
Besides, the various shapes inside do not
Block the perimeter from being square.
But difference in color will bar the way, prevent
A thing from having one gleam overall.
As a result, the reason that lures us on
To attribute color to the first-beginnings
Falls; since white things are not made from white atoms,   790
Nor black from black; from various seeds they come.
In fact, white things would far more readily
Be born from colorless atoms than from black,
Or from any other that blocks white and resists it.

Besides, since without light no colors can
Exist, and since no atoms stand in the light,
You must admit they can't be robed with color.
In the blind dark, what color can there be?
Why, it changes with the light itself! Its glimmer
Depends on whether it's struck by the light aslant   800
Or direct-on—as the plumes of doves in the sun
That crown the throat and neck with a gleaming ring.

For sometimes it's a brilliant red, like garnet,
While then, by a strange sensation, it seems to mingle
The sea-blue lapis with green emeralds.
And the fan of a peacock, when it's filled with light,
Shifts color likewise as it turns full view.
Since the colors are born when the light has struck just so,
You must conclude, they can't occur without it.
810 But since the pupil catches and takes in
A certain impulse when it senses "white,"
And others when it senses "black" and the rest,
Yet you touch a thing and it doesn't matter what color
It happens to have, rather the shape's what counts,
This proves there is no need for colored atoms,
And different shapes make different sorts of touch.

Suppose we say that each atomic shape
Isn't assigned a *certain* color, but
Each shape may come in any color at all—
820 Well then, why aren't the things they make the same,
All things poured out in colors of all kinds?
It would be natural, then, for the crow in flight
To cast at times a white gleam from white feathers,
Or natural for black seeds to turn swans black
Or whatever color you like, or parti-colored.
More proof: rip a thing up—the finer its parts
The sooner you will see its color doused
Little by little, and slowly fade away,
Like eastern purple shredded into bits.
830 Tyrian scarlet of surpassing splendor,
Torn apart thread by thread, will squander it all;
This shows you, these small parts give up the ghost
Of color, before they crumble into atoms.
Finally, you'll concede that not all things
Emit a sound or smell, so you're correct
Not to attribute sound or smell to them.
But then, we don't sense everything by sight,
So surely as many things are color orphans
As are odorless or withdrawn from sound; yet the mind,

Keen-scented, can know these as easily   840
As it marks those, devoid of other things.

Don't think that of color alone the first-beginnings
Are plundered; for they're also shut apart
From warmth and utter cold and the steaming heat,
Tossed about, barren of sound and desert-dry,
Not casting any odor of their own.
Just as, when undertaking to prepare
The soothing balm of marjoram or myrrh
Or the flowery spikenard with its breath of nectar,
You need to find—as much as you can—the oil   850
Of the odorless olive, that sends no whiff to the nostrils,
That loses little of the mingled scents
It helps distill, unsullied by its tang,
For the same reason the first-beginnings ought
Not make their smell cling to what they produce,
Or their sound (indeed, they have none to give off)
Or, by the same logic, any taste at all,
Or cold or heat that steams or the moist warmth—
Nothing. For since these qualities all perish—
The pliable soften, the brittle crumble, the hollow   860
Grow riddled—the atoms must be free of them,
Must, if we wish to lay an immortal base
For the topmost tower of life and health, if all
Your world shall not return to nothingness.

Now of necessity you must admit
That sensate things must even so consist
Of insensate atoms. Things at hand, in plain view,
Do not refute or countercheck this; rather
They lead you by the hand and prove my point:
From the insensate, animal life is born.   870
Notice that worms will spring forth fully living
From raw manure, from the rotten stench when earth
Is sodden with unseasonable storms.
Besides, all things turn into something else.
Rivers and leaves and the glad pasture turn

Into cattle; the cattle turn their substance into
Our flesh, and often from our flesh the vigor
Of beasts is fed, and the winged might of the birds.
So Nature turns all food to living flesh,
880   And from that food gives birth to animal senses,
In much the same way as she makes dry tinder
Explode in flames and turn all into fire.
Don't you see now how much depends upon
What order the atoms assume, where they are placed,
How mixed, what motions they can give and take?

Now, what's the sticking point? What moves your mind
To muster sensible arguments against
Belief that from the insensate sense is born?
It's this: if you blend stones and wood and earth
890   They won't give rise to living, sensing things.
As regards that, remember, I'm not claiming
That sentient things are born immediately
From every sort of stuff that makes for sense,
But much depends first on how very tiny
The sense-making atoms are, and how they're shaped,
Then the motion and order and shuffling they allow.
None of which traits we see in wood or soil,
Yet even these, half-rotten with the rains,
Give birth to the tiniest worms, as the atoms are scrambled
900   From their old order by the new condition
And ally to produce animal life.
But those whose law is "Sentient things are made
Of the sentient," who derive their sense from other . . .

When they make their atoms soft. For sense inheres
In muscle, veins, flesh, all of which we see
Are soft, formed out of perishable stuff.
But go on, we'll say they could persist forever.
Why, still, they'd have to sense as does a part
Or be considered like whole animals.
910   But by themselves parts have no sense—they can't.
Parts, when they sense, rely upon some other,

And a severed hand or any body part
Alone, cannot at all retain sensation.
What's left? They must be like whole animals.
Then everything we sense, they too must sense,
Sharing with us all of our life's sensation.
How then can these be called the seeds of things,
How can they shun the road to Death, since they're
Alive, and everything alive must die?

But if they're such, their union, their alliance   920
Would only make an animal-herd or mob;
Beasts, men, and cattle, after all, give birth
To nothing by *their* mixing all together.
Maybe the atoms lose their own sense, only
To catch another? But why should we grant a trait
To take it away? Besides, we've clinched the point:
Because we see eggs turn into feathered chicks
And the earth froth with worms when heavy rains
Afflict it with the rot, we should know for certain
That from the insensate sense can be produced.   930

But if someone says that, insofar as it can,
Sense rises from un-sense by natural change
Or by a sort of birthing that brings it forth,
This law will serve to prove the simple truth:
All birth requires alliance first, and union;
No alteration without coalition.

First of all, bodily sense cannot exist
Before the animal itself is born;
No wonder, for all the atoms would be scattered
In air and rivers and earth and the products of earth,   940
And not assembled in a fitting way
To give the motions of life, by which is kindled
All-watching sense that guards each living thing.

Second, a pounding harder than nature can bear
Instantly knocks an animal flat and garbles

All of its sense, both of the soul and body.
The arrangement of the atoms comes unraveled,
Snagging the inmost motions of life, jarring
The matter in every limb till it lets slip
950   Those knots of soul that knit the body's life,
Cast through the pores to scatter and be lost.
For what else do we think a blow can pack
If not the power to shatter or undo?
And sometimes, when the blow lands with less force,
The motions of life remaining may prevail,
Prevail, and settle the battering rioters,
Calling each back to his course; then warlord Death,
Campaigning through the body, is shaken free,
And the senses, nearly lost, blaze up anew.
960   How else can creatures at the brink of Death
Rally to life with senses gathered, and
Not run the last short stretch and pass away?

Furthermore, pain occurs when the atoms are whipped
By a force that stings through living flesh and limbs;
These atoms go on a rampage through their quarters,
But when they settle down, pleasure returns.
This proves that atoms of themselves cannot
Be gripped by pain, or feel a single pleasure,
As they are not composed of first-beginnings
970   Whose motions, in revolt, might make them stagger
Or help them seize the sweet fruit of delight.
The atoms can't, then, be endowed with sense.

Well, if to have a living, sensing creature
We have to grant the atoms all its sense,
What of the atoms that make people grow?
They'd be struck by something funny, I guess, and they'd shake
With fits of laughter and wet their cheeks with tears;
They'd be so bright they'd discuss the blending of things—
No, more, they'd delve into their own beginnings,
980   Since, being just like every mortal thing,

They too ought to consist of things more basic,
And these of others in turn! You don't dare stop!
I'll dog you till it's "Anything talking and laughing
And thinking is made of others that do the same."
But if we see that that's stark raving mad,
And that laughing men can grow from the nonlaughing,
And thinking and expounding in wise words
From ignorant and inarticulate seeds,
Why can't whatever we know possesses sense
Then be a blend of seeds that lack sensation?   990

And so we all arise from sky-born seed.
There is one father for all. When the fostering earth,
Our mother, takes within her his moist droplets,
Grown big, she bears the glossy corn and the orchards,
The human race and every kind of beast,
Proffering food for all to feed their bodies
And live sweet life and branch out into offspring.
Therefore she justly earns the name of "mother."
What springs from earth will turn again to earth,
What was sent down from the shores of heaven will be   1000
Brought back into the temples of the sky.
Death does not spend things utterly, cannot crush
The atoms; merely loosens all their bonds.
Thence it joins atom with atom and brings about
That everything shifts shape and color, catches
Sense, and then in a moment yields it up;
So you must know it matters how those atoms
Are held together, and with what other atoms,
And how they can move each other or be moved;
And never think that atoms, everlasting,   1010
House qualities that ripple on the surface,
That now are born and now have passed away.
Why, it matters, even for our verses here,
Where they are placed, with which, and in what order,
For the same letters signify the heavens,
Sea, earth, sun, streams, grain, farmland, living things.

By far the greater part are similar;
Order of elements makes the words distinct.
So too in things themselves; when the atomic
1020   Order, position, shape, and combination
Are shuffled, things must change accordingly.

Apply your mind now, hear the truth of reason!
A new fact fights to clear its way, to accost you
And show you a new aspect of the world.
Nothing's so very easy to believe
Which at first does not seem incredible;
So too nothing's so great or wondrous, whose
Wonder will not diminish, little by little.
The purity and brilliance of the sky— .
1030   Observe it first, and all that it encloses,
The planets that veer, the moon, the splendor of sunlight—
If all these, out of the blue, now hurled themselves
For the first time before our human sight,
What could be called more wonderful than they?
What would we less have dared to prophesy?
Nothing. We'd have beheld this sky with awe.
Now no one even deigns to lift his eyes
To the light-filled temples of heaven, so stuffed, so weary
We are with its sight. Leave, then, this terror of mere
1040   Novelty, cease to spit up the truth, but rather
Weigh with a keener judgment; if it seems true,
Surrender; if false, strap on your armor against it.
For the mind seeks to know: if boundless space
Stretches beyond the battlements of the world,
What lies at last where thought desires to glimpse,
Where the hurl of the mind soars far at liberty?

We start: in every section, everywhere,
On either side, from above or below, the All
Is endless, as I have taught, as the thing itself
1050   Cries out and sheds its light upon the deep.
In no way now can it seem plausible

That while space yawns in every direction, endless,
And numberless seeds in seas unfathomable
Fly this way and that, driven on in ceaseless motion,
Our world and sky should be unique creations,
And all those seeds out there accomplish nothing!
When after all our world is made by nature,
Of her own, by chance, by the rush and collision of atoms,
Jumbled any which way, in the dark, to no result,
But at last tossed into combinations which   1060
Became the origin of mighty things,
Of the earth and the sea and sky and all that live.
So again I say you must confess that elsewhere
Atom-assemblies like this world exist,
Like this, held fast in the jealous embrace of heaven.

Furthermore, since a wealth of matter is ready
And space stands waiting and not one cause whatever
Delays, things must of course be made and done.
Now if the atoms are so plentiful
That not all the eons of life on earth could count them,   1070
And if their nature and force remain the same,
So that the seeds can be caught anywhere
Just as they're caught on earth, you must admit
That in other regions other worlds exist,
With different kinds of men and animals.

And more: there is no one-of-a-kind in the All,
Nothing uniquely born, uniquely bred;
It must belong to a race with countless more
Of its kind. Direct your thoughts to animals first:
You'll find it's true of the beasts that wander the mountains, 1080
True of the human family, of all
The scaly and soundless snakes and the birds of the air.
By the same logic you must then allow
That the sky and earth, sun, moon, and sea and the rest
Are not one-of-a-kind, but past all number,
Even though the boundary stake of life is driven

As deep into the bodies they are born with
As it is here for any abundant race.

Grasp this truth, and at once you'll see that Nature
1090 Is free, unfettered from those haughty lords;
Rid of all gods, she works her will herself.
For, by the quiet and holy hearts of the gods,
By their calm lives and everlasting peace,
Who can direct the unmeasured All, or grip
With a firm hand the reins to rule the abyss?
Who can wheel all the starry spheres, and blow
Over all land the fruitful warmth from above,
Be ready in all places at all times,
Gather black clouds and shake the quiet sky
1100 With terrible thunder, to hurl down bolts which often
Rattle his own shrines, to rage in the desert, retreating
For target drill, so that his shafts can pass
The guilty by and slay the innocent?

After the time the world was born, and the first
Day of the sea and the earth and the sun had dawned,
Much matter was added from beyond, seeds added
Around us, which the great All flung into union;
From these the sea and the earth can grow, from these
The heavens extend their demesne and lift still higher
1110 Their lofty towers; from these the winds arise.
For driven from all quarters the atoms are sorted
Each to his own, and settle into kinds:
Water settles with water, from atoms of earth the earth
Grows; fire flints out the fire and air the air;
Until to the utmost limit of growth all things
Are led, made perfect by Creating Nature.
That happens when no more is fed into
Life-giving veins than that which ebbs away.
This is the age at which all things must stand,
1120 When mighty Nature reins in all increase.
For whatever you see grow big with hearty addition,

Mounting the steps to maturity one by one,
Takes on more atoms than it loses while
The veins are freely fed, and their bodies are
Not yet so tattered they lose their atoms and
Expend more than their time of life restores.
You must surrender the point, that atoms flood
Into and ebb from things. But more must enter
Till things have touched their pinnacle of growth.
Then slowly and softly the solid trunk of adulthood   1130
Breaks, and we melt into the lesser age.
And that's no wonder: the fuller and broader a thing
When you exhaust the source of its increase,
The sooner will it scatter and lose its atoms,
Nor will its veins be nourished easily,
Nor is there enough to shore up and restore
The ample exhalations of the old.
By rights they pass away, made thin and porous
In the dwindle of atoms, laid low by blows from without,
When finally in their great age all food fails them   1140
And the outside atoms, hammering, never cease
Till they rule with their rain of pounding and crush the thing.

So also the great battlements of the world,
Besieged and battered, will crumble into ruin.
For food it is that makes things whole and new,
Food shores them up, holds all things in repair —
In vain; enough will not be suffered to enter
The blood; Nature will not supply what's needed.
And now, so crippled is our age, that the earth,
Worn out by labor, scarce makes tiny creatures —   1150
Which once made all, gave birth to giant beasts.
For I find it hard to believe that a golden cord
From heaven let living things down into the fields,
Or they were made by the stone-splashing waves of the sea;
The same earth gendered then that now gives food.
What's more, at first she made, of her own prompting,
The glossy corn and the glad vine for us mortals,

And gave, of her own, sweet offspring and glad pasture.
Yet these now hardly grow for all our work:
1160   We sweat our oxen thin and the strength of our farmhands
We crush; for our fields the plow is not enough.
So full of labor and so spare of birth!

Now the old plowman shakes his head and sighs
That all of his hard work has come to nothing,
Compares the present days to days gone by
And over and over touts his father's luck.
Disheartened, the planter of stooped and shriveled vines
Curses this bent of our age, and rattles on
With his reproach: our elders, full of reverence,
1170   Managed to live with ease in narrow bounds,
With much less acreage to a man; he doesn't
Grasp that, slowly, wasting away, all things
Go to the tomb, worn out by the long years.

BOOK THREE

Out of such darkness you who were first to raise
So brilliant a light to show us the best of life,
I follow you, glory of Greece, and in the deep
Print of your traces I now fix my steps,
Not eager to strive with you, but longing in love
To imitate your work. For how can the swallow
Contend with the song of the swan, or the spindly kid-goat
Gallop around the track with powerful horses?
You, father, are the founder of truth, you confirm us
With a father's lessons, and from your pages, sir,   10
As bees sip all in the brambles decked with flowers,
So we partake of all your golden words,
Golden, and worthy of eternal life.
For once your teachings, sprung from a godlike mind,
Begin to trumpet the nature of things, the soul's
Terrors flee, and the battlements of the world
Sunder; I see vast space and all its works.
The quiet dwellings of the gods appear,
Which winds can never lash nor storms defile
Nor the fall of biting snow and its hard sleet   20
Mar with their gray; one still and cloudless sky
Is canopy, and laughs in a bath of light.
Nature supplies their every need besides,
And nothing nibbles at their peace of mind.
But the halls of the dead—nowhere do *they* appear,
Nor does the earth obstruct our looking down
On what occurs in space beneath our feet.
When I think of these things, I am seized by a godlike pleasure

And I shudder with awe; for by your power, Nature's
30   Veil is stripped free, and all made manifest.

I've taught of the first fabric of all things,
And how of their own the atoms of various shapes
Fly driven along in endless motion, how
All things can be created out of them;
Next, in my verse, it's clear I should shed light
Upon the nature of the mind and soul,
And pitch that fear of the underworld headlong
Which troubles human life from the inmost wells,
Muddying all our affairs with the black of death,
40   Leaving behind no pleasure pure and clear.

For though men preach that sickness or a life
Of infamous vice ought sooner to be feared
Than the realm of death, and say they know their souls
Are nothing but blood (or air, if the fancy strikes them),
And don't need our philosophy at all,
Turn your thoughts this way and you'll see it's just
Swagger and bluster and not firm belief:
Men driven out of their country and kept far
From human sight, men tarred by crime and scandal,
50   Wretched in every way, still hang to life,
Pathetic, and invoke ancestral shades,
And slaughter black cattle and send the spirits down
To the gods of the dead. In bitter times
They turn their minds more keenly toward religion.
All the more, in danger and doubt, when things go wrong,
We should keep our eye on the man, see what he is —
For that's the spell that snatches his mask and makes him
Cry out at last from the heart. The truth remains.
And greed and the blind craving for rank, which drive
60   Pitiful men to overleap the bounds
Of law, drive friends-in-evil and their henchmen
To struggle night and day with the utmost strain

To fight to the heights of wealth—these sores of life
Are fed in no small part by fear of death.
To be despised, to feel the pinch for money
Are ills that seem to linger at Death's door,
Far from the sweetness of a steadfast life.
And so, spurred on by groundless fears, men strive
To escape, to hustle themselves far out of their reach,
And from the blood of countrymen they forge   70
Riches, and double them, heaping slaughter on slaughter.
With a bloodthirsty glee they bury their own brothers
And hate and fear to eat at a cousin's table.
In the same way, from the same fear, men often
Grow lean with envy. There he is, that powerbroker,
That rising star attracting every gaze
While *they're* bogged down in the mud (they whine) and darkness.
Some waste away for statues and a name.
And often from fear of dying, men will be
Seized with disgust for life, will hate the light,   80
So with sorrowing hearts they pass their sentence, death,
Forgetting that all their cares spring from this fear—
This puts their shame to rout, this breaks the bonds
Of friendship and subverts all piety.
And men have sold the land that gave them birth,
Sold their dear parents, to shun the underworld.
For as little boys tremble and fear whatever's lurking
In the blind dark, so we in the light of day
Tremble at what is no more terrible than
What little boys dream in the dark and fear will come.   90
And so this darkness and terror of the mind
Shall not by the sun's rays, by the bright lances of daylight
Be scattered, but by Nature and her law.

First I say that the soul, which we call "mind,"
The site of judgment, governor of life,
Is one more human part no less than hands
And feet and eyes are part of the whole creature . . .

The mind's sense is not situate in one place
But is a certain life-giving state of the body
100 Called "harmony" by the Greeks, enabling us
To live and feel, without a part for "mind,"
As often it's said good health belongs to the body
And yet health's no one part of the healthy man.
So they place the mind's power in no certain part—
But I think they veer far off and stray from truth.
For often the body—and that's in plain sight—suffers
While we feel gladness in some hidden part,
And the reverse in turn is often true,
That a man's soul-sick with a body whole and glad,
110 Just as when, though the gout should pinch your foot,
Your head may meanwhile feel no pain at all.
More: when the limbs are poured out in soft sleep
And the laden body lies insensible,
There still is something else in us which then
Is tumbled this way and that, and takes inside
All the turns of gladness and idle cares of the heart.
Now, to show you that the "anima," the life spirit,
Is a body part, and that bodies do not feel
By virtue of harmony: cut away much of the body
120 And often life still lingers in our limbs,
But that same life, when the tiny atoms of heat
Flee, and the mouth releases its last breath,
Deserts the blood at once and leaves the bones.
This ought to show you that not all atoms play
The same parts, with the same sustaining powers;
Rather the seeds of air and the moist warmth
Take care that life may linger in the limbs.
So there's a vital breath and warmth in the body,
Which, when it leaves us, leaves us full of death.
130 Therefore, as the mind and soul are found to be
A sort of bodily part, let the musicians
Keep that "harmony" name they've filched from Helicon
Or from wherever they've dragged it and applied it

To something which had lacked a proper name.
Let them have it, whatever. You attend the rest.

Now I assert, the spirit and the soul
Are held conjoint and form one common nature,
But the captain, so to speak, and lord of the body
Is the judgment, which we call the soul or mind.
It sits fixed in the center of the breast.   140
Here alarm bucks loose, and dread, and round these regions
Gladness caresses. Here, then, is the mind, the soul.
The other, the spirit, sown broadcast through the body,
Obeys and moves to the mind's sway and will.
The mind thinks by itself, joys in itself,
Even when nothing is stirring the spirit or body.
And as when our head or eye is stricken with
Some trying pain, we're still not torture-crossed
Throughout the body, so the mind itself
Will grieve or flourish in gladness while the spirit,   150
Spread through the frame, is touched by nothing new.
But when the fear that troubles the mind is more
Vehement, we see the spirit in all the members
Agree, and the body blanches and beads of sweat
Break out all over, the tongue-tied voice cracks, falters,
It's dusk with the eyes, ears ring, limbs buckle and give,
And yes, we see men terrified in mind
Crumple—so anyone should easily learn
That the spirit and mind are one, for when spirit is struck
By the force of the mind, it thrusts and hurls the body.   160

This reasoning also shows that mind and spirit
Are corporeal. When they can shove the limbs,
Snatching the sleeping body and discomposing
The features, wheeling and steering the whole person
(None of which, we see, can come to pass without
Touch, and all touch implies a body), must
You not confess, the soul's corporeal?

And more: you'll notice the soul, as one with the body,
Is affected the same and shares the body's feeling.
170   If your life's not dashed by the force of a quivering lance
Thrust home to split the bones and muscles open,
Still languor will follow, and the soothing swoon to the earth,
And as you lie on the ground your mind's a whirl
With willing and not willing to arise.
The soul must therefore be corporeal, since
Corporeal lances jab it and make it stagger.

What sorts of atoms constitute the soul
And where they come from, I'll explain to you.
To start, I say that the soul is super-subtle,
180   Composed of tiniest particles. Consider,
To prove the truth of my hypothesis,
That nothing we see can happen so swiftly as
The mind imagines and initiates.
Quicker therefore the mind will spur itself
Than anything we see before our eyes.
But since it's so quick to move, it must consist
Of the roundest and tiniest seeds, so that a small
Impulse can drive them forward into motion.
For water will ripple under the littlest impulse,
190   Made up of tiny and turnable tumbling figures.
By contrast, honey stands thick, sticks, won't budge,
Its juice more sluggish, motion more reluctant.
For all its wealth of atoms clogs and clings
Together; no surprise, as it's not made
Of atoms so smooth or subtle or round and rolling.
And a puff—half-held and light—can send your mound
Of poppyseed spilling and scattering down from the summit;
By contrast, a rock heap or cornstalk rick
Won't. And so the smaller the bodies and smoother,
200   The more a thing enjoys mobility.
But then whatever you come upon that's heavy,
Rough, sharp—to that extent these things stand stable.
Now, therefore, since we've found the soul to be

Exceedingly mobile, it must then consist
Of atoms awfully tiny and smooth and rolling.
This knowledge, my good reader, you will find
Useful and opportune in many matters.

This too will help establish the soul's nature,
How finely woven it is and what small space
Would hold it, if it could be gathered up: 210
That as soon as the imperturbable peace of Death
Lays hold of a man, and the mind and soul have departed,
You detect nothing dwindling from the body,
Nothing to see or to weigh. Death guarantees
All, save life-giving sense and the moist warm breath.
Thus all the soul must of necessity
Be made of the tiniest seeds, be interwoven
So fully with veins, flesh, muscle that when it leaves
The body deserted, the outer contour is
Preserved intact and not a jot the lighter.   220
It's like bouquets of wine that evanesce,
Or the sweet breath of perfume that floats away,
Or savors that abandon any body.
Still to the eyes these things look none the smaller
And not a grain of weight seems drawn away:
No wonder, for many and tiny seeds create
Aroma and savor, diffuse through the whole body.
So again and again I say the mind and spirit
Are made up of the tiniest, tiniest seeds,
For when they flee they steal no weight away.   230

But don't think that our souls are one and simple.
A sort of light breath leaves us when we die,
Breath mingled with heat, and heat in turn with air;
No warmth at all without a mix of air.
For since warmth's thinly woven, there must be
Many air-atoms moving in and through it.
So then we find three elements in the soul.
Yet, all told, will these three suffice to make

Sensation? The mind grants none of them the power
240   Of sense-bearing motion—still less the power of thought!

Therefore to these we're forced to add a fourth
Element—this one has no name at all,
There's nothing finer or more readily moving,
Nothing made up of smaller or smoother atoms—
And *this* first deals to the limbs the sense-bearing motions.
For its small atoms are the first to stir;
Then warmth and the invisible power of breath
Are moved, then air, then everything falls into motion,
The blood is shaken to life, all the flesh tingles
250   With every sensation, and last, the bones and marrow
Feel joy (if it's joy they feel!) or burning passion.
And it's no harmless matter if sickness seeps
Or pain cuts to the marrow; for such brawls
Will follow, that life will have no room, and the soul
Will fly, torn up through all the pores of the body.
But usually the skin's a sort of shield;
That gives us strength to keep our hold on life.

And now, how these are jumbled, in what manner
They are arranged and thrive, I wish to explain—
260   Checked though I am by our spare native tongue.
What I can briefly touch upon, I will.

The atoms race between and amongst each other,
Each element with its motion, so none can ever
Be sundered and set aside to do its work;
Instead they're like four forces in one body.
As in the flesh of any living creature
There are color and smell and taste, yet all of these
Add up to make the single finished body;
So warmth, air, and the invisible power of breath
270   Mingle and make one nature, along with that
Quickest of elements that moves the others,
Then sense-bearing motions in our flesh arise.

This fourth is subtle, hidden, penetrating;
There's not a thing more subtle in our bodies;
It is itself the soul of all the soul.
As mingled throughout the frame of the whole body
Are the hidden powers of the soul and spirit,
Since they are made of small and scanty atoms,
So too your nameless element, made of the smallest
Atoms, lies hidden and itself is as   280
The soul of the soul, and sweeps like a lord through the body.
In just the same way, breath and air and warmth
Must mingle in the limbs and blend their powers,
One more withdrawn than the next, or thrust to the fore,
So that a uniformity appears;
Lest warmth and breath and the power of air, of their own,
Sunder and separate and destroy sensation.

There's that warmth too in the soul, which it puts to use
When it seethes in rage and the dagger-eyes flash fire.
There's the chill breath, that chattering friend of fear,   290
Which rattles the limbs and sets the bones to shaking.
There's finally that state of the calm air
For the easy heart and countenance at peace.
More heat's in the forging of those whose hearts are keen
For anger, and come to a quick and raging boil;
The prime example is the truculent lion
Who bursts his ribs with the growl, whose big roar often
Can't make the anger of his heart subside.
But the soul of a deer is shaken in the breeze,
Quivers through all his flesh and stirs cold breath   300
To make the members tremble into motion.
While cows, by contrast, live in the calm air;
No smoking firebrand ever sears their hearts
With anger, spewing soot and darkness; they
Are not transfixed or frozen into fear;
Their place, between the deer and the savage lions.
So too with men. Take them and train them alike,
Make them polished and learned; there will still remain

The first and native traces of each soul.
310 You can't yank up these vices by the roots:
This man careers headfirst into fits of rage,
While that man's sooner pinched with a little fear,
And a third takes it all too placidly.
And in many other matters the natures of men—
The various habits that hound them—have to differ.
I cannot now expose the unseen cause,
Or find as many names as there are shapes
Of atoms, whence these differences arise.
But this I can affirm: so picayune
320 Are the traces of those natural faults which reason
Can't clear away, that nothing hinders us
From leading calm lives worthy of the gods.

And so the soul's enclosed by the whole body;
It is the body's guard and cause of health.
They twine together with common roots, nor can
One be plucked loose without destroying both.
As easily could you tear the aroma from
A lump of myrrh, and not destroy its essence,
As you could draw the soul and spirit from
330 The body, and not have it all dissolve.
For from the beginning they share the seat of life,
Their atoms so interwoven; nor, it's clear,
Can the body or the soul, all by itself,
Without the power of the other, feel sensation,
But from those common motions sprung from both,
Sensation is kindled and fanned high in our flesh.
Furthermore, body is never born alone,
Never grows alone or lasts long after death.
It's not like heated water that releases
340 Its heat as steam, while the water remains intact,
Not rent by the release—not so, I tell you,
Can the limbs, abandoned, suffer the soul's separation,
But rent to the core they die and rot away.
From the earliest age the mutual touchings of

The soul and body learn the vital motions,
Even while dwelling deep in the mother's womb,
So that divorce must sicken and kill both;
Then, since their wedlock brings them health, you should
See that their natures also must be wedded.

Next: if someone denies that the body feels,   350
But trusts that the soul diffused through the whole body
Catches that motion we've been calling "sense,"
Well, he just fights the plain facts and the truth.
For how can the body's feeling be explained
Unless the facts of that experience teach us?
"But the body lacks all sense when the soul's departed."
So? It loses what in life was never its own,
And loses much besides, when it's thrust from life.

And worse, to say the eyes can't see a thing,
But the soul peeps through them as through open doors,   360
That's hard to do when vision itself refutes it—
Sense ropes us and hustles us down to the eyes themselves—
When in fact we sometimes can't see dazzling things,
The light of vision fettered by the light.
That can't happen with doorways. If they're open
We can see through them—and they're not distressed.
Finally, if our eyes are really windows,
The soul's sight should be all the keener when
The eyes—those very windows—are removed!

Don't assume, in these matters, what the holy   370
Words of the great Democritus propose:
That atoms of body and soul, matched one by one,
Alternate thus and link themselves together.
For as the atoms of soul are so much smaller
Than those which constitute our flesh and body,
They yield in number too, so sparsely sown
Throughout our frames that you can vouch for this:
The intervals in the fabric of soul-atoms

Are no smaller than the smallest bodies which
380   Can stir up sense-bearing motions when they strike us.
For we can't always feel the cling of dust
Or of chalk kicked up and settling on our limbs,
Of the night fog or the slender filaments
Of a spider's net that tangle us on our way,
Or an old cobweb settling upon our heads,
Or a bird's feather or floating thistledown,
Which are so light they find it hard to fall,
Nor do we feel at once the passage of
Any and every animal, or each footfall
390   Upon our skin of midges and such things.
Much in us must be stirred up first before
The seeds of the soul, diffuse through all our frame,
Can feel that the body's atoms have been jolted,
And hammering, jarring in those nooks and crannies,
Can dash for each other and ram and ricochet.

And the soul's the haughtier lord of life than the spirit,
Keeping tight-barred the battlements of life.
Not for the fleetest moment can the spirit
Reside in us without the soul; it follows
400   Like a meek friend, and scatters to the wind,
Leaving the cold limbs to the chill of death.
But if the soul remains, then life remains.
Lop off a man's limbs all about and leave him
A mangled trunk, his members spiritless—
Yet he survives, and breathes the breath of life.
So a man cut off from spirit (in large part,
Not wholly) will yet hang on, will cling to life,
As in a torn-up eye if the pupil's still
Intact, the power of sight's alive and well,
410   So long as you don't rupture the whole eyeball,
Or cut the pupil off from the rest of the eye—
That too must bring about the sight's destruction.
But let the pupil, as tiny as it is,
Be eaten away—light falls, the darkness follows,

Though the rest of the ball is whole and full of light.
Such bonds have ever bound the soul and spirit.

Listen: to show you that a living thing's
Soul is as light as air, is born, must die,
I shall lay forth my hard-won labor of love
In verses worthy of your noble life.   420
Make sure you merge these two under one term,
So if I need a word and I teach that "spirit"
Is mortal, trust I've said that "soul" is too,
Since the two are conjoint in unity.

To begin, then. Since I've shown that the soul, so thin,
So light, is made of the tiniest atoms, much
Smaller than those which make up the clear water
Or clouds or smoke (for in mobility
It far excels and moves at the slightest touch,
Why not? When it's moved by the *shadows* of cloud and
        smoke,   430
The sort we see as we lie asleep and dream
Of the breath high over the altar, the drifting smoke—
Such things, no doubt, bring images to our minds),
And now too since you mark that when a jar
Is smashed the water spills away and scatters,
And since clouds and smoke will scatter to the winds,
Trust that the soul spills too and perishes
The sooner and melts the quicker into its atoms
Once it's been drawn away from the human body.
In fact if the body—the soul's jar—is smashed   440
Or so attenuated by loss of blood
It can no longer hold the soul inside,
What air do you think will hold the soul, when air
Is slighter than the body and less confining?

What's more, we see the body and mind are born
Together, and grow old and weak together.
For as babies toddle about with bodies soft

And tender, so their minds are wobbly too;
But when the trunk grows ripe with the strength of adulthood
450   The mind is better endowed, the reason stronger;
And last, when the might of Age has crushed the body
And the limbs have fallen, strengthless, beaten down,
Then the native talent hobbles, the tongue wanders,
Thoughts lapse—all powers fail at the same time.
It follows then that soul and spirit too
Dissolve like smoke into that sea of air,
For soul is born with the body and grows with it
And, as I've shown, cracks under the weight of age.

Here we should note that as the body itself
460   Is racked with violent sickness and sharp pain,
So the soul's seized with trouble and fear and sorrow.
It follows that the soul will share in Death.
For when the body is ill the soul will often
Wander; he loses his train of thought, he speaks
Astray, while drowsiness sinks him into a deep
And lasting coma—the head nods, the lids fall.
Where he is, he can hear no voices, recognize
No faces of those who surround him and call him back
To life, dewing their cheeks and lips with tears.
470   Admit, therefore, the soul dissolves—you must,
When the touch of sickness penetrates so far.
And pain and disease are both Death's artisans,
As we've learned so well from watching many die.
Yes, why is it then, when wine has stung a man
To the quick, his blood aglow with the heat it lends him,
The limbs, as a consequence, grow heavy; tripped, tangled,
Legs stagger, the thick speech lags, the thoughts are soused,
Eyes swim, and roaring and sobbing and brawls break out?
And all the rest of this sort of thing that follows,
480   Why is it? If not that the thrust and throttle of wine
Makes a habit of whipping the soul—and this, in the body!
But whatever can be throttled or trip-and-tangled,
Shows us that if a little rougher force

Finds a way in, it will die, its future lost.
Why, the sudden power of sickness before our eyes
Will sometimes strike a man like a thunderbolt—
He crumples, froths at the mouth, moans, thrashes, raves,
Stiffens and wrenches his muscles, writhes and gasps
Fitfully, arms and legs flung to exhaustion.
Sure enough: the violent sickness spreads through the body,   490
Disorders it, drives the soul out, frothing—as waves
Of the salt sea seethe and foam in the battering wind.
Groans are wrung out because the limbs are racked
With pain, but chiefly because the vocal-atoms
Are spit up in a mass on the lips outside,
On the road, you might say, where they're used to go.
The raving comes when the powers of soul and spirit
Are jarred and, as I've shown, wrenched one from the other,
Sundered and torn apart by the same poison.
Then, when the illness has broken, and the black bile   500
Returns to its dens in the corrupted body,
He staggers to his feet, a little queasy,
Returns to his senses and takes the soul back in.
So if these are thrown for a fall—while in the body—
And torn and bruised so badly by such diseases,
Why then do you think that in open air, alone,
They can survive the battering of the wind?
And since we see that the mind, like a sick body,
Can be brought round by medicine and made whole,
That's our prognosis: souls live but to die.   510
You've got to add parts or scramble the order around
Or lift a jot directly from the whole
If you would undertake to change the spirit
Or bend the nature of any living thing.
But what's immortal allows no shuffle of parts,
No jot to trickle in or be skimmed away,
For change that leads a thing beyond its limits
Is instant death to the original.
So if the soul falls ill or is brought round
By medicine, those are signs that it must die,   520

As I've taught. The facts charge on to block the path
Of false reasoning and head off its retreat,
Routing it with a double-pronged rebuttal.

Yes, often we watch a man die by degrees,
Member by member losing the sense of life:
The toes and the toenails first turn black; then the feet,
The legs die; then creeping through all the other limbs
The chilling pace of Death will make its way.
Since the soul is sundered here and doesn't come out
530   Unscathed or in one piece, it must be mortal.
What if you think the soul can draw itself
In from the limbs, contracting its parts into
One, and there stow away the members' senses?
And yet that place where so much soul's collected
Should be super-sensitive! That never happens;
Don't wonder if, as I've said, the soul is sliced
To ribbons and scattered away. Conclude: it dies.
Even if we concede what is flat wrong
And grant that the soul can shrink into one lump
540   As the dying, little by little, lose the light,
Still we must then admit the soul shall die;
Let it die scattered to the winds, grow dull, blank,
All its parts clumping up—it doesn't matter,
When the senses fail him everywhere more and more
And less and less of life remains behind.

And since the mind is just one part of a man,
Fixed in its proper place, like eyes and ears
And the other organs of sense that steer our lives,
And just as a hand or an eye or nose if severed
550   From us, can neither sense nor even be
(Rather resolves directly into rot),
So by itself the soul can't live—it needs
The body, the man who is its vessel, or
Whatever image you can find that joins
More intimately, for the body is bound fast.

Indeed, the living powers of body and soul
Join in their strength, delight in life together.
For without the body, alone, the soul cannot
Make motions that bring forth life; if stripped of soul
The body can't last long or use its senses.   560
Know then, as an eye that's plucked out roots and all
Sees nothing, torn away from the rest of the body,
So too, alone, the spirit can do nothing.
Of course—for mingled in the veins and flesh,
In bone and muscle, the atoms of soul are held
By the whole body and can't leap free in flight
Over great intervals; shut in, they stir
The sense-bearing motions, but cast by death from the body
Into the winds they cannot make those motions
Because they're not confined in the same way.   570
A body, a breathing thing—air would be *that*
If it could bind the soul and lock it into
Motions that stirred in the sinews once, in the body.
So again I argue, if the sheltering body
Is undone, and the breath of life is cast away,
The soul and sense—you must admit—dissolve;
Conjunction is the cause of life for both.

Well then, if the body can't outlast the departure
Of soul, but dwindles into the stench of rot,
Why hesitate to say that the soul is gathered   580
And seeps away like so much smoke spilled out,
That the body, now altered, crumbles into ruin
And falls apart, foundations jolted from
Their proper places, letting the soul seep out
Through all the limbs and winding passageways
And chinks in the wall? So many proofs should show you
That when it leaves the limbs the soul's been split,
Torn into pieces first in the very body
Before it slips out, floating in the wind.
Look, when the bonds of life within are shaken,   590
Though the body is whole, still something will stagger the spirit

So that it strains its moorings to the body;
And the face goes blank as at the final moment,
And all the limbs fall limp and drained of blood;
As when they cry, "He's fallen unconscious!" or
"He's fainted dead away!" and in the panic
They clutch at the last cable of his life.
For the faculties of the mind are cracked and crazed
And reel to the earth with the body—if the stroke

600   Were slightly heavier, they might be destroyed.
How, then, can you doubt that the soul, cast out of the body,
A weakling, in the open, its shields removed,
Not only can't outlast the ages, but
Can't for the tiniest moment stand intact?
Nor does a dying man sense that his soul
Takes its leave of the body safe and sound,
Making its way up the gullet into the throat;
Rather he feels it failing where it dwells
As he knows the other senses in their organs

610   Are slipping away. But if our souls were deathless
He wouldn't wail that he was slipping away—
No—going to shuck his old skin, like a snake!

Then, too, why aren't mind and judgment born
In the head alone or the feet or the hands, but cleave
In all of us to one sure dwelling place?
It must be, every human part is given
A certain place to be born and to endure,
Partitioned among all the various parts,
Not wrong-end-up or cart-before-the-horse!

620   For effect follows cause reliably;
We don't get fire from rivers or frost from flame.

Besides, if the soul by nature is immortal,
And can sense although it's severed from our body,
We'd better, I think, equip it with all five senses.
How else can we imagine for ourselves
That the souls stroll about in the underworld?

Painters and poets have for generations
So introduced those souls, complete with senses.
But separate hands for the soul cannot exist,
Or nose and eyes, or separate ears and tongue —   630
Then by themselves these souls can't feel — or be.

And since we feel that the sense of life belongs
To all the body, and all is filled with soul,
If a sudden stroke should chop us clean in two,
Each part divided wholly from the other,
Surely the force of the soul would be divided
And, severed, along with the body be destroyed.
But whatever can be sliced to fall in halves
Surely denies that it can never die.
Men tell of sickle-wheeled chariots that in a flash   640
Lopped members off and gleamed in a welter of slaughter,
And while the lopped limb lay on the ground and twitched,
The soul of the man himself, alive and strong,
Could feel no pain, so swift was the attack,
His mind so zealously devout to fight;
He seeks with what's left of his body the battle and slaughter,
Nor grasps that his left arm and shield are lost,
Dragged off by the horses and wheels and hungering sickles,
Or his right is fallen, as he mounts to charge.
Another tries to rise on a missing leg   650
As his dying toes lie scrabbling in the dust.
And a head lopped off from a glowing, living trunk
Preserves its face alive, eyes open, till
It renders up the remnants of its soul.
Or take a serpent — the flicking tongue, the tail
That menaces, body arched to strike; if you please,
Chop its trunk with an axe into many parts;
You'll see those separate hacked-off snake parts writhe
From the sudden wound and spatter the earth with gore,
And the head of the snake will twist about and try   660
To strike at the tail, or gnaw the searing wound.
Say all the soul's in each of the little parts?

But from that line of reasoning this would follow:
One living thing possesses many souls.
Therefore what once was single is now divided
Along with the body, and therefore both must die,
For into many parts they're cut alike.

Besides, if the soul by nature stands immortal
And slips into the body right at birth,
670   Why can't we recall as well the times gone by,
Preserving traces of our former lives?
But if the spirit's power is so altered
That all its hold upon past actions fails,
Well, that, I think, strays not too far from Death.
Therefore you must confess: what once existed
Has died; what now exists was just now formed.
Moreover, if the living power of soul
Is first installed when the body is complete
And we are born and come to the shores of life,
680   It's hardly fitting that it grow together
Along with the members, in the very blood;
Instead it ought to live cooped up, alone,
And somehow flood the body with sensation.
So again I say it: never think the soul
Is free from birth, or from the law of death.
For if it were slipped in from without, it couldn't
Fasten itself to us so thoroughly
(The reverse causes that—the facts are plain,
For soul is so enmeshed with veins, flesh, muscle,
690   And bone, that even the teeth share in sensation,
As the toothache shows and the bracing of ice water
And the harsh crunch of a stone in a loaf of bread),
Nor, so sewn up with the body as it is,
Could it depart intact and loose itself
Safely from all the bones and joints and muscles.
But should you think that, slipped in from without,
The soul seeps through our members, all the more—
So blended with the body—shall it perish.

Whatever seeps will dwindle; therefore death.
It would be strained through all the pores of the body.   700
As food when sent to all the limbs and members
Dies, and shores up another from itself,
So the spirit even if it's whole and new
When it enters the body at birth, must still break down
As all its particles are being sifted
Into the limbs, to make up a new spirit,
This one, the lord of our bodies now, born from
That first which died, dealt out to every joint.
Therefore the soul is not without its day
Of birth, nor shall it lack its funeral.   710

And are there or aren't there soul-seeds left behind
In a lifeless body? If some are lodged inside
It's hardly just to think the soul immortal,
For it retreats, diminished of its parts.
But if its limbs are sound when it escapes,
Not one of them remaining in the body,
Out of what atoms do corpses, the guts gone rancid,
Sigh forth their worms? How can such an army of creatures,
Boneless and bloodless, swell like a tide through the members?
Maybe the souls are slipped from without into   720
The maggots, a soul for each maggot body? If
You think so, you haven't reckoned on why so many
Thousands of souls converge where one retreats!
This research problem it would seem to pose:
Whether, see, all the seeds of the maggot souls
Arrive and build themselves their homes-to-be,
Or are slipped into maggot bodies ready-made.
And you can't prop things up by telling why
They'd bother to do such work. They've got no bodies!
They'd flutter free of hunger and cold and illness!   730
These are the plagues that weary the body—and soul,
Its neighbor, catches many of its evils.
Ah, but let's say they make that awfully useful
Body they enter! How? No way appears.

Thus souls do not make bodies for themselves.
And they don't slip into finished bodies either,
For that will not allow the subtlest weave
Of body and soul, the touch that makes sensation.

Yes, why does violence stalk the sullen brood
740   Of lions? Or fraud, the fox? And the deer's forefathers
Bequeath them their flight and their family limbs that tremble,
And so on and so forth? Why are they all born
With traits and talents proper to each kind,
If not that in accordance with the breed
One sort of soul develops with each body?
But if souls never died and could swap bodies,
All creatures would become a welter of cross-traits:
Noble Hyrcanian hounds would scoot away
From the charge of the antlered stag; trembling in flight
750   The hawk would flee the swooping of the dove;
Men would be foolish and fierce creatures wise.
It's all illogic when they say the soul
Is deathless, only changed by the change of body.
What alters must dissolve. Conclude: it dies.
Its parts are shuffled, straying out of order;
Hence in the members it must also dwindle
And at last die together with the body.
Now if they say that human souls will always
Pass into human bodies, let me ask:
760   Why does that wise soul make a foolish boy?
Why isn't the foal as cunning as the stallion?
Sure, they'll wriggle out, "The mind in a weakling body
Becomes a weakling too." Well then, they must
Admit that the soul dies, since it's so changed
It loses all its prior life and sense.
How can the mind along with the body too
Grow firm and attain that longed-for flower, adulthood,
Unless it was its consort from the first?
And why would it want to leave its wasted limbs?
770   Afraid to be trapped inside a rotting body?

Or its house will cave in, heavy with old age?
These pose no danger—to a deathless thing.

And then, what a laugh! to think that souls stand waiting
When beasts are born or during the rites of Venus,
Innumerable immortals taking numbers
For mortal limbs, crowding, elbowing to see
Who'll be the first to slip himself in or the strongest—
Oh, maybe all the souls are bound by contract:
Whoever swoops in first to be installed
Is first; no scuffling, and no arguments!   780

There are no trees in the sky, in the ocean plains
No clouds; no fish can live in the fields, no blood
Can dwell in a wooden stock, no sap in stone.
Each thing has one sure place to grow and dwell.
Soul cannot spring alone without the body,
Nor, far away from flesh and blood, survive.
For if it could, far sooner might that soul
Dwell in the head or the shoulders or the heels
And be born into whatever part you like—
So long as it stays in the same man, the same "jar."   790
But since there's a certain place inside our bodies
For the spirit, set apart, to dwell and grow,
All the more reason why you must deny
That it can be born or endure outside the body.
Admit then, when the body passes, so
The soul must pass, torn up throughout the body.
Really, to yoke what's mortal to the eternal,
Thinking they can agree and work as one,
Is silliness. For what can be reckoned more
Disjoint, discrepant, dissonant, than that   800
What's mortal, bound with the lasting and immortal,
Should bear up under the storm-whipped surge of life?

More proof: whatever's everlasting must
Either (solid of matter) spit back the punches,

Not suffering anything to pierce and split
Its tight-packed parts within (so durable are
Atoms, whose nature I have shown above),
Or persevere through all eternity
Not struck by a single blow (as empty space
810   Remains unacting and untouchable),
Or last because no wealth of space surrounds it
Where its loosening parts might break away and scatter
(As the everlasting All-in-All), for there
Is no Beyond to fly to, or atoms which
Could loosen it and destroy it with their pounding.
Should the soul be thought immortal all the more
In that it's fortified by living things,
Because the foes of health never invade it
Or the invaders for some reason yield,
820   Repulsed before we can feel what harm they'd do . . .

Besides the fact that the soul falls sick with the body,
A thought of things to come will strike the soul
And starve it hollow, harass it with worry and fear,
While the remorse for old sins gnaws away;
Add the mind's own madness and forgetfulness;
Add that it drowns in the black depths of coma.

Death, then, is nothing to us, no concern,
Once we grant that the soul will also die.
Just as we felt no pain in ages past
830   When the Carthaginians swarmed to the attack
And under the sky's high shores the whole world shook,
Struck by the shocks of war and alarm and riot,
All mankind over land and ocean in
The balance, whether to fall to the rule of either—
So too, when we no longer are, when our
Union of body and soul is put asunder,
Hardly shall anything then, when we are not,
Happen to us at all and stir the senses,
Not if earth were embroiled with the sea and the sea with heaven!

And even if the soul, ripped from the body,   840
Retained the power to feel, that still would be
Nothing to us, whose beings have been fashioned
By one fit marriage of one body and soul.
And if the Ages should collect our matter
After we die and return our present forms,
Lending us once again the light of life,
Even that won't mean anything to us,
Once our continuation has been snapped.
Who we once were can't touch us now at all;
Nor are we gripped with care for who we'll be.   850
When you reflect on the unmeasured span
Of ages past, how many and various were
The motions of matter, you may rest assured
That the seeds at times were placed in the same order
As these seeds which compose us now; a fact
That the mind can't retain in memory.
There's been a halt—hiatus—in our lives,
And all the motions of sense have gone astray.
Thus if your future is misery and sickness
You've got to exist in that same future time   860
For the ill to catch you. But since death clears the deck,
Forbidding that would-be sufferer to exist,
Nothing at all have we to fear from death;
He who cannot exist cannot feel pain,
Or care if he's never born again, once death
That does not die has seized his dying life.

Now if you happen to see someone resent
That after death he'll be put down to stink
Or be picked apart by beasts or burnt on the pyre,
You'll know that he doesn't ring true, that something hidden   870
Rankles his heart—no matter how often he says
He trusts that there's no feeling after death.
He doesn't grant the premise or conclusion,
Can't pluck himself out of life by the roots and chuck it;
He posits, unknowing, a bit of himself left over.

For when anyone living puts it that his body,
Dead, will be laced by the birds and the wild beasts,
It's himself he pities! He can't cut himself free
From the castoff body—no, he dreams it's him,
880 Stands by, infects it with his own sensation.
So he resents that he was formed to die;
Can't see that when he dies there'll be no other
Him living to moan that he's bereft of him,
Weeping because he's lying scorched or mangled.
If in death it's bad to be treated to wild beasts
And the jaws that rip, I don't see why it's not
Bitter to lie there roasting in brilliant flames
Or to smother in balm and honey or grow stiff
With cold as you lie on your ice-hard bed of stone,
890 Or be squashed flat by the earth's crushing weight.

"Now—now—no happy home, no darling wife
Will greet you, no sweet children race to steal
Kisses, and touch your heart with quiet joy.
You'll never rule the roost or watch your business
Flourish. From you, poor boy, poor boy," they say,
"One bad day's stolen all life has to win."
"Not one desire for any of these things,"
They don't add, "will beset you anymore."
If they could see *that,* and speak accordingly,
900 Their souls would slip the tight strong clench of fear.

"Sure, you enjoy the sleep of death—you're free
Of all the bitter pains that were to come.
But we stand shuddering by your pyre of ash,
Insatiably lamenting; nevermore
Shall this great grief be lifted from our hearts."
Better ask this fellow: what's so very bitter
If the whole business comes to sleep and quiet?
Why waste away with his everlasting tears?

When men lie back and shade their eyes with garland
910 And tip a few too many, they love to utter

Such heartfelt stuff, "Ah, we only go round once, boys!
Soon over the hill—and there's no turning back!"
As if the worst of death were really this,
That the poor souls would be so dry they'd parch
With thirst, or that some other want would catch them!
But no one searches for himself or life
When body and mind together rest in sleep.
For all we'd care, that sleep could be eternal;
No longing for our waking selves would move us.
Yet when we sleep our atoms never stray   920
Far from the sense-bearing motions—for a man
Can snatch himself from bed and gather his wits.
Much less, then, should we be concerned with death,
Less than the *nothing* that we think of sleep!
For greater is the whirl and scatter of atoms
Which follows death; no one will wake and rise
Once the cold halt in life has caught him up.

Yes, if Nature herself should suddenly raise her voice
Against one of us, and rebuke him in this way,
"What's the matter, mortal, with you, that you coddle yourself   930
With all this sorrow? Why moan and wail at death?
If your life's been happy and blessed, and all those blessings
Haven't been poured into a leaky pot
To spill away, with nothing left to give thanks for,
Why not, as a man who's feasted full of life,
Retire contented—fool!—and rest in peace?
But if all the blessings squandered on you are gone
And life's so hateful, why add still more? What use?
They'll all turn sour again and come to nothing!
Why don't you strive instead to end your life?   940
For what else can I find or make to please you?
There's nothing—all things always stay the same.
If your body's not shriveled with years and your arms and legs
Still don't hang nerveless, well, things stay the same,
The same, should you go and outlast generations,
Just more of the same, if you never happen to die—"
What shall we say in defense, if not that Nature's

Complaint is just and her indictment true?
And if some high and mighty older man
950 Should whimper, poor fellow, too sadly that he must go,
Let her cry the louder and lash out in reproof!
"Get your sobs out of here, scoundrel, and quit your whining!
You mope—though you've rifled all life has to win;
But since you scorn what's here and crave what's not,
Your life—unfinished, thankless—slips away,
And so you're shocked that Death is waiting now
Before you're stuffed and ready to leave the table.
Give it up, old man, it doesn't become your years.
Come, be content! Give way to your heirs! You must."
960 Just, would her charge be! Just, her rebuke, her outcry!
The old, shoved out, must always cede to the new,
One thing restores another; it must be.
And no one's flung to the pit or the pains of Hell.
We need those atoms for our progeny
Who, though they live life full, shall follow us.
Before you came, men died—and they will die.
One thing gives rise to another, incessantly;
Life's given to no one outright; all must borrow.
Reflect how the span of the endless ancient past
970 Before our births means nothing at all to us.
Here Nature has provided us a mirror
Of the time to come when we at last have died.
Is there horror in the prospect? Any sorrow?
Isn't it freer from care than the sweetest sleep?

But the things that are said to exist in the depths of Hell
Are all, to no surprise, part of our lives.
No fairy-tale Tantalus, frozen in empty fear,
Pathetically shudders under a teetering stone;
Rather here, in life, an empty fear of the gods
980 Looms, and it's chance that brings the fall we dread.
No birds delve into a Tityus flat in Hell
Or prick for a morsel left in that huge liver
Throughout time everlasting—really now!

Let him stretch out, if you like, immense in bulk,
His splayed limbs spanning not nine acres merely
But the whole globe; nevertheless, he'd not
Be able to suffer everlasting pain
Or offer the food of his body forever and ever.
Our Tityus is here—a man laid flat by love,
Whom the birds peck apart—that's gnawing worry   990
Or other cares that tear us with desire.
In life we've Sisyphus too, before our eyes,
Drunk with campaigning for the rods of power,
And always the people send him home to sulk.
To canvass for power—unattainable, useless—
And ever to sweat and suffer hardship for it,
That's to push and push up a mountain a heavily-leaning
Boulder—which tumbles right back down from the summit
Anyhow, bouncing and bounding down to the plain.
Then to feed forever your ingrate heart, to take   1000
Your fill of the good things, stuffed but still not full
(As the returning seasons in their rounds
Bring us fresh life and harvest and delight,
The fruits of life that never seem to fill us)
That's the old tale, I think, of the ripe young virgins
Gathering water in a leaky pot
That couldn't be filled no matter what they did.
And Cerberus and the Furies, see, and the darkness,
Tartarus belching blasts from his horrible maw,
Really, they can't exist and never have!   1010
But in life infamous fear of punishment for
Infamous crimes is how we pay for evil.
Prison, and being flung from the frightful Rock,
Flogging and chopping, racking, tarring, torching,
Take these away—still the man who knows his sin
Anticipates, and whips himself hot with terror,
And never sees where misery can have
Its terminus, and punishments their limit;
He fears they may grow heavier still in death.
This life of fools, then, *this* is the true Hell.   1020

Sometimes you should remind yourself, "For shame!
The good king Ancus lost the light of day
And he was a far better man than you.
And many other kings and potentates
Have fallen, once commanders of great nations.
Even that ruler who over the ocean once
Laid down a road for legions to bridge the deep,
Taught them to go over the salt gulfs on foot,
Who scorned with a trample of hooves the hissing sea,
1030   Robbed of light, from a dying body poured his soul.
And Scipio, the battle-lightning, the terror of Carthage,
Gave his bones to the earth like the meanest slave.
Include discoverers of truth and beauty,
Include the poets—among whom solely-sceptered
Homer sleeps just as soundly as the rest.
And when ripe age had warned Democritus
That the motions of his memory were fading,
He accosted Death and offered his own head.
Even Epicurus died, his light of life
1040   Run to the finish; the mind who bested all,
Who doused their light as the sunrise dims the stars.
Who are *you* to be reluctant about dying?
You with your half-dead life still kicking about!
You fritter most of your last years asleep,
You snore when you're awake, and you're always dreaming,
Carrying around a mind that's touchy, panicky,
But you can't tell what's the everlasting trouble,
You're so groggy and worried and jostled on all sides,
And you wander and drift along you don't know where."

1050   If, when men sense a weight upon their minds,
A trouble deep within that wearies them,
They could but recognize the source, and know
Why such huge misery masses in the heart,
They'd never lead their lives as we see now—
As men who never know what they want, who move
From place to place to lay their burden down.

Out of his mansion he's got to go, that fool,
Home bores him to death, and yet he turns right back,
Finding that things are just as dull outside.
Swift, to the villa he spurs his galloping ponies,   1060
Bringing relief—you'd think—to a house afire.
But soon as he touches the villa door, he yawns,
Tries to forget, falls heavily asleep,
Or hurries out to see the town again.
We flee ourselves, whom we can never flee.
Against our will the self we hate clings tight
For we are sick and do not grasp the cause.
If he could see it, he might leave his worries
And strive to understand the nature of things,
For not an hour but all eternity   1070
Is here at issue: what the state will be
Of the time left for each man after death.

What vicious yearning for life, then, makes us hurry
In such a panic, attacked by doubts and dangers?
This much is sure: the end of life awaits us,
The summons must be answered; we must die.
As it is, we lurch in the same ruts; no new pleasure
Is forged for us from drawing out our lives.
Whatever we lack, we want, we think it excels
All else, but when we've grabbed it something new   1080
We thirst for, always panting after life.
Yet we don't know what fortune the years will bring,
What luck we'll have, and what our end will be.
And long life won't allow us to pluck out
One moment from our span beyond the grave
That we might spend a shorter time in death.
Survive this generation and the next—
Nevertheless eternal death awaits,
Nor will the man who died with the sun today
Be nonexistent for less time than he   1090
Who fell last month—or centuries ago.

BOOK FOUR

The trackless haunts of the Muses I explore,
Where no man's foot has trod. What joy to drink
Deep from those pristine fountains! What joy to pluck
New flowers, to weave a garland for my temples
Which the Muses have never veiled anyone with before!
Let the fame be mine, for I teach great things, stride forth
To free the soul from the stranglehold of religion;
Also, I sing dark matters into the light,
Spicing all with the grace of poetry.
10   I have good reason too for doing this:
When doctors try to coax children to take
Foul wormwood, first they brush the rim of the cups
All round with the sweet and golden juice of honey,
To fool their short-sighted years, fool them all the way
To the lips, so they drink down those bitter drops
Of wormwood, and are tricked but not betrayed,
For all the sooner is their health restored.
So I now, since this doctrine seems so harsh
To many who have never sampled it,
20   Since the mob shrinks back in horror—I have desired
To reveal our doctrine in sweet-throated song,
Touching it with the honey of the Muses,
That I might hold your mind by this device
To attend to my verse, until you grasp the entire
Nature of things, and see its usefulness.

Because I've shown you what the soul is like,
What makes it thrive united with the body,

How, torn apart, it melts into first-atoms,
Now I shall show you—and the point is crucial—
That ghosts of things, which we call "semblances,"   30
Exist, which like light films shucked from a surface
Flutter this way and that through the air. These films will strike
Our minds when we're awake, but in our dreams
They terrify, as we behold the bizarre shapes
And semblances of those who lack the light,
Who rouse us with a shudder when we lie limp
In sleep—so let's not think that shades from Hell
Have flown the coop and flutter among the living,
Or that there's anything left of us after death,
When soul and body are destroyed together,   40
Sundered, resolved into their first-beginnings.
So, I say, thinnest images and forms
Peel away from the utmost skin of things.
A dullard could understand this from what follows.

Since I've taught of the first fabric of all things,
How of their own the atoms of various shapes
Fly in a whirlwind, whipped by ceaseless motion,
And how all things can be created from them,
Now I shall show you—and the point is crucial—
That what we call the "semblances of things"   50
Exist; the "films" or "peels," as you might say,
Since all these wandering images still bear
The likeness of the things from which they're shed.

To start, since many bodies in plain sight
Shed substances, some fleeting and diffuse
(As oakwood gives off smoke, or as fires heat),
Some stitched more closely and tightly (as sometimes crickets
Slough off their slender tunics in the summer,
Or calves just coming out of the womb will shed
The cauls that covered them, and the slippery serpent   60
Strips his skin on the thorns—for we often see
Briars festooned with snake hides dangling there),

Since that's the case, a slender image also
Must be shed from the surfaces of things.
These specters sooner fall away from things
Than the slight skin or smoke, and it's no wonder,
Since first of all on objects' surfaces
Lie many tiny bodies that can be
Cast forth in their former pattern and preserve
70   The object's shape—the swifter, since they're placed
In the front rank, too few to tangle badly.
And we can surely see that many things
Pour out their wealth, not only from deep in the core,
But from the surface too; for instance, color—
As awnings, saffron-yellow or iron-blue
Or russet, stretched taut over wide theaters,
Ripple above the beams and the poles and the people.
Beneath from the bleachers down to the boxes and all
The stage itself and the senators in their regalia,
80   They dye it all and make it ripple in color.
And the closer the walls are huddled around the theater,
Catching the sunshine, the more will all within
Laugh in a wash of colorful delight.
So just as canvas draperies from their surface
Send color, things in general must send slender
Images—slung from the surface in both cases.
Thus certain husks or shells of things exist,
Subtle as filaments, fluttering everywhere,
So thin that you can't see them one by one.
90   What's more, all smoke and odor and vapor and
Other such things gush out in a confusion
Since as they work their way from deep inside
They're grated by the winding passages;
There are no fine straight roads for them to march.
But when a delicate film of surface color
Is released, there's nothing in the way to rend it,
Since it stands ready-placed in the front rank.

Next: in mirrors and glassy pools and shiny things
Whatever semblances appear to us

Must, since they give the likenesses of things,   100
Consist of images those things transmit.
Thus slender forms of things, their replicas,
Exist; although no one can make them out
One at a time, yet hosts of them, ever assailing,
Repulsed, fling what we see in the flat of the mirror;
They clearly have no other way to be
Preserved, to give us likenesses so true.

Listen, and learn how slender the images are.
For starters, since the first-beginnings lie
So far below our senses, so much smaller   110
Than the smallest thing the eye begins to see,
Learn—for this will bolster my point—in few
How subtle is the texture of all things.

First, there are animals so tiny, if
You split them in thirds they'd be invisible.
What do you think a bit of their innards is like?
The ball of the heart or the eyes? The limbs? The bones?
How tiny they are! But what of the atoms then
Which of necessity compose their souls?
Isn't it clear how subtle and small they'll be?   120
And consider things that give off pungent odors,
Like the heal-all, the evil-smelling absinthe,
Southernwood thick and nasty, foul centaur-weed,
One of which should you happen ever so lightly . . .
Why not admit that hosts of images wander
Everywhere, impotent, insensible?

Don't think that only images released
From actual things go wandering about;
For there are some spontaneously born,
Produced alone in the lower heavens, in the air.   130
These, shaped in many ways, are carried high;
Their shapes melt one to another and never cease,
Turning to any sort of contour as
Easily as the clouds in the deep blue sky

Gather, and mar the view of the heavens at peace,
Caressing the air as they drift; sometimes it seems
The forms of Giants are soaring and trailing broad shadows,
And now it's all huge mountains or gouged-out boulders
Sweeping in succession beneath the sun,
140   Then some monster pulls and drags more clouds along.

Now just how swiftly and easily they're begotten,
Flowing from things forever and passing away . . .

For things are always firing off a stream
Of surface atoms. When they reach something else
They pass as through a veil; but if they hit
Rough stones or wood, well, there the atom-stream is
Split—and there's no more image to be sent.
But if their obstacle is dense and shiny,
As mirrors especially are, these things don't happen,
150   For then they can neither pass as through a veil
Or be cut—the smoothness keeps their health in mind.
That's why the semblances flood back upon us.
No matter when or how quickly or what thing
You place before a mirror, the image appears;
That shows you, surfaces shed an endless stream
Of the slenderest cloth of things and slenderest shapes.
So in a flash there are many images born
And it's correct to say their rise is quick!
And as the sun in a moment must send forth
160   Many rays of light that fill and fill the world,
So semblances must of necessity
Also be sent from things in a single instant,
Many, in many ways, in every direction,
Since wherever we slant the mirror everything in it
Replies with all the objects' forms and colors.
Besides, when the skies are fine and stream with light,
Suddenly they can roil with a storm so filthy
You'd think the gloom of Hell was gushing out
And flooding the vast caverns of the sky;

And everywhere you look specters of Fear   170
Surge in the grim cloud-night to hang above us.
What tiny part of these are semblances
Sent by the clouds, one can't begin to say.

Listen: how swiftly semblances are swept,
What ease of motion they're endowed with as
They swim through the air and wear away an hour
Crossing a vast gulf; where they're inclined to turn,
I'll give you in verses, eloquent and few,
Like the swift but lovelier song of the swan, and not
The honk of a mob of storks in the south wind.   180

First off, things made of light and tiny bodies
Most often appear to be the speediest.
Of this sort are the warmth and the light of the sun
Made up of tiny first-beginnings which
Are hammered along, as it were, through the gulf of the sky,
Thrust on by the blows to follow and never pausing.
Supplies are there in an instant, light for light,
Lashed on in a sort of long train, dazzle and dazzle.
So of necessity semblances likewise
Can speed across an inexpressible space   190
In a single moment. First, though the force is tiny,
There's something far behind that spurs them on;
Then too, they're whisked along as light as wings;
Last, they're sent off so sheer and finely woven
They can pierce easily into anything,
And thus, if you will, they pour through the gulf of space.

Besides, if you grant that substances deep within
Are sent to the world outside, like the light and warmth
Of the sun—they're seen in an instant as day breaks
Streaming throughout the space of all the heavens,   200
On the wing over lands and seas and flooding the sky—
What then of the atoms ready in the front rank,
When they're flung forth and nothing's there to delay them?

Why, don't you see, they'll go farther and more swiftly
And speed across the same space multiplied
In the time the light of the sun will fill the sky?
This, notably, will give you a good look
Into how swiftly semblances are driven:
Place a tray of glittering water beneath the sky;
210 At once the quiet stars in the spangled pool
Reflect the radiance of their world above.
Then do you see how the image, in an instant,
Sails from the shores of heaven to the shores of earth?
So again I say, you must admit there are
Bodies released that strike the eyes and the eyesight.

From certain things there are odors ever streaming,
As chill from brooks, or warmth from the sun, or spray
From the surf at the shore, that eater-away of stone;
Sounds flutter through the air and never rest;
220 And, last, our tongues are touched by the salt taste
When we take a turn by the sea, and when we watch
The watering-down of wormwood, we're touched by the bitters.
To that extent do such things stream away
From other things and scatter everywhere.
They're never given a pause or a rest from flowing,
For our sensation is continual—
All may be seen, smelled, heard at any time.

What's more, since when you handle a shape in the dark
You recognize that it's the very same
230 You see in the clear bright light, it must be true
That sight and touch are moved by the same cause.
Take a cube and test it in the dark: the shape
Moves our sensation. Then, in the light, what cubic
Thing could accost our sight, if not its image?
In images, therefore, lies the cause of vision;
Without them nothing can be seen at all.

Now what I call the "semblances of things"
Are scattered everywhere, flung in every direction.

But since it's only through our eyes we see,
The result is that wherever we turn our sight   240
All things—their shapes and colors—strike us squarely.
And the image causes us to see and judge
How far away from us an object is.
When it's sent off, at once it thrusts and drives
All the air that lies between it and our eyes;
And the air glides gently over our vision and washes
The pupils, so to speak, and passes by.
By this, we see how far an object is:
The greater the stream of air it stirs before it
And the longer the breeze that washes over our eyes,   250
The more remote the object will appear.
These films, of course, whiz by so fast that we
At once see what the thing is and how far.

Along these lines it's not a bit surprising
Why semblances that strike our vision can't
Be seen alone, though we see the things themselves.
Think of the wind when it whips up little by little,
Or when the nip of the chill seeps in—we can't
Feel single particles of wind or cold
But rather all in one as they collide   260
Against our body, like a thing that strikes us
To let us sense *its* body there, outside.
Or when we stub our toe on a stone, we touch
The surface and outer color, and yet we can't
Feel those by touching. What we feel instead
Is the deep hardness at its stony core.

Listen, and learn why images appear
Way back in the depths of the mirror, far removed.
It's like when doors are open and you can see
Across the room and through to the outside   270
To look at many things beyond your walls
(The airstream for these sights is twice as long;
First it's the air on your side of the posts,
Then follows your sight of the doorway, right and left,

And last, the light outside sweeps over your eyes
With that far air and the objects past the door),
So too when the face of the mirror itself is first
Flung to our sight, it drives and thrusts before it
Whatever air's between it and our eyes,
280   Thus causing us to sense the air before
We see the mirror. But when we look inside
That mirror, at once our image, flung from us
Into the glass, returns, revisits our eyes,
Rolling before it a second stream of air
Which we see before we see our own reflections
That seem as deep in the mirror as we are far.
So again I say, there's hardly a cause for wonder . . .

   . . . Sight of those given back from the level mirror,
For both are formed from double streams of air.
290   Now here's the reason why our right sides seem
To be on our left when we see them in a mirror:
When the image rushes against the flat of the mirror
It doesn't just turn about untouched, but straight
Backwards it's dashed—just as a moist clay mask,
If you should mash it against a post or beam,
Preserves the proper shape it had in front
By pushing it out and squeezing it back behind.
That's how it happens that your right eye is
Now on the left, and the left's on the right in turn.

300   And when an image is passed from mirror to mirror
You may get as many as five or six reflections.
For whatever's stashed in the back rooms of a house,
No matter how far, no matter how crooked the path,
Can be teased out through a zigzag access of
A series of mirrors, and appear anywhere.
So fully do images shine from mirror to mirror;
When the left's passed along, it's back to the right,
And back again reverses and returns.
Now a mirror whose small side-panels or side-curves

Are turned at the same angle as our flanks   310
Sends back the right on the right, and this is why:
Either the image is shunted from mirror to mirror
And flies to us twice reflected, or it's not been
Bounced back at all, but twirls as the curve of the mirror
Teaches it how to turn about toward us.
Further, you think our images stride with us,
Step as we step, and copy all we do,
Because as you move aside from one part of the mirror
At once no image can return from there,
Since Nature forces all rebounding things   320
To carom and ricochet at equal angles.

The eyes shun things that dazzle, they flee the light.
The sun blinds if you hold your stare, because
Its power is great, and from the pure deep sky
It sweeps along an avalanche of air
And batters the eyes and sends their structure reeling.
Furthermore, any piercing brilliant light
Will sear the eyes, for it's got seeds of fire
That dart into the eyes and cause them pain.
And a jaundiced man sees all things greenish yellow   330
Since a lot of jaundice-seeds stream from his body
And strike the images in their way; besides
Many seeds of the sickness mingle in the eyes,
Touching and tainting all with yellow pallor.

From a dark place we can see things in the light;
Here's why. Though the near air, gloomy and dark, is first
To enter and seize our open eyes, at once
There follows a clear and brilliant stream of air.
This, so to speak, burns off the smoke and scatters
The shadows of that air. For its atoms are   340
Far smaller and move more swiftly and pack more power.
And once they've cleared the way—which the dark air
Had held in blockade—and filled our eyes with light,
Immediately the semblances of things

Placed in the light will follow, and strike our vision.
By contrast, we can't do that from the light
Into the dark. The smoke-thick stream of air
Follows the light and clogs up all the pores,
Blocking the way to the eyes; no images,
350   Though hurled in force, can make their way within.

When we see square city towers from far away
They often appear to be rounded; it's because
Any angle at a distance will look blunt,
Or, better, it can't be seen, its image dies,
Can't follow through on the punch to strike our sight,
For since it's carried along through so much air,
Air dulls it and makes it stagger with all its joltings.
Each angle eludes our senses in this way,
Rounding the rock towers off as if turned on a lathe—
360   Not like what's truly round and seen nearby
But like a roundish shadow or far resemblance.

Our shadows seem to move with us in the sun,
To follow our traces, copy all we do—
That's if you think the air, deprived of light,
Can stride and follow the motions and acts of men,
For what we're used to calling "shadow" can't
Be anything but the dead air, robbed of light.
Areas on the ground in definite sequence
Are robbed of sunlight as we stroll along
370   And stand in its way, but when we leave they fill
With light, and that of course is why what was
The shadow of our body follows us.
Ever-new rays of the sun come pouring down
And the old perish—like wool drawn into the fire!
It's easy, then, for the earth to be stripped of light
And then to be filled and wash away the shadows.
But still we won't concede the eyes are fooled.
Their job's to note wherever there may be light
Or shadow. Whether the light's the same or not,

Or the shadow here is the same that crosses there,   380
Or if it's all as I've just said above,
That's what the reason must at last discern—
Eyes cannot come to know the nature of things.
Pin the blame on your weak mind, not your eyes!

We're swept along on a ship—but seem to stand,
While ships at anchor all go passing by.
As we let fly the sail and shave the coast
The fields and mountains seem to flee astern.
And the constellations set in the vault of the sky
Look still, at rest, yet are all in tireless motion,   390
Rising to see their distant fall, when they
Have measured all the sky with their pure light.
So too the sun and moon seem to stand still,
And yet the simple facts show that they move.
Far mountains rising out of the whelm of the sea,
Through which a fleet might steer a wide free passage,
Seem to be joined to form one single island.
And the halls spin and the posts whirl round and round—
So real it all seems to boys when they themselves
Stop spinning, they can hardly think the roof's   400
Not tipping over to tumble down upon them!
And when Nature begins to raise high over the hills
The brilliant rose of the dawn with its trembling fire,
You'd think the sun was tussling with those hills,
Brushing against them with its very flames—
Hills that can't be two thousand flights of an arrow,
Can't be five hundred javelin-flings from us,
And from them to the sun there lie the measureless plains
Of an ocean shored by the vast coasts of heaven,
With thousands of other lands along the way,   410
Where various sorts of men and creatures live.
Yet a pool of water of but one finger's depth,
A puddle between two stones in the open street,
Offers a sweeping vista underground
As vast as the depths of heaven that yawn above,

And you seem to be looking down on the clouds and sky,
On things in a wondrous heaven below the earth.
When a swift horse halts, balks in the river's current
And we look down on the water rushing away,
420 The horse—at a standstill—seems to be swept upstream
By some force, seems suddenly thrust against the river,
And if we cast our glance to either bank
Everything seems to sweep along with us.
Although a colonnade is parallel
And stands with columns always of one height,
When the whole long stretch is viewed from the upper end
Little by little it draws into the narrows
Of a cone, joining right with left and roof with floor,
Contracting to the disappearing point.
430 It looks to sailors at sea that the sun rises
From the waves, and sets in the waves to hide its light.
(So what? There's nothing to see but sky and ocean!
Then don't blithely assume the senses' failure.)
Landlubbers think that a ship in port looks hobbled,
Its stern broken and bucking against the waves.
For the part of an oar above the sea's salt spray
Is straight, and straight too is the helm above;
What's plunged in the water below seems broken backwards,
All switched and shifted belly-up, bent round
440 And rippling nearly to the water's surface.
When the wind scatters a few far clouds at night
The constellations in their splendor seem
To wheel against them and arise above,
Carried into a distant part of the sky.
Press your hand from below against one eye:
By a quirky sensation it's as if all things
We see, we see them double; double are
The flowering torch-flames in the evening lamps,
Double the furniture twinning down the halls,
450 The faces of men are two and two their bodies.
When the soothing sway of sleep sets the limbs free
And all the body lies in deepest ease,

Then even so we seem to be awake
And moving, and in the visionless gloom of night
We think we see the daily light of the sun;
Shut in our rooms the sky, seas, rivers, mountains
Melt by, and we think we're crossing fields afoot
And hear a sound—though the night is stern in silence
All round us; we reply, with not a word!
Many such marvelous things we see, which all   460
Seek, as it were, to stain our faith in the senses—
In vain, for most of these illusions are
Due to the added suppositions of
The mind; we see what we have never seen.
Nothing's as tough as to set things in plain sight,
Apart from the instant errors of the mind.

And whoever thinks that knowledge can't be had
Can't know that either—as he says, he knows nothing!
So against this man I'll cease to plead my case—
Let him stand on his head if that's his wish.   470
But let's suppose he knows this; still I'll ask,
Seeing that truth could never be found in things,
How he knows what it is to know or not to know,
What gives him a sign of the true and false, what tests
And separates the doubtful from the sure?
You'll find that truth's criterion first proceeds
From the senses—which can never be proved false.
For something more worthy of trust would have to be found
Which of its own subdues the false with truth.
What then should be held more worthy of trust than the senses?   480
Or can reason arisen from false senses speak
Against them, arisen wholly from those senses?
If they're not true, all reason must be wrong!
Can the ears accuse the eyes? Or can touch blame
The ears? Or a taste in the mouth refute this touch?
Or the nose or the eyes defeat the taste in court?
I think not. For their powers are separate,
Whatever power they have; therefore what's soft

Or icy or boiling hot has to be sensed
490 By itself, apart; as the various colors of things
And all things joined to color are sensed apart;
Separate too is the power of taste, and smells
Rise separate; separate, sounds; so it must be
That senses cannot prove each other false.
What's more, they can't accuse themselves of falsehood;
They're always to be trusted equally.
So if a thing seems true to them, it is.
And if reason hasn't a clue as to what causes
An object to look square close up but round
500 From afar, that reasonless man had better give
Blundering explanations for both shapes
Than to fling away what's clear, at hand to grasp,
Polluting the prime faith and ripping up
The basis for the tower of solid life.
Not only would reason fall, but life itself
Would instantly crumble unless you dared to trust
The senses, and not build on the edge of cliffs—
Seeking the sure, shunning the dangerous.
Therefore make ready your host of words against
510 The senses, marshal all your force! In vain.
If for a building the first rule is wry,
And the joiner's T strays from the square and true,
And the plumb line wobbles a little on any side,
The whole thing must end up crooked, wrong—roofs warped,
Bulging, pitched forwards, backwards, off-key, ill-fitted,
Looking like they'll be falling—and they fall,
Done in from the beginning by bad judgments;
So too your reasoning on things must be
Crooked and false, if it's founded on false senses.

520 Now how the different senses sense their objects
Is not a rocky matter to explain.
To start, each sound or voice is heard when its atoms
Have slipped into the ears and struck the sense.
Voice is corporeal—this must be admitted—

And sound, since they can strike and stir the senses.
After all, the voice will scrape the throat, and hollers
Make the windpipe hoarse as they troop upstairs and out.
Of course—when the vocal-atoms begin to gather
In a big crowd to squeeze through the cramped exit,
That throng has got to scrape the gates of the mouth.   530
No doubt, therefore, that words and voices are
Made up of matter, of atoms: they can hurt!
And don't forget what matter is drawn from a man's
Muscle and flesh and very health, when he
Gushes an everlasting sermon from
The rising gleam of dawn to the gloom of night,
Especially if it's at the top of his lungs.
Voice, therefore, is material; it must be,
For the long-winded loses part of his matter.
Harshness of voice results from harshness of atoms,   540
As polished smoothness makes for smoothness; nor
Do like-shaped atoms penetrate the ears
When the big trumpet bellows its deep roar
And the roused barbarians boom the rebounding cry,
As when on Helicon in the cool of night
Birds from the garden warble their sad songs.

So when from deep within we press those sounds
Out of the body and send them through the mouth,
The artful tongue saws them up into words
And the lips round them into final form.   550
Thus when a voice has no great space to travel
The words must also of necessity
Be clearly heard, distinct and separate.
They keep their order of sounds, they keep their form.
But if too long a distance intervenes
The words must garble in the air, the voice
Be scrambled to confusion in its flight.
That's why you'll hear a sound but fail to grasp
Distinctly what the words are, what they mean—
So turbid is that (and so tangled) voice.   560

Then too, a single word sent from the mouth
Of the public crier will sting the ears of the people.
That shows that a single voice will suddenly
Disperse into many, dividing with every breeze,
Stamping its shape and clarion call with words.
But the part of the voice that doesn't find the ears
Floats past in the wind and perishes in vain;
Part dashes against a hard place and hurls back
Its sound, the empty mockery of a word.

570   If you grasp that, it's easy to explain
To yourself and others how, in lonely places,
Cliffs will return our words in form and order,
When wandering the dark mountainsides we search
For our scattered friends, and call them with loud cries.
I've seen a place give six or seven echoes
For every cry you send, as the hills themselves
Dash the words back and forth and back again.
That's where the Nymphs and the goat-foot Satyrs live—
So the hill-dwellers imagine, and say and swear
580   That there are Fauns whose boisterous night-prowling
And merry play disrupt the peace and quiet,
With the strum of lute strings and the sweet sad songs
That the pipe pours forth at the fingering-pulse of the players,
And the farmfolk far and wide can hear when Pan,
Shaking his shaggy head and its wreath of pine,
Sweeps with his pursed lip over the holes in the reed
That it may pour its forest song forever.
Other such signs and wonders they relate,
Unwilling to think that even the gods won't dwell
590   In a land so desolate. So they boast of marvels,
Or maybe (like all people everywhere)
Their ears are eager for the tallest tales.

Next, it's no wonder how sounds penetrate
Places that block the eyes from seeing things
Otherwise in plain view, and strike the ears.
Behind closed doors we'll "see" a conversation;

Sure, for the voice can twist itself intact
Through the winding tunnels in things, while semblances
Refuse. They'll be sliced to ribbons unless the tunnels
Are straight, like windows, through which all sight can fly.   600
A sound, moreover, divides in every direction,
For each produces another as soon as the first
Sound rises and bursts into many, as often a spark
Will spray and scatter and set fires from itself.
That's how the back rooms fill with sound; they're in
A boil and a bustle with all the racket round them.
Images, though, take aim for the straight paths
Soon as they're sent. Over a high wall no one
Can see—but he'll hear voices from beyond.
Yet even these sounds that pass through the doors in a house   610
Are blunted and make their garbled way to the ears
So we hear the noise rather than hear the words.

The tongue and the palate, that lend us the sense of flavor,
Involve a little more reasoning here, more work.
We feel the juice of flavor in the mouth
When we crush food in the chewing—like a soaked sponge
That someone squeezes in the hand to dry.
What's squeezed all soaks into the pores of the palate
And the winding spongelike tunnels in the tongue.
So when the atoms of the oozing juice   620
Are smooth, they sweetly touch and sweetly stir
The moist and sweaty precincts of the tongue.
By contrast, if the atoms are rough, bitter,
They rather surge to sting the sense and slash it.
Now the pleasure of flavor is bounded by the palate.
For really, when food slides down the gullet, there's
No pleasure, and none when it all spreads into the limbs.
Nor does it matter what meal you serve the body—
So long as what you take, you can give to the limbs
Cooked and digested, and keep the stomach moist.   630

Now I'll explain why every creature needs
Its special food—why what to some is loathsome

Can yet seem full of sweetness to another.
Things stand apart so far and differ, that
What's food for one is poison for another.
There's a snake that at the touch of human slaver
Perishes, chewing and champing itself to death.
Hellebore, too, is venomous for us
But quails and goats can fatten on the stuff.

640   That you may grasp how such a thing can be
You should recall first what I've said before:
Things contain many seeds, mixed many ways.
Consider every living thing that eats.
As their outward features are dissimilar,
The cut of the limbs according to their kinds,
They must be made of seeds of varying forms.
Now if the seeds are different, then the gaps
And ways—which we call passages—must differ,
In every limb, in the mouth, in the palate too.

650   Some must be smaller then, some larger; in
This creature, square, in that, triangular;
Many are round, and many multicornered.
For as the atom-patterns and their motion
Demand, shapes must be matched with passageways
Which vary according to atomic texture.
So if what's sweet to one to another is bitter,
In the one for whom it's sweet the smoothest atoms
Must glide with ease into the palate's pores,
While others find the same food bitter, since

660   Rough and hooked atoms pierce into their jaws.
This line of reasoning's easy to apply.
In fact, in a man whose fever is high from jaundice,
Or in whom some other disease has surged somehow,
The whole body is thrown into such confusion,
All of the atoms' places scrambled up,
That atoms once quite suitable to sense
Are now unsuitable, and the rougher atoms
More apt to pierce and bring up bitter tastes.
Both sorts are mingled in the flavor of honey,

670   Which I have shown you several times above.

Aroma is now my topic and how it wafts
To the nostrils. First, there must be many things
From which the rolling and ever-rippling stream
Of smell can flow and scatter abroad and spray.
One smell's more fit for a creature than another
Because of the various shapes of atoms. Bees
Are drawn by the scent of honey no matter how far,
As buzzards by carcasses; the dogs lunge on
To wherever the cloven hooves of game may lead,
And man is sensed from afar by the white goose,   680
The savior of the Roman citadel.
Various smells lead various creatures each
To its proper food, and make them leap away
From the foul poison: so their breeds survive.

Now of the various smells that strike the nostrils,
One may be sent much further than another.
Yet none will carry nearly as far as sound,
And I don't even need to mention things
That strike keen eyesight and excite the vision.
Like laggards they loll along and perish first,   690
Slowly and easily tugged apart in the breeze,
Mainly because they issue from deep inside
And hardly make it out (there are sure signs
Of such deep trickling: a thing split open smells
Stronger, or ground in a mortar or crushed in fire),
Also, because its atoms naturally
Are bigger than those of sound; smell cannot pierce
Stone walls, while sound will carry through and scatter.
That's why you see it's not so easy to
Trace a smell to its origin. It dallies,   700
Losing its force as it cools off in the breeze;
No couriers rush to the senses with hot news.
So hounds will stray and try to find the traces!

This property is not peculiar to
Odor and taste; the look of things, their colors
Don't all agree with every creature's senses;

Some things will be more painful to behold.
Why, the cock, whose huffed wings hustle the night offstage,
Who calls the dawn in with his clarion cry—
710 The savage lions can't stand up against him
Or look him down; they scamper away at once!
That's no surprise. In the cock's body are certain
Atoms which, when they strike the eyes of lions,
Bore into the pupils and bring stabs of pain
That the lions, though big and bold, just can't endure—
While these can't bruise our eyesight in the least,
Either because they don't pierce through, or if
They do pierce, there's a free way out, so that
At no point will their lingering hurt the eyes.

720 Listen and learn, in few, what moves the soul,
Whence those things come that come into the mind.
First I say this: the semblances of things
Go drifting all over, millions, in all directions,
So slight that when they cross in the air they join
Easily, like gold leaf or gossamer.
In fact, they're far more subtly woven than
What seizes and incites the eyes to see;
They pierce through the pores of the body and deep down
Arouse the slender soul, and stir the senses.
730 Then we "see" Centaurs and the legs of Scyllas,
The jowls of the hell-dog Cerberus and the shades
Of those whose bones the earth has clasped in death,
Because all sorts of replicas go floating
Here, there, some popping up in the air itself,
Others released from various things, and others
Amalgamating several semblances.
For surely, the image comes from no live Centaur—
Never did such an animal exist!
But when horse- and human-images meet by chance,
740 Right off they stick, and easily, as I've said,
Because of the subtle and slender weave of atoms.
Other such things are formed in the same way.
And any one such image, subtle and swift

To move, as I've shown above, or exceedingly light,
Will easily stir the soul with a single stroke.
Mind too is slender and wonderfully swift to move!

What follows, I think, will help you understand:
So far as what we see with eyes is like
What the mind sees, their causes must be like.
Now since I've shown that I see, let's say, a lion   750
Through semblances that strike the eyes, it follows
That the mind must be aroused in the same manner,
By lion semblances or what-all it sees
Alike with the eyes, though what it sees is slighter.

When the limbs are all poured out in sleep, the mind
Watches; the reason is, that the same shades
Arouse the soul as when we wake, so that
We'd swear we're seeing those who have left their lives,
Who now are in the power of earth and death.
Nature so brings it about that all the body's   760
Senses rest dull and quiet in the limbs,
And cannot conquer falsehood with the truth.
The memory, too, lies drowsy and dull in sleep,
Cannot protest that death has in its power
Him whom the mind believes it sees alive.

Moreover, it's no surprise that semblances
Should move their arms and other parts in rhythm.
(Images seem to do that when we dream.)
You see, when the first one's died and a second is born
In another pose, that first will seem to have moved.   770
Of course you must suppose this happens swiftly:
There's such a wealth of films so quick to move
And such a wealth of atoms to supply
The instantaneous images we see.

Here there are many questions to be asked,
Points to make clear, to set the plain facts forth.
First we ask why, as soon as the mind pleases,

It can reflect upon the thing it wants.
Do the semblances stand watch over our wills
780　So that, as soon as our hearts desire, an image
Comes running to us, of the sea or the earth or heaven?
Processions, congregations, banquets, battles,
Nature prepares them all, I suppose, on order,
That too when other men in the same spot
Can have far different sorts of things in mind?
And when we see the shadows in our dreams
Stride on in measure and move their supple limbs,
Do those supple shadows swing their easy arms
And match their footsteps, all for us to see?
790　Those wandering shades are sure well-trained, just soaked
With skill, to play such nightly tricks on us!
Or maybe what follows is true? Within one moment
Of our sensation (say we hear a sound),
Many tinier moments are hidden whose existence
Reason discovers; so too, at any moment,
All the shadows are ready and waiting in their places.
There's such a wealth of them, so ready to move.
So when the first has died and a second is born
In another pose, that first will seem to have moved.
800　And since they're slender, unless the mind takes aim
It can't perceive them sharply. So all the rest
Die, if the mind has not prepared itself.
It does so focus itself then, hoping to see
Whatever will follow the image — and it sees.
Consider that even the eyes must be prepared
To strain to see things that are slender-woven,
And if they're not, we can see nothing sharply.
Yet you can learn from things in plain sight too;
If you don't focus on them they will seem
810　To have been far off the whole time, by themselves.
Why is it strange then that the mind should lose
All else but what it concentrates upon?
So we draw huge conclusions from small signs
And snarl ourselves in error and self-delusion.

Sometimes it happens too that the image isn't
Backed up by one of the same sort. Women turn
To men right in our very grasp, old, young,
One face, another—yet we're not amazed.
Oblivion and sleep have seen to that.

Here I most violently want you to   820
Avoid one fearful error, a vicious flaw.
Don't think that our bright eyes were made that we
Might look ahead; that hips and knees and ankles
So intricately bend that we might take
Big strides, and the arms are strapped to the sturdy shoulders
And hands are given for servants to each side
That we might use them to support our lives.
All other explanations of this sort
Are twisted, topsy-turvy logic, for
Nothing is born in us that we might use it,   830
But what is born produces its own use.

Sight was not born before the light of the eyes,
Nor were words and pleas created before the tongue;
Rather the tongue's appearance long preceded
Speech, and the ears were formed far earlier than
The first sound heard. To sum up, all the members
Existed, I should think, *before* their use,
So use was not what caused them to have grown.
By contrast, struggling in hand-to-hand combat and mangling
The limbs and dabbling them all with gore were here   840
Long before the flight of the shining lance,
And Nature urged a man to duck a wound
Before the left hand parried with its shield.
Of course! Laying one's weary bones to rest
Is far more ancient than soft coverlets,
And slaking the thirst was born before drinking cups.
Thus we can trust that these were first conceived
To use—for life displayed their usefulness.
In a separate class are all those things born first

850 Which afterwards showed how they might be used—
Our limbs and senses in particular.
So again I'll say it's far-fetched to believe
They have been made for usefulness and service.

Nor should it cause amazement that the bodies
Of every living creature seek for food.
Many atoms, as I've shown, in many ways
Stream into and ebb from things—but most of all
From living creatures. Spurred to strenuous motion,
Many are huffed out from the short-of-breath,
860 Many are squeezed and sweated from deep down.
That thins the body away and undermines
All its supports; the consequence is pain.
So food is taken—to prop the joints, restore
Strength when the food's doled out, to stuff the gaping
Craving to eat that grips each limb and vein.
Water too seeps away into all the places
That call for water, and the many massed-up atoms
Of steam that set our stomachs all ablaze
Are quenched and dissipated by a drink,
870 So that the arid heat won't scorch our organs.
Now you know how panting thirst is washed away
From the body, and lean hunger is fulfilled.

How we can take a step whenever we wish
Or move this way or that, what gives a shove
To this huge weight, our body, and always has,
I shall explain. You listen to my words.

I say that images of walking figures
First fall to the mind and push it, as we've seen.
From them comes will. For no one begins to act
880 Before the mind first sees what it would do.
The image of that act is what it sees.
So when the mind first rouses itself to go
And take a step, at once it jogs the spirit,

That power diffused throughout each part and limb.
Easy to do, since spirit and mind are joined.
Then at last that rouses the body, and its whole bulk
Is pushed, pushed gradually ahead, and moves.
The body's pores gape wider then, and air
(As it should, of course, for it's always ready to move)
Comes flooding in to fill the open pores   890
Dispersing to the smallest parts of the body.
So it happens that two separate causes drive
The body—it's like a ship, with oars and sails!
Nor in these matters is it all so strange
That this huge body of ours with all its weight
Can be jerked and steered by bodies so very tiny.
For in fact whenever a slight and subtle breeze
Thrusts a ship of enormous bulk along,
One hand can steer it, no matter the ship's momentum,
And one lone tiller can turn it anywhere;   900
And a small machine, a pulley or block-and-tackle,
Can lift great weights—and with the lightest strain.

Next, sleep: how its peace can trickle through the body
And dissolve all the troubles of the heart,
I'll give you in verses, eloquent and few,
Like the swift but lovelier song of the swan, and not
The honk of a mob of storks in the south wind.
Lend me your subtle attention and keen mind,
And don't shout "That can't be!" at what I say,
Driving the truth away, defecting from us,   910
Though you're the one at fault and just can't see it.
First of all sleep occurs when the spirit's force
Is discomposed; some spirit is cast outside
And some retreats to crowd in the depths of the body.
Finally all the limbs flow loose and free.
No doubt about it, since our senses are
The work of the soul, when they're blocked back by sleep
Our soul must then be scrambled up or cast
Outside—not all, for then the body would lie

920   Steeped in the everlasting chill of Death.
     Why, if no part of the soul were left to hide
     In the limbs, like sunken fire in a heap of ash,
     How could the senses be suddenly fanned again
     Like flames that blaze up from an unseen spark?

     But by what means this change occurs, and how
     The body will lie faint and the soul be scrambled,
     I'll explain. Don't have me toss my words to the wind!
     To begin with, since the body's surface is
     Exposed to the touch of air, it must then be
930   Pounded and thumped by the air's constant blows.
     (That's why nearly everything is covered with
     Hide or hard horny skin or shells or bark.)
     And the inner parts of animals are lashed
     By this same air drawn in and then blown out.
     So since the body is flogged on both sides, since
     Blows thrust into our tiny pores and reach
     Our fundamental parts and elements,
     Our limbs slump, so to speak, to a slow ruin.
     For jumbled and knocked about are all the atoms
940   Of body and soul. And so a part of the spirit
     Is cast outside, and a part yields, tucked deep down,
     And another part distracted through the limbs
     Cannot connect or join in mutual movement.
     Nature walls off their paths to unity.
     With such deep change of motion, sense submerges.
     And since there's nothing that might prop the limbs
     The body grows feeble, all the members droop,
     Arms dangle, eyelids fall; we stagger to bed
     As the knees buckle and melt their strength away.
950   And sleep will follow a meal, for what air does
     Food does the same, as it spreads into the veins.
     Our drowsiness is deeper and heavier when
     We're stuffed or weary, for most of the atoms then
     Are jumbled, knocked about by the hard work.

As a result part of the soul sinks deeper
And part is projected further out of the body;
Within, it's more divided, more distracted.

And whatever we'd been terribly busy with,
Wherever our mind's been drawn as tight as a bow,
In general, what study each of us is glued to,   960
We often seem to dream we're going at it.
Lawyers plead cases and cite precedents,
Generals have at the fighting and the battles,
Sailors sign on for a life at war with winds,
I work at this—seeking the nature of things
And setting what I find in Latin verse.
So other arts and studies seem to grip
The minds of men in empty dreams and shows.
And if for the many days of festival
You devote all your attention to the plays,   970
We see that when they've stopped seizing the senses
There are still open ways left in the mind
For those same semblances of things to enter.
Then for days on end these things present themselves
Before our eyes, and even when we're awake
We see the dancers moving their lithe limbs,
We hear the liquid music of the lute,
The strings so eloquent; we see the audience too
And all the brilliant glories of the stage.
So much depends on study, on what we make   980
A habit of giving our minds to with a will—
That's not just men but all the animals too.
For when the limbs of a thoroughbred rest asleep,
You still will see him sweating in his dreams,
Puffing hard, striving with all his strength for the prize,
Or eager to fly when the stalls are finally opened.
And sometimes setters sprawled out in soft sleep
Will suddenly twitch their paws and let out yelps,
Flaring their nostrils and sniffing over and over

990   To hold to the traces of the game they've found,
And when they're rousted up they'll often race
After phantoms of deer, as if they'd seen them fleeing—
Till they shake off the error and come to.
And the cuddly lapdogs reared up in the home
Will leap to their feet with a sudden shake, as if
They'd caught sight of some stranger breaking in.
And the fiercer the stock from which a creature springs
The wilder and more savage are its dreams.
But the dappled birds will suddenly take to wing,

1000   Flapping away in the sacred groves at night,
If in their pleasant dreams they see a hawk
Flying in hot pursuit of battle and warfare.
And the minds of men, that do big things in thought,
Will often act out big things in their dreams:
They'll slug it out with kings, be caught, pitch battles,
And holler as if their throats were cut, in bed;
Many lose title bouts and groan in pain,
And as if ripped and champed by a panther's jaws
Or a fierce lion, fill the house with cries;

1010   Many in dreams will speak of grave misdeeds
And often testify against themselves;
Many will die; many, as though they were
Plummeting from sheer mountains to the earth,
Are seized with terror and wake like madmen, hardly
Returning to themselves, in the seethe of the body;
A thirsty man will sit by a pleasant spring
And gulp almost the whole brook down his throat;
Gripped by their dreams, innocents think they're lifting
Their nightshirts at the latrine or on the pot,

1020   Spilling the fluid filtered through the bladder,
Soaking their splendid Persian coverlets.
When the surging channels of youth, when the ripeness of time
Fashion the semen and slip it into the members,
Then, from any body whatever, images strike,
Heralding youth's fresh rose and radiant features.

These things so tickle and rouse the seed-swollen place
That it gushes out—as if the job were done—
In the flow of a mighty stream and soils the linen.

As I have said, the seed's provoked in us
When full-grown age makes the limbs strong and sturdy.   1030
Things stir or set the spurs to different things.
Only human power will urge up human seed.
This seed, as soon as it's cast out from its place,
Passes through members and limbs and the whole body,
Collecting in that knot of muscle, inciting
At once the part of the body that makes life.
The genitals, roused, swell big with seed, long to
Expel it into the place of fierce desire.
The body seeks what wounds the mind with love.
Fighters fall where they are stricken, the blood spurts   1040
In the direction from which we suffer the hit;
In hand-to-hand combat the red gush strafes the enemy.
And so whoever is shot by the arrows of Venus—
Whether pierced by the womanly limbs of a young boy
Or a lady darting love from her whole body—
Strains toward the archer, shudders with joy to come
Close, to shoot into that body his body's juice.
Silent desire gives hints of that wild joy.

Such is our Venus, our love, our "amor" and "umor";
From here those first sweet drops of Venus trickle   1050
Into our hearts. The chilling care comes next.
Your love's not around, for a change? But still her image
Is, and her sweet name echoes in your ears.
But we ought to flee these shadows and scare off
The food of love, and turn our thoughts to another—
Shooting the juice into any available body,
Not holding it all in for a single lover,
Saving up for ourselves sure pain and sorrow.
If you feed the sore it'll put down roots and fester

1060 And blister over and drive you mad with trouble—
Better write off the old wounds with new business,
Stroll after a street-strolling trollop and cure yourself,
Shift your thoughts to another while you still can!

The man who shuns love can enjoy sex still—
More, for the goods come with no penalty.
Certainly, pleasure is purer in the sane
Than in the lovesick. Though they've got each other
The torrid lovers are tossed in a storm of wandering,
Never settling on what first to see or feel.
1070 What they hunger for, they squeeze hard, tight, and cause
Pain, often nipping the lips between their teeth
And inflicting kisses, for the pleasure's not
Pure; there are spurs beneath that prick them on
To hurt whatever it is that makes them rave.
But Venus sweetly allays their pain in love,
And a dash of gentle pleasure soothes the sting,
So they hope that the same body that gave rise
To the heat of love can put the flame out too.
Nature objects—this cannot come to be.
1080 Love is unique; the more of it we have
The hotter our hearts burn with their fierce desire.
Water and bread we take into our bodies—
Once they have occupied the proper places
Our hunger or thirst is easily fulfilled.
But from the lovely and fresh human face
The body feeds on nothing but those slight
Images—poor little hopes that are lost in the wind.
As a thirsty man will dream of drinking, but
No water is there to quench his parching body—
1090 He strives for the shadow of water and struggles for nothing,
Gulping the rush of the river and yet still thirsty,
So lovers are fooled by Venus and her shadows,
Never having their fill of seeing the nude beside them
Nor able to glean the sleekness from its limbs,
Their vague hands roaming wildly over the body.

And now, limbs locked in the embrace, they taste
Life's flower, and the body can feel the joy to come,
And Venus is poised to plow the womanly fields,
And they rush and fasten their bodies and let the spittle
Mingle, and mingle the breath, teeth bruising lips— 1100
In vain, for they can't scrape a thing away
Or penetrate and bury body in body.
That's what they seem to want and fight to do:
So eagerly do they tangle in Venus' snares,
Till delight lets their members melt and fall.
When the massed-up longing at last spurts out of the muscle,
There's a lull in the violent blaze—the briefest lull.
But the same madness returns, and the fury too,
They long to attain they don't know what, and can't
Find any trick to master this disease: 1110
They waver, and pine away from the hidden wound.

Add that they spend their strength to the point of exhaustion,
That they waste their time at another's beck and call!
Their duties fall faint, their fame grows sick and totters,
Their business fails and their wealth is turned into
Ointments from Persia and sweet Sicyonian slippers.
Sure! and great emeralds with their grass-green shine
Are enclosed in gold, and the seaside robe's worn sheer
From the constant rubbing, soaked and stained with sex.
Father's hard-earned estate? Bonnets or scarves 1120
For whores—or long lush robes or lingerie.
Then formal dinners and delicacies and games,
Goblets all round, crowns, garlands, lotions, all
For nothing: from the very fount of pleasure
The bitter will surge and in love's flower beds
Clutch—for regrets bite back at the conscious mind,
To have lost his years to idleness and whoring,
Or maybe the girlfriend's tossed some two-edged word
That sticks in the lover's heart and blooms like fire,
Or her roving gaze has lit on another lover— 1130
He thinks—he sees the traces of her smile.

These evils, though, attend the luckiest, most
Successful love; but for the crossed, or for those
Who come up empty, the evils—and these you can see
With your eyes shut—are countless! As I've shown you,
Better stay awake and watch out for the snare.
For to shun the hunting nets of love is not
So hard as, once being caught, to free yourself
From Venus' mesh and break through her tough knots.

1140   You're bound and tangled? You can still flee the hunter
Unless your stubbornness gets in your way
And you overlook all of the blemishes
Of body and mind in her you crave so much.
For men are blinded by their appetites
And grant their loved ones graces they don't have.
The vile, the crooked—these, we see, are sweethearts
And are honored in the highest by their lovers.
Men laugh at a fellow who's stuck with an ugly girlfriend,
"You better go keep your Venus happy!" Fools!

1150   Their own troubles are worse, and they can't see them.
She's black as soot? "Honey-tan." She never washes?
"Casual!" Cat-eyed? "Like Pallas!" She's knobby and wiry?
"A gazelle." A dwarf's "ma petite," "my little charmer,"
A big bruiser's "one who'll take your breath away";
The stammerer "lisps," the stock-still, she's just "bashful,"
While the spiteful little spitfire's "a real sparkler";
Then it's "svelte" for a woman too withered to keep alive,
And the half-dead hacker's got "a delicate frame,"
But a "diva" she is with the great gargantuan boobs,

1160   And Fat Lip is "one big kiss," Pug Nose "my puppy."
I could go on forever with such stuff.
But all right, all right—she's as gorgeous as you say,
The glory of Venus glowing in every limb—
Hey, there are others; hey, we've lived without her;
And she does (we know it!) just what the homely do,
Douches herself, poor lady, with smelly perfumes
While her maids scurry away and chuckle in secret.
But the weepy locked-out lover buries the steps

Under flowers and wreaths, and oils the snooty posts
With marjoram, planting kisses on the door—   1170
Pathetic. Just let him in and let him take
One awful whiff! He'll look for a decent reason
To get out; the whiny poem he's got by heart
Falls, and he curses himself for being a blockhead,
For granting her more than is just to grant a mortal.
Our goddesses are no fools. No! They themselves
Guard all the secrets of the hoary deep
From those they want to hold in the bonds of love;
In vain, for you can guess and drag it all
Into the light, and ask them what's so funny.   1180
And if she's good-hearted and not shrewish you
Can overlook for that her human failings.

A woman won't always sigh with put-on passion
When she entangles her lover in the tight hug
Of bodies, sucking his lips in with wet kisses.
No, she'll do it with spirit, looking for mutual joy,
Spurring his steed along on the track of love.
What allows the birds and the cattle and wild beasts
And sheep and horses to squat and submit to the male,
Unless their moist parts burn in heat themselves,   1190
And eagerly thrust against the mounting godhead?
Those linked by mutual pleasure—don't you see
How they are tortured in those chains they share?
How dogs in the crossroad, trying to go their ways,
Tugging and straining in opposite directions,
Stay stuck instead in the strong cement of sex!
If it weren't for mutual joy they'd never do it—
A joy that sets the trap to shackle them.
So I say it again: the pleasure goes two ways.

And if by chance in the mingling of the seeds   1200
The female's the victor and masters the male at climax,
Then the mother's seed bear children like the mother
As the father's the father. But those who look like both,

Their faces mingling the features of both parents,
Grow from the father's body and mother's blood,
When mutual heat fanned high and the stings of Venus
Dash all their roused-up seeds against each other,
So neither is the victor nor the vanquished.
And a child at times can look just like his granddad,

1210 Or even recall more distant ancestors,
Since many atoms mixed in many ways
Will lurk within the body of the parent,
Straight from the stock that the fathers pass to the fathers.
At random Venus picks them for our looks.
And they're crucial too for the hair and the voice and the manners,
For these no less than facial features or
Our frames are fashioned from specific seeds.
And the father's seed can give rise to a daughter,
And sons have grown from the seed of the mother's body.

1220 For the baby always comes from the seeds of both,
And will be more than half of whichever parent
He most closely resembles—as you can observe,
Whether the sprout's a boy or a little girl.

The gods don't scare the seed from any man
So that he'll waste his life with a sterile Venus
And never be called "father" by sweet children—
Though many sad people think so and splash the altars
With a lot of blood and set the incense smoking,
So that their wives will come home full of seed.

1230 They pester gods and oracles, in vain.
If a man's sterile his semen is just too thick
Or too thin and runny to be suitable.
If it's runny it can't cling fast to the right organs,
And trickles back out of the womb abortively.
As for the thicker, too-clumped-together semen,
Either it doesn't shoot out far enough,
Or it can't get in or if it does get in
It mingles too feebly with the woman's seed.

For the organs need to be in tune together:
He will fill *her* more readily, and from him   1240
She'll sooner grow heavy and bear the burden of children.
And many a barren and often-wedded woman
Will find the man to enable her at last
To carry the sweet treasure of a child.
And men whose wives, though fertile, could never bear
Children, have found concordant women too
To fortify their age with progeny.
So much it matters that the seeds can fuse
In the fit way to cause conception: thick
Most suitable for the runny and vice versa.   1250
And for that, it matters what you eat to live.
Some foods make semen clump in the members while
Other foods thin it out into decay.
And the methods for transacting your delight,
They've a bit to do with it too. For women, it's thought,
Conceive the sooner from the custom of
Wild beasts or horses; with her breasts beneath
And the buttocks high, the womb can take the seed.
As for pleasant tricks, they're not required for women.
For a wife prevents conception, fights against it,   1260
If she gleefully clamps his god between her hams
And writhes away with all her boneless flesh.
That shoves the plowshare out of the proper field
And furrow—the seeds shoot out and miss their place.
It's how whores move, for their own benefit,
So as not to grow heavy with children all the time,
But to make sex more delightful for the men—
A thing which *our* wives never seem to need!

It's not an act of god or the arrows of Venus
That makes a homely little woman loved.   1270
She brings it about herself by what she does,
By her yielding temper and her clean appearance;
You'll easily learn to spend your life with her.

For habit is the recipe for love.
A thing struck over and over, no matter how lightly,
Will give in at long last and totter and fall.
Notice how water dripping upon a stone
Bores a hole through that stone eventually?

BOOK FIVE

Whose potent mind can build a worthy song
For these discoveries and their majesty?
Who so muscular of words to shape the praise
To match his merits—his, whose mind brought forth
And left for us such a sought-after prize?
No mortal man, I think, could do him justice.
If we must speak as the majesty of nature
Now seen, demands, he was a god, great Memmius,
A god, the founder of that way of life
10 Called "wisdom" now; our skillful pilot, who   10
Steers our lives from such dark and tossing storms
To dwell in sunlight and tranquillity.
Bring the old inventions of those other gods!
For Ceres, they say, first brought us grain, and Bacchus
Gave mortal men to drink of the juice of the vine—
And yet life can go on without these things,
As we hear some nations still live nowadays.
Without a clear heart, though, no one lives well.
All the more does he merit from us the name of god
20 Whose way of life, by now spread worldwide, brings   20
Sweet soothing solace for the minds of men.
You think the labors of Hercules were greater?
You've drifted even further from the truth.
That big gaping maw of the Nemaean lion,
What's it to us? Or the bristly Arcadian boar?
What harm from the Cretan bull, or that pest of Lerna,
The hydra, fortified with poisonous snakes?
Or the triple power of three-breasted Geryon?

How badly could the Stymphalian swamp birds hurt us,
30   Or the fire-snorting horses of Thracian Diomedes
Hard by Mount Ismarus in Bistonia?
And the guard of the bright Hesperian golden apples,
The serpent of piercing eye and measureless body
Hugging a tree trunk—what harm could he possibly do,
Way off at the coast of the ruthless Atlantic, where
No Roman goes nor even the natives venture?
And all the other such monsters put to death,
If they'd won and lived, how could they hurt us, really?
Not at all, I think. Even now earth teems to the brim
40   With wild beasts filling all the woods with terror,
And the high hills and the deep wilderness,
All places we can shun, most of the time.
But if the mind's not cleansed, what dubious battles
Must we then stalk, and enter against our will!
How sharp are the lusts that tear a man in two
And trouble his life! How many fears will follow!
What insolence, filth, and shamelessness! How many
Disasters they deal! What sloth and debauchery!
Who conquered these and drove them out of the heart
50   With words alone, not weapons, is this man
Not worthy to be numbered with the gods?
Especially as he spoke much—and divinely—
About those same immortal gods; his words
Opened to us the nature of all things.

His is the path, his are the reasonings I
Follow and teach, how all things at their birth
Are treaty-bound and must remain so bound,
Not strong enough to tear the laws of time
(As in particular the soul's been found
60   To be born and grow and stand fast with the body,
Unable to outlast long time intact,
But it's semblances that fool the mind in dreams,
When we seem to see someone whom life's abandoned).
The train of reasoning leads me now to this,

That I likewise expound the law that all
The universe was born too and will die;
And how the assembly of matter fashioned first
The earth, the heavens, the sea and the stars and sun
And the round moon; what animals then on earth
Sprang up, and what earth never bore; how mankind   70
First began in their interchanges to
Use language's variety for naming,
And how into our hearts that dread of the gods
Stole its way, with its awe throughout the world
For temples, altars, lakes, groves, holy idols.

Besides that, I'll make plain how the helmsman Nature
Steers the course of the sun and the wanderings of the moon,
Lest we think that, gliding of their own free will
Between earth and heaven, they light their annual way,
Compliantly swelling the grain for living things,   80
Or that they're turned by any plan of the gods.
Men may learn well that the gods live free of care,
But if they wonder anyway how all things
Can come to happen, especially what they notice
Looming above their heads in the shores of the sky,
They slide back into their old religions, calling
Upon those pitiless masters, whom the poor fools
Believe almighty; they don't know what can be,
What cannot, what law grants each thing its own
Deep-driven boundary stone and finite scope.   90

Now then—not to waste your time with promises—
Begin by observing the earth and sea and sky!
Whose threefold nature—Memmius, three bodies,
Three forms so far unlike, three sorts of stuff—
Will be put to death in a day; the vast world's structure,
Upheld through many years, will fall to ruin.
And well I know how strange to the mind, unsettling,
It is that heaven and earth will be destroyed.
Hard for my words to overcome that doubt!

100   As when you hear of some unusual thing
        Which you can't place within the scope of sight
        Or toss in the hand—the shortest road to usher
        Faith into the reaches of the human mind.
        Yet I shall speak: events themselves may lend
        Faith in my words, and in earth's deepest quake
        You may soon see how all the world is crushed.
        Let the helmsman Fortune steer that far from us!
        Let reason and not the actual fact persuade us
        That the world's walls can fall with a thunderous crash!

110   Before I prophesy about this matter,
        Truths holier, founded on far surer reason
        Than what the laurel-toking Priestess utters,
        I'll give clear comfort in my learned verse
        Lest bridled by religion you suppose
        That the earth and the sun and the sky, sea, stars, and moon,
        Divine in substance, must be everlasting,
        And therefore think that, just as the Giants did,
        We all shall pay for our tremendous sin
        Whose doctrines breach the battlements of the world
120   Or snuff the brilliant sunlight in the sky,
        Slandering immortals with mortality—
        Objects which stand so far from divine will,
        Unworthy to be numbered with the gods,
        That they rather give you an idea of
        Insensibility and lifelessness.
        And really, it's not the case that the mind and spirit
        Can dwell in any kind of stuff you like,
        As a tree can't dwell in the sky, or clouds in the salty
        Plains of the sea, or fishes live in the fields;
130   No blood in wooden blocks, no sap in stones.
        Each thing must dwell and grow in one sure place.

        The soul can't spring alone without the body,
        Nor live alone, far off from flesh and blood.
        For if it could, far sooner might that soul

Dwell in the head or the shoulders or the heels
And be born into whatever part you like—
So long as it stays in the same man, the same "jar."
But since there's a certain place inside our bodies
For the spirit, set apart, to dwell and grow,
All the more reason why we must deny   140
That beyond the body and form of a living thing,
In the crumble of earth-clods or the fire of the sun,
In the sea or the shores of the sky, the soul can last.
These things can hardly be blessed with a god's sensation
If they can't be quickened by the breath of life.

Just so, don't think that the holy seats of the gods
Are found in any region of the world.
Our minds can hardly see, remote from sense,
The slender substance of their deities.
As they ever elude the touch and the strike of our hands   150
They cannot touch a thing that we can touch.
A thing can't touch if it's not touchable.
Therefore their dwellings also must be different
From ours, and be as subtle as their bodies.
I'll prove this to you later, at some length.
Further, to say that for man's sake the gods
Wished to prepare this glorious world, and therefore
It's only right to praise their handiwork
And think it will be deathless and eternal—
Shocking, that what the gods in their timeless wisdom   160
Founded for mankind to outlast the ages
You should ever shake from its base by any force,
Pound it with words and topple it—Memmius, to
Invent such errors and paste them one to the next
Is stupid. What gain can our grateful hearts bestow
Upon the blessed immortal gods, that they
Might take one step to act on our behalf?
What innovation after such long peace
Can lure them on to wish to change their lives?
Only someone whom the old order thwarted   170

Takes joy in a new one; but if nothing irksome
Has ever befallen you down the beautiful ages,
What could enkindle a love for novelty?
Their lives, I suppose, lay sunk in sorrow and darkness
Until there dawned the birthday of the world?
And what did it hurt, that *we* had not been made?
Now whoever's been born, he ought to want to stay
Alive, so long as pleasures keep their charm.
But for him who's never tasted the love of life—
180   Never been on the roster—what harm, in not being born?
The model, moreover, first planted in their minds
For the very idea of man and the birth of the world,
Where did they get it? How could they see what to make?
How could they ever find out about first-beginnings,
What those might make when you shuffle their order, if
Nature herself had given them no peek?
But many atoms jumbled in many ways,
Spurred on by blows through the endless stretch of time,
Are launched and driven along by their own weight
190   And come together and try all combinations,
Whatever their assemblies might create;
No wonder then, if into such arrangements
They happen also to fall, the tracks that would
Bring forth and still restore the universe.
But if I knew nothing of atoms, of what they were,
Still from the very ways of the heavens, from many
Other things I could name, I'd dare to assert
And prove that not for us and not by gods
Was this world made. There's too much wrong with it!
200   To start, what the vast sweep of the sky vaults over,
Mountains take up the lion's share and forests
Full of wild beasts, and sloughs and rocky cliffs
And the sea that holds the headlands far apart.
Worse, torrid heat and the constant fall of snow
Remove from mortals two-thirds of the earth.
And what's left to farm, Nature, through her own force,
Would choke with briars; man's strength must stand against it,

Inured to groan over the iron mattock,
To scratch a life by leaning hard at the plow.
The clods are rich, but the plow must turn them over,   210
Loosen and work them, prod them to give birth;
Crops won't spring up in the air all by themselves.
And now that our hard work has paid off in crops,
Breaking into leaf and flower over the fields,
The sun in the sky will scorch them in its rage
Or sudden storms will kill, or frost and ice,
Or the blasts of bullying winds will batter them down.
And the wild beasts that set your hairs to bristle,
Hostile to man, on the land, in the sea—why should
Nature create and feed them? Or why should the seasons   220
Bring pestilence? Why should early Death come stalking?
And then, a baby, tossed up like a mariner by
Fierce waves, lies naked on the beach, dumb, helpless
To save its life, when Nature has spilled it out
Of the clench of its mother's womb to the shores of light,
And fills the place with wailing—as is proper
For one whom so much suffering awaits.
But the various flocks and cattle and beasts grow up
And don't need rattles, or the kindly wet-nurse
Teasing with her sweet broken baby talk;   230
Don't need to change their clothes for the changing sky;
They need no weapons or high walls to guard
Their own, for the earth herself and artful Nature
Bring forth abundantly for all their needs.

First of all, since the stuff of earth and water,
And the soft breath of the air and the brilliant fire,
The four that make this universe, are all
Composed of bodies that are born and die,
We must conclude the world is born, and dies.

For in fact, whatever we see whose parts and members   240
Are of a form to suffer birth and death,
Invariably these things must also die

And be born. Then since I see that the world's chief parts
And members are destroyed, and then reborn,
Surely the heavens and earth must also have
A time of origin and time of death.

Don't think that for my own sake in these questions
I've hustled it in as given that earth and fire
Die, and been sure of the death of water and air,
250   Claiming they'd all be born and grow again.
For starters, a good part of the earth, parched
By the relentless sun, stampeded under,
Is breathed forth in a wraith of floating dust
Which high winds scatter in the atmosphere.
And part of the soil is called to wash away
In storms, and the streams shave close and gnaw the rocks.
Besides, whatever the earth feeds and grows
Is restored to earth. And since she surely is
The womb of all things and their common grave,
260   Earth must dwindle, you see, and take on growth again.

For the rest, that the sea and springs and streams abound
With ever-new water, flowing throughout the year,
Needs little argument: great rollicking brooks
Make it clear everywhere. And yet the water
Is skimmed away, so the flow won't swell to the brim,
Partly because high winds that sweep the sea
Diminish it, and the shearing rays of the sun;
Partly because it soaks into the earth.
There its brine is filtered out and the sweet water
270   Seeps upward and at the source of every stream
Collects—then it's fresh assailing over the land,
Feet cutting a watery way for the waves to follow.

Let me now tell of the air, whose transformations
Each hour are total and innumerable.
For all that ever flows from things is carried
Into the sea of air. But if that same matter

Never washed back to restore the things in ebb,
All would by now have melted into air.
It never ceases to rise from things and fall
Back into them, for the world's a tireless flux.   280

And that brimming fountain of light, the brilliant sun,
Never ceases to flood the sky with its fresh dazzle,
With new supplies in an instant, light for light.
For the first of its flashes dies wherever it falls—
And the following shows you why this must be so.
As soon as the clouds have stolen beneath the sun
And snapped, so to speak, in two the rays of light,
The lower halves die off at once, and the earth
Is cloaked in shade wherever the clouds are riding.
Know then that things will always need fresh light,   290
For each first sling of the flashing sun shall die;
Nothing at all could be seen in the sun unless
That well of light restored the stream forever.

Why, all of your earthly lights you use at night—
The hanging lamps and the torches rich in smoke,
Oil-sleek and quivering into brilliant light—
Rush as the sunshine rushes, with courier-fire
Supplying fresh light, hurtling on to fork in flame,
On, that no places are left in the dark by the interruption,
    so swiftly is light's ruin hidden   300
By the quick rise of flame from all the fires.
So we conclude that the sun and the moon and the stars
Hurl light from a constant rising and rising of light,
And always lose what fire they had to start.
Don't think they live and thrive inviolable.

Then, don't you notice that stones give way to age,
And high rock-towers crumble into ruin,
And the shrines and the forms of the gods grow weary and crack,
The sacred Will unable to prolong
Their destiny, or buck the laws of Nature?   310

Don't we see fallen monuments of men
Ask if we don't believe *they* grow old too?
And torn-loose granite tumble from high mountains,
Unable to suffer or outlast the stress
Of a *finite* time? Nor could their fall be sudden
If for an endless age they had held fast
Against time's battering rams, without a crack.

Now look at what above and around us holds
All the earth in embrace. If, as some say,
320   Out of itself it bears all and takes back
All that have died, it must be born, must die.
For a thing that feeds another from itself
Must dwindle, and be restored by what returns.

And if there's been no first dawn for the world
And the skies above have stretched eternally,
Why did no poets sing of other deeds
Before the Theban war and the death of Troy?
Where have so many brave deeds fallen, not
Grafted to flower in lasting monuments?
330   The truth, I think: the universe is new,
The weave of nature's not long since begun.
That's why some crafts are just now being polished,
Just now developed; innovations in
The naval art, in melodies that sing;
Even the nature and order of things have been
Recently found, and I myself am first
To turn them into Latin poetry.
Now if you think this all's been here before,
But the human race died out in a scorching fire,
340   Or their cities fell in some great cataclysm,
Or from relentless rain the hungering rivers
Spread out to bury every little town,
So much the more you're beaten and must confess
That there shall come an end to heaven and earth.
Supposing things were roughed up by such stress,
If a fiercer danger had borne down hard upon them

They would have fallen into utter ruin.
A clear proof of our own mortality
Is that we all fall ill of the same diseases
As those whom Nature has removed from life.   350

Besides, whatever is everlasting must
Either (solid of matter) spit back the punches,
Not suffering anything to pierce and split
Its tight-packed parts within (so durable are
Atoms, whose nature I have shown above),
Or persevere through all eternity
Not struck by a single blow (as empty space
Remains unacting and untouchable),
Or last because no wealth of space surrounds it
Where its loosening parts might break away and scatter   360
(As the everlasting All-in-all), for there
Is no Beyond to fly to, or atoms which
Could loosen it and destroy it with their pounding.
But, as I've shown, the world does not consist
Of solid matter—for void's mixed into things;
Nor is it void; and there's no lack of bodies
To rise by chance out of the infinite
And reel annihilation for all things
Or smuggle in some other threat of ruin;
What's more, no place is missing, no deep gulf   370
For the wreckage of the universe to rain,
Or something else can batter and destroy it.
Death, therefore, has not shut its gates against
Heaven, or sun and earth and the depths of the sea,
But gapes wide open with its empty maw.
And so you must admit, these things were born,
And nothing made of perishable stuff
Could, from the endless stretch of time till now,
Have mocked the vigorous might of the boundless ages.

And then, since the chief elements of the world   380
Fight with each other, stirred to unholy war,
Intestine strife, don't you see that an end can come

To their long struggle? Maybe the sun and the heat
Will overwhelm and drink up all the water—
For that's their aim, though they've striven in vain so far.
So large is the river-army, so strong their threat
To drown all things in the deep whirl of the ocean—
In vain, for the winds that sweep the plain of the sea
Diminish it, and the shearing rays of the sun;
390   They're confident they could dry it up before
The water has clutched the end of its design.
Flaring such spirits of war, in deadlocked battle,
They strive with each other over the great spoils,
Though fire, for a time, once gained the upper hand,
And once, they say, the water reigned in the fields.

For fire was lord with its licking and charring flames
When the hungering might of the sun-god's horses swept
Phaethon astray over all the sky and the earth.
But the almighty father, stung to anger,
400   Flung with a bolt of lightning the big-minded
Phaethon from his horses to earth, and Apollo
Relayed, and caught that timeless torch of the world,
Rounded the team run wild and reined them, trembling,
Steered them along their track and restored all—
That is, as old Greek poets used to sing.
This far-fetched nonsense reason must reject.
Fire can prevail when out of infinite space
More fiery seeds than usual have gathered,
Then somehow their might fails and they're beaten back,
410   Or all the world is scorched up in the blazes.
And water once rose up to overwhelm,
So they say, when it plunged cities in its wake.
But all its force arisen from endless space
Somehow receded then, was turned aside,
And the rains were stilled and the rush of the waters abated.

But in what ways the hurly-burly of matter
Has founded the earth and the sky and the depths of the sea

And the tracks of the moon and sun, I shall set forth.
For surely the atoms did not hold council, assigning
Order to each, flexing their keen minds with   420
Questions of place and motion and who goes where.
But because many atoms in many ways,
Spurred on by blows through the endless stretch of time,
Are launched and carried along by their own weight
And come together and try all combinations,
Whatever their assemblies might create,
In just this manner, scattered through the ages,
Chancing upon all combinations, motions,
They at last tossed together and suddenly fused
Into the origin of mighty things,   430
Of the earth and the sea and sky and all that live.

Not the wheel of the sun high-soaring and full of light
Could then be seen, or the stars of this great world,
Or sea or sky; no, not the earth or the air
Or anything like what we now see about us,
But rather a strange tempestuous medley, arising
From all the sorts of atoms whirled in discord,
Their walls and ways and tangles and weights and punches,
Clashes and motions, all mixed up in battle,
Which, due to their various shapes and unlike forms,   440
Couldn't stay yoked together in every way
Or allow motions suitable for each other.
At that point the parts scattered; like with like
Were joined, and the world began to shear away,
Assign its members and arrange its parts,
That is, to sift the heavens from the earth,
Open the secret hollows of the sea
And set apart the realm of perfect fire.

Now, first of all, since the atoms that made the earth
Were heavy and interstitched, they came together   450
In the middle and were situated lowest.
And the more they sank together into that tangle

The harder they squeezed out atoms that would make
Sea, stars, sun, moon and the world's great battlements.
All these are made of smooth and roly-poly
Atoms, far more than the earth, and their components
Are smaller. So, bursting through the pores of the earth,
The ether was first to carry itself aloft,
Ferrying flames, the many fires of heaven —
460   Not so far otherwise than when we see
The golden dawn in the greenery gemmed with dew —
Those radiant spokes of sunlight — blushing red,
And the pools and the ever-flowing streams breathe out
Their mists, and even the earth will sometimes smoke,
All of which when assembled and collected
Above, compose the clouds that veil the sky.
And so when the slender and easily spreading ether
Coalesced into a body and domed the world,
Spilling and spreading wide in every direction,
470   It walled all other things in tight embrace.
There followed then the inchoate sun and moon,
The spheres that turn between the earth and stars.
Earth turned them away, and so did the vast ether,
Not heavy enough to sink and press to the bottom,
Not light enough to glide on the highest coasts;
Rather they're in the middle, and whirl their lively
Bodies, and form parts of the universe —
Just as for us some members can remain
Standing in place while others move about.
480   These elements withdrawn, at once the earth,
Where now the vast blue tract of the ocean stretches,
Subsided, and the salt sea filled the trenches.
Time passed, and the more the seething surf of the ether
And the rays of sunlight with their constant lashing
Made the earth's outer surface more compact,
Molded and pushed to its center, packed, condensed,
The more did the salt sweat, squeezed from the earth's body,
Seep into the ocean swell and the sailing plains,
And the more did many seeds of fire and air

Slip free and fly away, and far from earth   490
Sow thicker the high and flashing fields of heaven.
The flatlands settled down; slopes of tall mountains
Grew steeper. For the rocks could not all settle
Or sink together in one level plain.

Thus coalesced, the weight of earth stood firm;
This sludge, if you will, of all the universe
Sank heavily to the bottom, as sediment.
Then the sea and the air and the fire-bearing ether itself,
Fluid of substance, were all left undefiled,
One lighter than the next, and the lightest of all   500
Was the fleet ether that flows above the air,
Nor does it mingle its liquid body with
The tossing waves of the air. It allows all things
To be whirled in the breakers below and the fitful surge.
But in sure pace its own fires wheel along.
That the ether can flow at even speed and force
The Black Sea shows us, gliding in one sure current,
Keeping the steady tenor of its flow.

Now let us sing what causes stars to move.
To start, if the great sphere of heaven turns,   510
We'll say it's air that presses upon both poles,
Clasping the axis, locking it in place;
One current then flows above and bends toward where
The stars of the ageless World roll on and shine,
One sweeps the World from below, in the other direction,
As we see streams turn waterwheels and dippers!
Or it may be that all the heavens stand
In one still place, while the brilliant signs sweep on—
Maybe swift surges of ether are dammed inside,
And seek a way out and as they turn, here, there,   520
Their flames roll through the thundering fields of night;
Or maybe, from somewhere beyond the World, a wind
Impels the fire to turn; or the stars themselves
Mosey to where their grazing lands invite them,

Feeding their flame-forms scattered in the sky.
To settle upon what's certain in this world,
That's hard. But what might possibly apply
In various worlds arranged in various ways,
That I can show, and set forth many causes
530   Of stellar motion through the universe.
One of those anyway must be what stirs
The stars to move; but to find which it is
Is not for our slow, step-by-step advance.

For the earth to settle and rest in the cosmos' center,
It's fitting that it slowly dwindle in weight
And evanesce; that it have some other substance
Below, joined with it from its birth and living
As one with the air, like a well-grafted limb.
Earth's not a burden then, won't press air down,
540   As a man's members are no weight to him,
Or the head to the neck; nor, really, do we feel
The whole weight of the body in our feet.
But heap a weight upon us from without,
That hurts—though it's often lighter far than we.
So much depends on what each thing can do.
So the earth is not some sudden stranger brought
Upon the air or cast from some strange source,
But it was born with the air at the world's beginning,
Is part of the world, as our limbs are part of us.
550   More: when the earth is battered by big thunder
It batters what lies above it with its motion,
Which it could hardly find a way to do
If it weren't bound fast to the air and the sky above.
They twine together with common roots, and are
Made one in wedlock from the dawn of time.
And don't you see how the great weight of our bodies
Is lifted by the lightest touch of soul,
They are so neatly wedded and united?
Now what could lift a vaulter over the bar
560   If not the strength of the soul, which steers the members?

Then do you see how strong the slightest substance
Can be when joined with heavier matter, as
The air that's one with the earth, and the soul with the body?

The wheel of the sun can't be much bigger than
It seems to our senses, or its light much dimmer.
For however far the space from which a fire
Can cast its light or blow its warmth to us,
That interval of space culls nothing from
The fire, and thus cannot contract its image.
Hence, since the warmth of the sun and its spill of light   570
Come flashing upon our senses and the world,
From here then too the shape and the size of the sun
We should see — adding nothing — as they are.

And the moon that glides in its solemnity
With a bastard light, or maybe it casts its own,
Whichever it is, is of a size no greater
Than what appears before our very eyes.
First, all we see that's far removed from us
Across great currents of air sooner looks blurred
Than shrunk. And therefore, as regards the moon,   580
Since she offers a bright appearance and sharp outline,
However large she is, whatever the marks
On her utmost shores, from here that's what we see.
And last, what fiery stars we see from here,
Can be, you know, the tiniest wee bit smaller,
Or just a very little larger, since
All of the fires we notice here on earth
(While they flicker brightly and their flames burn clear)
Will sometimes seem to change size just a little,
Bigger or smaller according to the distance.   590

And it's no wonder how that sun of ours,
So tiny, could ever send out such great light,
Welling, and filling the seas and sky and all
The earth, and soaking everything with warmth.

Maybe from there one universal spring
Spills broad and free and gushes its burst of light,
Because it's there that heat from the whole world
Can mingle all its tributary streams
So that the fire flows to us from one source.
600   For look now, even a little brook can soak
Wide meadows, brimming over into the fields.
Or maybe the fires of the sun, themselves not large,
Can seize the air with the feverish flush of warmth,
If the time is right and the air is suitable
To be enkindled by its little flares,
Sort of like straw and cornstalks that we see
Go up in flames from a single random spark.
Or the ruddy sun as it lights its lamp on high
Possesses a vast reserve of flames around it
610   Which we can't see, not marked by the flash of light—
And this surf of heat adds force to the sun's rays.

No reason, simple and direct, appears
For how the sun from his summer quarters swerves
To his midwinter turn in Capricorn
Then veers back into Cancer and its standstill;
Why the moon goes that distance every month
For which the sun's race uses up a year.
One simple cause, I say, cannot be found.
Most probably the truth has been set forth
620   In the holy judgments of Democritus:
The closer a heavenly body is to earth
The less it's swept along by the whirling sky.
Down there the speed and the fierce drive of heaven
Dwindle and disappear, so little by little
The sun lags into the rear of the zodiac,
Since it's far lower than those fiery signs.
Worse yet for the moon: as its course is so much humbler,
Farther from heaven and closer to the earth,
So much the less can it race that zodiac.
630   For in proportion as the moon is lower

And dragged more sluggishly along, so will
The signs catch up with it and pass it by.
So it looks as if the moon returns more nimbly
Into each sign, but *they* revisit it.
Or it may be that seasonal crosscurrents
Of air can flow athwart the sun, and push it
Clear out of the summer constellations to
The winter solstice and its stiffening ice,
Then sling it back from the chill shades of winter
All the way to the stars of warmth and light.   640
Also it may well be that the moon and stars,
Rolling vast revolutions through the years,
Can move in cross-directions with the air.
You see how lower and higher clouds are tossed
By different winds, and are blown to different places?
Why can't the stars in the great vault of heaven
Also be swept by different tides of ether?

Night plunges the earth in a deep gloom and darkness,
Either when from its long race the sun reaches
The last of the west and, limp, puffs its last fires,   650
Weary of the trek and roughed up by the air,
Or that same force which vaulted the disk above
Turns it along its course beneath the earth.
And the Goddess of Morning, at a certain time,
Fills the wide shores of the sky with rosy light;
It's that same sun returning from under the earth,
Charging to take the sky and set it akindle,
Or it's fires that merge and the many seeds of flame
That always flow together at just that time,
Renewing the light of a sun born every day.   660
As, rumor has it, from Mount Ida's heights
You can see scattered fires in the eastern dawning
Collect into one roundish mass or ball.
And as for that, it shouldn't seem so strange
That at a certain time these fire-seeds could
Fuse, and restore the splendor of the sun.

For we see many properties of things
Occur at certain times; the woods in season
Blossom, and lose their flowers in season too;
670   Baby teeth fall at the right time's command,
And the bare boy's furred with the down of growing up,
Letting his hair sprout softly upon each cheek;
Lightning, besides, and snow, storms, clouds, high winds,
Occur in rather regular times of the year.
Since from the dawn of the world causes have been
The same, and things have fallen out the same,
They'll now recur in sequence and sure order.

The days may lengthen and the nights decay,
And the light dwindle when the nights increase,
680   For the sun as it treks above and below the earth
Splits the shores of the sky into unequal arcs,
And into unequal sectors cuts its circuit,
So that what it takes from one side, to the other
It gives the same when it comes round again,
Till it reaches that sign in heaven, the node of the year,
Which makes night's gloom equivalent with day
(When the path lies midway between North and South
The sky then keeps its turnposts equidistant,
Due to the placement of that wheel of signs
690   Through which the sun moves slowly till at year's end
It shines on lands and sky with its slant light,
As those explain who map the heavenly regions
And deck them all with signs in the proper places);
Or maybe in certain areas air is thicker,
And the radiance flickers under the earth, gets stuck,
Can't easily pierce or swim up to the dawn
(And so the long nights in the wintertime
Lag, while they wait for the spoke-wheeled badge of the day);
Or maybe at different seasons the sun's flames,
700   Which make the sun arise in a certain quarter,
Just always flow together faster or slower,
And therefore it appears they tell the truth . . .

The moon can shine when it's struck by the rays of the sun
Insofar as it withdraws from the sun's orbit,
Turning the daylight roundabout to face us
Till, opposite the west, its full light gleams
And the moon arises to see the falling sun.
Then little by little likewise it must hide
Its light again, the nearer it glides to the sun's
Fire, from the opposite part of the zodiac;   710
That's what they say who imagine the moon's just like
A ball whose track's between us and the sun.
Yet there's reason to think that with its own moonlight
It turns, and gives us various shapes of splendor.
Another body might glide as one with it,
Obstructing it in every way, occluding,
Invisible because it doesn't shine.
Or it could be turned like a ball, perhaps, that's bathed
In a brilliant white light only on one side,
So that the turning ball gives various phases   720
Till that full side—the one endowed with fire—
Turns to our faces and our gazing eyes.
Then little by little it spins and flings away
The light-bearing side of the roundish mass or ball,
As the Chaldeans teach triumphantly
Against the art of Greek astrologers—
As if these boxers both could not be right!
And why should you dare accept this but not that?
And really, why the new moon can't, each night,
Be made in a certain order of certain phases,   730
Failing and disappearing every day,
Restored by another moon to take its place,
Is hard to show by reasoned argument,
When so much of creation follows sequence.
Spring comes, and Venus, and the pennoned herald
Of Love who prances before her, and close on the heels
Of the West Wind mother Flora strews their way,
Filling the world with marvelous color and fragrance.
Then follows the hot dry Summer and his companion

740   Ceres of harvest-dust and the northerly rains.
    Then Autumn's here, and—hallelujah!—the Wine God,
    Then other seasons follow and winds and storms,
    Volturnus of deep thunder and lightninged Auster.
    Then at last the Shortest Day brings snow, and the Winter
    Its stiff chill, followed by teeth-chattering Cold.
    All the less wonder if at a certain time
    The moon is born or is destroyed; so many
    Things are created at successive times.

    The solar eclipse too and the moon's hideout
750   Can, you should think, arise from many causes.
    For if the moon can shut the sunlight out,
    Its head thrust high between the sun and earth,
    An orb, opaque, blocking those burning rays,
    Just then—consider—why can't some other body,
    Some gliding, lightless object, do the same?
    Or the languid sun might even lose its flames
    At a certain time—why not?—and resume its light,
    As it moves through places hostile to its flames,
    That make them gutter for a time and die?
760   And if earth, in turn, can rob the light of the moon,
    Hold, by itself, the sun in check, while on
    Her monthly course through the sharp cone of night
    The moon glides, just then why can't some other body
    Race under the moon or glide above the sun
    To interrupt the rays and the shower of light?
    Yet if the moon shines with its own gleam, why
    Can't it lag in a certain part of the sky, a zone
    Unfriendly to its light, while passing through?

    For the rest—now that my reasons have untangled
770   How things occur in the great deep blue of the sky,
    That we might know what force or cause impels
    The shifting tracks of the sun and the roving moon,
    How they can fail too when their light is thwarted,
    Shrouding the earth with unexpected darkness,

As if they'd sort of winked, and then, lights open,
Seen all the brilliant places shining clear—
I return to the newborn world, and the soft-soil fields,
What their first birthing lifted to the shores
Of light, and trusted to the wayward winds.

First the Earth gave the shimmer of greenery   780
And grasses to deck the hills; then over the meadows
The flowering fields are bright with the color of springtime,
And for all the trees that shoot into the air
It's a growing contest—and the reins are free!
As feathers or bristles or hair are the first to form
On birds' strong wings or the limbs of galloping horses,
So the new earth sent the grass up first, and the brush,
Then made the many mortal animals,
Various kinds arising in various ways.
They were land dwellers, and so they couldn't have fallen   790
Out of the sky or swum from the salt lagoons.
That leaves the earth, which justly assumes the name
Of mother, for from earth all things are made.
Many animals even now spring out of the soil,
Coalescing from the rains and the heat of the sun.
Small wonder, then, if more and bigger creatures,
Full-formed, arose from the new young earth and sky.
The breed, for instance, of the dappled birds
Shucked off their eggshells in the springtime, as
Crickets in summer will slip their slight cocoons   800
All by themselves, and search for food and life.
Earth gave you, then, the first of mortal kinds,
For all the fields were soaked with warmth and moisture.
And then, whenever the land was suitable,
Wombs grew deep down and clutched the earth with roots.
These, when the time was ripe, were broken open
By babies fleeing the soaked earth, craving air,
And Nature channeled the pores of the earth their way,
Making its open veins drip with a juice
Like milk, just as a woman now grows full   810

With that sweet milk when she has borne a child,
Nourishment welling up into her breasts.
To the toddlers the earth gave food; the warmth of the sun
Was all their clothing; their beds, the wool-rich grass.
But the world in its childhood didn't provoke hard winters,
Heat waves, or hurricanes; like everything else
It had to grow, and take on the trunk of adulthood.

Justly therefore the earth assumes and holds
The name of mother, for it is she who made
820   Both man and beast, and in due time poured forth
All of those roaming revelers of the mountains
And the various birds of the air in dappled flight.
But since it had to end its birthing sometime
It stopped, like a woman wearied round the stretch.
For time will alter all the universe.
One state succeeds another and takes it all,
Nothing remains the selfsame; all things drift;
Nature shuffles them all and makes them turn.
One thing will molder, crumble with age, while another
830   Will shoot up unregarded in its place.
So it is that all the universe is changed
By time. One state will seize the earth from another,
So it can't bear what it could; can, what it couldn't.

For the earth, way back then, tried to bring forth many
Prodigies, strange of feature, monster-limbed,
The halfway not-this not-the-other hermaphrodite,
Some orphaned of feet, some widowed of both their hands,
Many even lacking a mouth, or blind and eyeless,
Or manacled up by the members clung together,
840   Unable to do a thing, go anyplace,
Dodge harm, grab hold of anything they'd need.
Other such freaks and monsters Earth created—
In vain, for Nature frightened off their growth,
They couldn't attain the wished-for flower of adulthood,
Or seek out food or join in the act of love.

For many things, we see, must coincide
So as to forge the generations; first
There must be food; next, ways for the genital seeds
To stream through the body from the slack-fallen members,
And, so that males and females may unite,   850
A way to exchange the mutual joys of love.

And many kinds of creatures must have died,
Unable to plant out new sprouts of life.
For whatever you see that lives and breathes and thrives
Has been, from the very beginning, guarded, saved
By its trickery or its swiftness or brute strength.
And many have been entrusted to our care,
Commended by their usefulness to us.
For instance, strength supports the savage lion;
Foxes rely on their cunning; deer, their flight;   860
But the watchdog, trusty of heart and lightly napping,
And all those beasts of burden bred to pull,
Along with the wool-backed sheep and the big-horned goats,
All, Memmius, are entrusted to man's care.
Gladly they fled their predators and sought peace,
Wide feeding grounds they did not work to find—
Rewards we give them for their use to us.
But those whom Nature had granted nothing (they
Couldn't survive out on their own or be
Of any use to us, for which we'd let   870
Their race feed safely under our protection),
Prone to be preyed on for another's profit,
All tangled in their fatal snares they lay
Till Nature had reduced their race to death.

But Centaurs there never were, and at no time
Creatures of two-ply nature or double body
Compact of members alien to each other
Yet matched just right to make a unity.
This the most sluggish mind could understand:
First, the high-spirited horse near three years old   880

Flourishes in his prime—but a boy? hardly—
Might yet be dreaming of his mama's milk;
But when the sturdy limbs of the horse sag, fail
In his old age, while life is fleeting fast,
Then at last the flower of young manhood blooms
And clothes the cheek and chin with a tender wool.
So don't think that from human and cart-horse seed
Centaurs can be compounded or even exist,
Or the semimarine Scyllas with their groins
890   Belted by froth-mouthed hounds—and other such
Whose parts are clearly in disharmony,
Which will not flourish together or grow sturdy
Or cast that vigor away in their old age,
Won't burn in the same love-heat or have the same
Habits; won't find the same foods nourishing.
Just look and see the bearded goats grow fat
On hemlock; for a man that's deadly poison.
And flames, you know, will roast and burn to a crisp
The lion's tawny body just as soon
900   As it burns anything made of blood and guts;
How, then, could one of those three-sectioned Chimeras—
A goat with a dragon's tail and the head of a lion—
Blow fire out of its mouth from deep inside?
Really, anyone who dreams that things like these
Could have been born from a brand-new earth and heaven,
This silly term of "newness" for their crutch,
Might blather about a lot in the same manner,
Might say that golden rivers used to flow
All over the earth, and shrubs budded out real jewels,
910   And men were born whose limbs could swing so far
They could plant their feet firm over the deep sea
And with their hands twirl the whole sky around.
Granted that when the earth first poured forth creatures
It did contain a host of seeds for things,
Still that's no sign it could have made these hybrids,
Mixed-cattle or fused-together animal parts,
Since things that spring from the earth in plenty now—

All sorts of grass and grain and the glad woodlands —
Can form no creatures intertwined in one,
But each proceeds in its own way; all things keep   920
Themselves distinct, by the sure bonds of Nature.

Yet the human race was hardier then by far —
No wonder, for the earth was hard that formed them —
Built upon bigger and tougher bones within,
Bowels and flesh sewn tight with well-strapped muscles,
Not easily overcome by heat or cold
Or by strange diet or bodily decay.
For many revolutions of the sun
They led the life of the pack, like beasts that roam.
There was no ruddy farmer to steady the plow;   930
Unknown were iron tools to till the fields,
How to plant out new shoots, or from tall trees
Prune away the old branches with the hook.
What the sun and the showers bestowed, what the earth created
Of its own doing, satisfied their hearts.
Often they met their bodies' needs by feeding
From the acorn-copious oak, and the berries you see
Ripen in winter, wild strawberries, purple-red,
Rose bigger and more plenteous from the earth.
Many other foods the flowering fresh earth bore,   940
Hard fare, but ample, for wretches born to die.
And springs and rivers called them to quench their thirst,
As now from the mountains clear cascades of water
Draw from afar the thirsty animals.
Those rovers found and dwelled in the sacred groves
Of the Nymphs, wherever the rush of a good deep brook
Spilled over to wash the wet and slippery stones,
The slippery stones, and trickled over the moss,
Or where streams sprung up bubbling from the fields.
They had no foundry skills, no use for fire;   950
They didn't know how to clothe themselves with skins
But lived in the wild woods and the mountain caves,
Stowing their dirt-rough limbs among the bushes

When driven to flee the wind's lash and the downpour.
They could not recognize the common good;
They knew no binding customs, used no laws.
Every man, wise in staying strong, surviving,
Kept for himself the spoils that fortune offered.
And in those forests Venus brought lovers together.
960   Mutual desire might win a woman over,
Or the man's violent strength and reckless lust,
Or a present: wild strawberries, nuts, or the choicest pears.
Trusting the marvelous strength of their arms and legs
They harried and pursued the woodland beasts
With stones for hurling and bludgeoning-clubs; they killed
Many; a few they hid from in their dens.
When the night caught them, just like bristly hogs
They flopped their uncouth limbs to the earth, naked,
Rolling about them a thatch of leaves and branches.
970   Nor did they wail for the day or wander the fields
To search for the sun, in fear of the shades of night,
But silently they waited, tombed in sleep,
Till the red torch of the sun brought in the light.
They'd grown used to seeing, from when they were little,
Darkness and light give birth to each other forever,
And so they took it as a matter of course
And didn't worry that eternal night
Would steal the sunlight away and seize the earth.
Poor souls, this worried them instead: wild beasts
980   Would terrorize the stillness of their sleep.
Cast out of their rocky dens, they fled the charge
Of the froth-snorting boars and the lions swift and strong;
Trembling, they yielded in the dead of night
Their leaf-strewn bedding to those savage guests.

Nor did those mortals much more often then
Lament their leaving the sweet light of life.
More often it happened then that someone snatched
By the fangs of a beast gave him living feed to gobble,
Filled hills and forests with his cry, alive

But watching his vitals interred in a living tomb.   990
And those who could flee to safety with half-gnawed bodies
Later would press their festering sores, their palms
In a palsy, and call for Death with dreadful cries,
Till the grip of lockjaw took their lives away,
Helpless, not knowing how to treat a wound.
But thousands of men led by the battle-standard
Were not wiped out in a single day; and the rolling
Ocean would smash no ships and men on the rocks.
And so in vain the ineffectual sea
Rose up and roared and pitched its empty threats,   1000
Nor could the calm conniving stretch of water
Lure anyone with its lies and laughing waves.
Presumptuous seamanship lay hidden then.
Lack of food gave their faint limbs up to death,
While nowadays we drown ourselves in plenty.
Poison they often drank unwittingly;
We are more skillful now—we give it to others.

Huts they made then, and fire, and skins for clothing,
And a woman yielded to one man in wedlock . . .

. . . Common, to see the offspring they had made;   1010
The human race began to mellow then.
Because of fire their shivering forms no longer
Could bear the cold beneath the covering sky;
Love sapped the strength of the men, and children tamed
Their parents' proud wills with their pleasing ways.
Then neighbors who wanted neither to harm each other
Nor to be harmed, began to join in friendship,
Setting aside as special the women and children,
Signaling with their hands and stammering speech
That the weak must be pitied, as was just.   1020
Harmony wasn't always the result,
But the better part kept faithful to their vows;
If they had not, our race would have all perished,
Not kept its shoots alive unto this age.

And Nature compelled them to utter the sounds of language,
And names were coined for their utility,
Rather as speechless infancy itself
Draws children on to gestures—when, for instance,
The babies point at things they see before them.
1030 For everyone senses how to use his powers.
Before the first horns sprout from the bull-calf's head
With it he'll butt in a fury, thrust, attack,
And the cubs of lions and the panther's kittens
Will tussle each other with pawing and clawing and biting,
Although their teeth and nails are hardly formed;
And we see callow birds trust to their wings,
Seeking a fluttering help from their young feathers.
So to think that someone in those days dealt out
The names for things, and taught men their first words,
1040 Is stupid. How could this person mark all things,
Utter the various sounds the tongue can make,
At a time when others couldn't do the same?
Besides, if others hadn't used their voices
Amongst themselves, what planted the idea
Of language's use? What gave him that first power
To know, to see in his mind what he wanted to do?
One master, too, to tame so many pupils,
Force them to learn by heart the names of things,
And teaching them, like making the deaf hear—
1050 Not easy to see how! They wouldn't stand it,
Wouldn't be able to bear the gobbledygook
Of noises drumming against their ears in vain.
And finally, what's so very strange, if man,
Whose voice and tongue are active and well-formed,
Should give things various names to suit his feelings,
When the dumb cattle, when even the wild beasts
Utter their various sounds and all unlike,
When they're scared or hurt or feeling the glow of joy?
Things in plain sight will show how true this is:
1060 Rile a Molossian bloodhound and right off
He growls from his great loose jaws and bares his teeth

In the menace of tight-drawn fury; a different sound
From when he finally fills the place with barking.
Or when they nuzzle and go to lick their puppies,
Or rouse them up with a teasing paw or a nip,
Pretending to gobble them, gently, their teeth held back,
They lovingly yip and yelp, a sound much different
From when they're left in the house to yowl all day
Or when they whine and slink away from a beating.
And isn't it clear that whinnyings differ too,   1070
When among the mare the young stud in his prime
Rages, struck by the spurs of the winged Love,
Neighing and flaring his nostrils for the combat,
And when he shakes and whickers, tense with fear?
Then too, the race of birds, the dappled fliers,
Hawks and bone-cracker ospreys and diving gulls
Seeking their food and life in the salt streams—
Far different calls they use at different times,
When they fight over food, or the prizes fight right back,
While some, in keeping with the weather, change   1080
Their croakish song, like the long-lived race of crows
And the flocking rooks, when it's said they warn of storms,
Or when sometimes they call the wind to blow.
Therefore if various feelings force these creatures,
Mute though they are, to utter various cries,
All the more plausible that men could mark
Dissimilar things with this or the other sound.

Likewise—in case you're wondering to yourself—
Lightning brought fire to earth for mortal men,
It was the first; all flames have spread from there.   1090
For we see many things dazzle like lightning
When the bolt from the sky laces them with fire.
Then too when a well-branched tree sways in the wind,
Sawing back and forth, weighing over another tree's branches,
Its great force crushes and grinds out seeds of fire
That sometimes flare up into heat and flame,
While the stocks and branches scratch against each other.

One or the other could have given men fire.
And how to use fire to soften and cook food
1100   They learned from the sun—for they saw fruits in the fields
Grow mellow under hot rays beating down.

Those of a clever and vigorous turn of mind
Soon showed their fellows how to adopt new things—
Like fire—for a new diet and way of life.
Kings founded cities then, and citadels
As garrisons for themselves or hideaways,
And parceled out the cattle and land according
To beauty or intelligence or strength.
(For strength and a lovely face were highly prized.)
1110   Then property was established and gold found,
Stealing the honor from the strong and handsome.
For the mob all flocks to the rich man's following,
Even those blessed with strength and lovely bodies.
But if true reason governs how one lives,
To have great wealth means to live sparingly,
With a clear heart: small wants are always met.
But men were avid for high rank and rule
To set their fortunes on a steadfast basis,
To prosper and to lead their lives in peace—
1120   In vain, for while men battled to the top
They left a road of treachery behind,
Then from off that summit as if thunderstruck
They'd be flung by Envy down to hell in scorn—
For as lightning strikes the summits in most cases,
So envy scorches the most prominent.
Thus it's far more satisfying to serve in quiet
Than to want to rule the world and hold a throne.
Let them weary themselves and sweat their blood for nothing,
Choking their way through the narrows of ambition,
1130   For all they know comes from what others tell them,
They trust in rumor and not in their own senses,
And that's the way it is, and was, and will be.

When the kings were slain, the ancient majesty
Of the proud scepter and throne lay toppled over
And that bright bloody crown of the Lord's head
Mourned its lost honor under the tread of mobs
Who gleefully trampled what they once had feared.
Thus the state returned to the mob and the lowest dregs,
And each man sought supremacy and power.
Then some men showed how to make magistrates   1140
And appoint courts—for they would live by laws.
Weary of living by brute force, exhausted
From lack of friendship, men, of their own will, fell
The sooner under the strict laws and the courts.
Embittered and angry men had sought revenge
Beyond what our fair laws would now concede;
But people grew sick to death of violence.
Then loot was spoiled by the fear of punishment.
The snares of injury snatch their engineer;
Force doubles back upon its origin.   1150
Not easy for one to lead a sweet calm life
Who violates the common bond of peace.
And even if he should fool the gods and men,
Still he can't trust the secret will last forever,
And in fact many, talking in their sleep
Or crazed with disease, are said to have dragged themselves
Out in the open and revealed their crimes.

How the idea of gods spread to all nations,
Stocking their cities with altars and making men tremble
To undertake the solemn rites, which flourish   1160
With all our luxury and magnificence
(Even now sowing in us the seeds of horror,
Urging us on to rear across the world
New shrines to the gods to crowd on festival days),
Is not hard to explain in a few words.
In those days mortal men saw while awake
The excellent countenances of the gods,

Or rather in dreams they gasped at their vast size.
Men lent sensation to these giant forms
1170   For they moved their limbs, it seemed, and spoke proud words
As arrogant as their beauty and great strength.
Eternal life they gave them, for their faces
And their physiques persisted ever-present,
And they thought that beings endowed with such great power
Could never be put to rout by any force.
They thought the gods preeminently blest,
For the fear of death could hardly trouble them;
Also because in dreams they saw them do
Miraculous things, and many, without an effort.
1180   Then too they saw the systems of the sky
Turn in sure order, and the changing seasons,
But could not understand why this occurred.
Their refuge, then: assign to the gods all things,
Have them steer all things with a single nod.
In the heavens they placed the holy haunts of the gods
For through the heavens wheeled the night and the moon,
The moon and the day, the night and night's stark signs,
And night-roaming torches of heaven and gliding flames,
Clouds, sun, storms, snow, high winds and hail and lightning
1190   And the sudden growl and great and menacing rumble.

Unhappy human race—to grant such feats
To gods, and then to add vindictiveness!
What wailing did they bring forth for themselves,
What wounds for us, what tears for our descendants!
It's no piety to be seen at every altar,
To cover your head and turn to the stone idol,
Or to flatten yourself on the ground and lift your palms
To the shrines, or to spray altars with the blood
Of cattle—so much!—or to string vow on vow.
1200   To observe all things with a mind at peace
Is piety. For when we look up to the heavenly
Shrines of this great world, the stars that glitter, the sky
Studded, when we think of the journeying sun and moon,

Then in hearts heavy-laden with other cares
That Trouble is roused to boot, and rears its head—
That the limitless power of gods, the power that wheels
The stars and planets, may be aimed at us.
Then ignorance assails the mind in doubt
About the universe's origin,
About the end, how long the walls of the world   1210
Can suffer the straining of such stir and motion,
Or whether, granted everlasting health
By the gods, they can in endless course disdain
The turning age and the vast strength of time.
And worse, whose soul does not contract in fear
Of the gods, whose limbs don't crawl with terror when
The scorched earth under the terrible lightning bolt
Quakes, and a grumbling rolls through the great sky?
Don't people and nations tremble, and arrogant kings
Cringe, stricken into shock by fear of the gods,   1220
Lest for some foul deed done or proud word said
The heavy time has come to pay the price?
When a high hard gale across the plains of the sea
Rakes a commander and his fleet along
With all his mighty elephants and legions,
Won't he beseech the "Peace of the Gods" in terror
And pray for peaceful breezes and fair winds?
In vain, for the whirlpool's got him anyway
And borne him down unto the shoals of Death.
So thoroughly is human grandeur crushed   1230
By a hidden force; the glorious rods and axes,
Those splendid mockeries, are trampled under.
Well, when the whole earth staggers underfoot
And cities are battered and fall, or threaten to fall,
What wonder if self-loathing seizes men
And they grant wondrous power over all affairs
To gods, to steer and rule the universe?

To the next topic: bronze and gold and iron
And heavy silver too, and good strong lead,

1240   Were found by man when fire in the high mountains
    Had burnt big woods; these may have been struck by lightning,
    Or maybe wood dwellers, waging war, brought fire
    Into the forests to frighten their enemies;
    Maybe, lured by the fat of the land, they wished
    To clear the rich fields, make them good for pasture,
    Or slay the animals for their costly spoils.
    (Hunting with fire and animal pits came first,
    Then fencing the thickets with snares and flushing with hounds.)
    Whatever, however it was that the flaming heat
1250   With hair-raising crackle had crunched on the deep woods
    Down to the roots, and charred the earth with fire,
    There oozed, through the boiling veins in the earth's pores,
    A river gathered up of silver and gold,
    Copper and lead. And later, when they saw these
    Solid and shining below in splendid color—
    How shiny and smooth they were—they picked them up,
    Each in its outlines like a little pool
    Shaped like the hollow which it left behind.
    It struck them, they could melt the metal down
1260   And make it run to the mold of whatever they liked,
    Then they could to draw it to however sharp
    And slender a point you want, hammering, honing,
    Giving them tools to fell the forests and
    Rough-hew the wood with an axe and plane the planks,
    Or bore with an auger or chisel through or gouge.
    At first they tried no less with silver and gold
    To make these things than with good rugged bronze—
    In vain, for all the metals' strength gave in,
    Not able to bear up under the same hard work.
1270   So copper was prized more highly, and gold lay
    Dull-edged and blunted in its uselessness.
    Now copper lies—gold's stepped to the highest honor.
    And so the roll of time brings change to all;
    What once was prized is now bereft of honor,
    Succeeded by another, once disdained,

But sought after in time, and among men
Blossoming out in praise beyond belief.

How men discovered iron and its nature,
Memmius, you yourself can easily see.
Hands, teeth, and nails—these were the weapons used   1280
In the old days, and rocks, and broken branches,
And fire too, after they'd discovered it.
Later they learned of the strength of iron and bronze.
They knew the use of bronze first, then of iron—
Bronze was more easily worked and more abundant.
With bronze they tilled the soil, with bronze they furrowed
The rivers of war and sowed vast fields with blood,
Despoiling lands and chattels. Unarmed, naked
Opponents fell before the soldiers' bronze.
Then gradually there came the sword of iron,   1290
And the brazen sickles were looked on with contempt.
They started to scrape the earth with iron; now wars
Were evenly matched, as dubious as the twilight.
And soldiers learned to mount a horse's flanks,
Curb him with reins and fight with the strong right arm,
Before they risked the chariots of war—
The two-horsed chariots first, then the twin-yoked four,
Then mounting high in the cars with sickle-spokes.
Then elephants, bulwark-bodied, fearsome, snake-handed,
Were taught to endure wounds by the Phoenicians   1300
And to put great enemy forces to confusion.
Harsh Discord thus makes one thing out of another,
Horrible weapons for humanity,
Increasing day by day the terror of war.

They even tested bulls in the thick of battle
And drove wild boars against the enemy.
Sometimes they sent ahead the robust lions
With their armed trainers and their savage masters
To curb and check them, hold them under the leash—

1310 In vain, for the savages, hot with the splash of bloodshed,
   Routed the squadrons indiscriminately,
   Everywhere tossing their heads, their terrible manes;
   And the riders couldn't calm their horses, gone
   Mad with the roaring, and rein them to turn and fight.
   And the she-lions, provoked, would crouch and spring
   Everywhere, lunging for the attacker's face
   Or ripping the unsuspecting from behind,
   Clamping them, mortally wounded, to the ground
   And fixing them fast with healthy bites and claws.
1320 Bulls threw their own men, trampled them to powder,
   With their horns guzzled the flanks and guts of horses
   And raked the earth up with the threatening hoof.
   And the boars, mighty of tusk, slaughtered their allies;
   They raged and they spattered their blood on broken lances,
   On lances broken inside them spattered their blood,
   Bringing horseman and foot soldier both to ruin.
   For the horses shied and veered from the fierce tusk's
   Lunges, and reared up, pawing at the air—
   In vain, for you might see them, their hamstrings sliced,
1330 Crumple, and cover the earth with their heavy fall.
   Some had been tamed enough at home, they thought—
   But these they saw froth in the heat of action,
   In the bloodshed and shrieking and flight and the terror and uproar;
   Not a single one of them could they round up.
   For all the beasts ran wild, as often now
   Elephants, pricked and slashed by the sword, will turn
   And maul their masters for it, and then scatter.
   But did men really do such things? I find it
   Incredible that they couldn't have seen it coming,
1340 Disgrace and the common-bad for everyone.
   In the All, perhaps, you could insist, "It happened!",
   In various worlds created various ways,
   Sooner than in one certain globe wherever.
   But *they* didn't act in hope of conquest—rather
   To give foes cause to weep, and to die themselves,
   Not certain of their numbers, lacking weapons.

First clothes were made by knotting, then came weaving.
Weaving came after ironwork, for looms
Are iron—the only way to make such smooth
Treadles and spindles, shutters and rackety yardbeams.   1350
And men were compelled by Nature to spin wool
Before the women (for in all arts the male
Excels by far in cleverness and skill)
Till the stern farmers called it a sissy thing
And passed that work along to the womenfolk—
For their own part, they'd tackle the tough jobs
And with hard labor make hands hard, limbs strong.

Nature herself, the first creator, was
The origin of sowing and engrafting,
The model; for fallen nuts and berries gave   1360
Their seasonal swarms of sprouts under the trees.
Thence came the whimsy too for grafting slips
And digging holes in the fields to set new shoots.
From there they tried to plant out this and that
In their little plots, and saw that gentle tillage
Pampered the wild fruits, made them milder and sweeter.
In a while they forced the forests to recede
Up to the mountain, and yield the land below
To farming. So they had, in the hills and the plains,
Pools, streamlets, gardens, grain fields, the glad vine,   1370
And a sea-gray sweep of olive trees to mark
The landscape, over hollow and hill and field,
As now you'll find a various charm mapped out
Wherever the land's adorned with apple orchards
And the glad vines that fence the land around.

And echoing the liquid warble of birds
Came long before men gathered together to sing
Fine polished carols to delight the ear.
And the winds whistling in the hollow of reeds
Taught them to play the rustic hemlock pipe.   1380
Then little by little they learned the sweet complaints

That the pipe pours forth at the fingering-pulse of the players,
Heard in the trackless forests, the shepherds' dells,
Places of sunlit solitude and peace.
After a hearty meal these songs caressed
And pleased them all—for then things touch the heart.
Often they lay at ease in the soft grass,
In the shade of a tall tree by the riverside,
Their bodies refreshed and gladdened, at no great cost,
1390 Especially when the weather smiled, and the season
Stippled the meadow with fresh and lusty flowers.
Then they had games, and talking, and sweet laughter,
For then the rustic Muse was in her prime;
Then prompted by merry Foolery they would garland
Their heads and shoulders with a crown of flowers,
And move their limbs in a rough rhythm and dance,
Pounding their mother Earth with their rough feet.
Then they would smile at themselves and merrily laugh—
It was all new to them then, and wonderful!
1400 And there were solaces for loss of sleep:
To troll out long notes, turn with the turn of the tune,
And race the pursed lip over the woodland pipe.
The night watch even now observe these ways
And learn to keep the various beats; nor do
They catch a sweeter pleasure, for all their learning,
Than did those soil-bred dwellers of the woods.
For unless we know of something more delightful
What's here at hand prevails and pleases best;
Later on something better will destroy
1410 That too, and change our views of all things past.
So acorns came to be hated; so the strewn beds
Of mounded grass and foliage were abandoned;
And clothing made from pelts fell into contempt,
Whose discovery, I'll bet, aroused such envy
That the first wearer was assassinated,
And, worse, the killers in their rivalry ripped
The blood-soaked hide to bits—so no one got it!
In those days it was pelts, now gold and purple

March men to war, and weary human life.
That makes me think the greater fault is ours.   1420
Naked, those sons of the soil were racked by cold,
But in our case it's no great harm to lack
Purple or gold or gaudy embroidery —
A commoner's coat will keep the cold away.
So people struggle blindly and in vain,
Wasting their lives on foolishness; no wonder,
For they can grasp no limits to their having,
No limit to the growth of true delight.
That, little by little, sets their lives adrift
In the deep sea and the seething tides of war.   1430

The great revolving temple of the sky,
The sentinel sun and moon that glide in light,
Taught watchful men the turnings of the year —
By a certain means things happen, in certain order.

Then they spent their lives walled up behind strong towers
And the earth was pieced and plotted to be farmed.
The the sea blossomed out with sail-winged ships.
With allies and confederates they leagued,
And they discovered alphabets, and poets
Began to pass their great deeds on in song.   1440
What happened before these histories, we can't now
Tell, unless reason helps us find the traces.
And agriculture and ships and walls and laws,
Weapons and roads and robes and all the rest,
All the luxuries, all the highest joys of life,
Poetry, painting, the artful polish of sculpture,
An alert mind and use have slowly taught us,
Little by little, advancing step by step.
So time, little by little, draws each thing out
Into the open, raised to the shores of light   1450
By reason. One thing shone upon the next
Till men had touched the pinnacle of art.

BOOK SIX

First from of old to scatter the gift of grain
To mankind born to die was glorious Athens;
She restored life with art, she voted laws,
And first gave human life sweet consolation
When she brought forth a man of such great mind,
A man—an oracle pouring forth all truth.
His light has set, but his divine discoveries
Have spread his fame, time-honored now, to the skies.
For when he saw that the things which life demands
Are, almost all of them, ready for men to take,
That life was as secure as it could be,
Saw men who swam in honor and praise and wealth
Enjoying eminent sons who did them proud,
While at home they felt the strangling in the heart,
Saw them abusing their lives with thanklessness,
Lashing out in a fury and never pausing,
He grasped then that the vessel caused the vice—
That even the best of blessings would be spoiled
By the vice of the soul that takes them in,
Partly because it's frail and riddled with holes
So that you'd never have enough to fill it,
Partly because whatever it takes inside
Is, so to speak, all fouled by its sour stench.
So he purged men's hearts with his truth-telling words,
Setting a limit for desire and fear,
Unveiling what that highest good might be
Toward which all strive, and he showed the narrow path
Whereby we run directly to that goal;

And what maladies there are in mortal things,
Which swoop upon us naturally by chance   30
Or by physical force—for these are natural causes;
And from which gates to charge to meet each foe.
And he showed that people, often and for nothing,
Were tossed by the storms of trouble in their hearts.
For as little boys tremble and fear whatever's lurking
In the blind dark, so we in the light of day
Tremble at what is no more terrible than
What little boys fear in the dark and dream will come.
And so this darkness and terror of the mind
Shall not by the sun's rays, by the bright lances of daylight   40
Be scattered, but by Nature and her law.
On, then, to weave my enterprise of song.

And since I've shown that the vast world will die,
That the heavens, made of matter, were born, and since
I have explained most of what there occurs
And must occur, attend to what remains,
As now I undertake to mount the chariot
Of glorious poetry . . .

The hard winds might be calmed and all the omens
Reversed, just as the fury is appeased;   50
So too with all that mortal men observe
In the sky, on earth, when their minds hang by a fearful
Thread, and they fall prone, flattened to the ground,
Sunken in shameful fear of the gods, because
Their ignorance of causes makes them yield
All power and rule to those divinities.
These rational causes they cannot discern,
So they suppose it's all the will of the gods.
Men may well learn that the gods live free of care,
But if they wonder anyway how all things   60
Can come to happen, especially what they notice
Looming above their heads, in the shores of the sky,
They slide back into their old religions, calling

Upon those pitiless masters, whom the poor fools
Believe almighty; they don't know what can be,
What cannot, what law grants each thing its own
Deep-driven boundary stone and finite scope.
So their blind reasoning carries them astray.
Spit out such thoughts, unworthy of the gods
70 And alien to their peace; leave off, discard them;
Or the sacred powers, by you yourself diminished,
Will do you harm. Oh, their godheads can't be so
Defiled, to crave the drink of retribution;
What's wrong is, you suppose that those calm gods
Are rolled by tides of anger, and this will hurt you,
For you won't then go to the shrines with a calm heart,
Nor will your mind be strong enough to take
Their holy semblances in peace, the heralds
Of godlike beauty sent to human minds.

80 Easy to see what sort of life will follow.   .
Reject it, cast it far away, and listen
To what we teach! Though many truths have issued
From me, much yet remains, to be adorned
In polished verse: the order and form of the heavens
Must be grasped, and the thunder sung, and the flash of lightning—
What these effect, what causes them to be—
So don't you scurry like a brainless fool
To check what zone of the sky the fire's been shot from,
If it forks left or right, what wall it enters
90 To lord it in the building and then pass through.
Men can't discern what causes things like these,
So they suppose it's all the will of the gods.

Show me the white chalk line at the end of the race,
Show me the course to run, you cleverest Muse
Calliope, pleasure of gods and man's repose,
Lead me to seize that crown of praise and fame.

To start: the deep blue heavens are thunder-stricken
Because there fly together in high collision

Clouds driven against each other by winds at war.
For there's no rumble when the sky is calm,   100
No, but where all the clouds move in thick troops,
There will you hear the growls and the big roaring.
Besides, the stuff of the clouds can't be so dense
As stones or wooden studs, yet even so
Can't be as slender as puffs of smoke or mist.
For they'd have to fall, thrust down by the brute weight,
Like stones, or else like smoke be too unsteady
To stand together or keep the snow pent up.
They sound above the spreading plains of the world
As a taut awning over the theater   110
Noisily flaps between the poles and the beams,
Or, roaring and tearing, is rammed by the boisterous winds
And crackles like a big roll of papyrus—
That kind of thunder too you recognize—
Or when sheets hung to dry or loose-flown papers
Are given a slap and are whirled and whipped in the wind.
Sometimes it happens too that the clouds don't race
To such a frontal attack, but from the flank
Shave, drag each other, scraping separate ways.
Then that dry friction noise grates on the ear   120
And drags on, till the clouds get free of the clinches.

Here's why the whole world, rocked by volleys of thunder,
Appears to tremble, and its vast battlements
To have been torn asunder, burst and shattered:
When the sudden gathering surf of a strong wind
Bores its way into the clouds, and there walled up
And spinning faster and faster it makes the cloud
Hollow inside, with a thick hull around,
Weakened and finally ripped by the sharp assault,
The cloud explodes with a terrible thunderous roar.   130
No cause for wonder. Blow up an animal bladder
Until it bursts: it gives its great big pop.

This will explain, when winds blow through the clouds,
Why noise results. For often we see clouds

Branched like the crowns of trees, or somehow jagged,
So it's as when the northwest wind blasts through
Dense woods—leaves rustle and branches groan and crack.
And sometimes too the riotous wind attacks
Head on in strength, and tears the cloud to pieces.
140   Facts in plain sight will show what wind can do,
When here on earth where the wind is gentler, tall
Trees can be torn and sucked up roots and all.
And there are waves in the clouds themselves, that break
And give their low hoarse grumble, as in deep rivers
Or the vast sea when the surges break on the shore.
Or it's when the flash of lightning from one cloud
Assaults another. Let the fire be caught
By a soaked-wet cloud, and at once, with a great outcry,
It's butchered—as white-hot irons from the furnace
150   Hiss, if you dunk them straight off in cold water.
What's more, if a drier cloud takes in the fire
It will flare like tinder and burn with a huge noise,
As when a fire whirled by the reckless wind
Chars in its fury the mountains tressed with laurel,
The laurel of Apollo at Delphi; nothing
Burns with a more terrific crackle of flame.
Last, often a loud crack of ice and the fall
Of hail will cause a racket in big clouds.
When the wind packs them solid, the heaped hills
160   Of cloud, hail-thick, crushed tight together, shatter.

Just so, the lightning flashes when many sparks
Are flinted out by the clash of the clouds—as stone
Or steel strikes stone—for then light leaps up too
And scatters scintillating sparks of fire.
And our ears catch thunder after the eyes have caught
The flash, for things that stimulate the ears
Are always slower than what rouses sight.
For example, if you watch a lumberjack
Chopping the trunk of a tree with his two-blade axe,
170   You'll see the stroke before the sound of the chop
Reaches the ears. So too we see the lightning

Before we hear the thunder, though both are sent
From the same cause, born in the same collision.

Here too is how the clouds can streak the earth
With light, in the quivering flash of a coming storm.
When the wind's rushed into a cloud and whirled about,
And has hollowed the cloud, as I've shown, and thickened its
    shell,
The motion boils it over, as everything
Grows hot by motion, burns—as a lead ball
Slung far into the air will liquefy. 180
So when the boiling wind has slashed the stormcloud,
It scatters at once, as if pressed out by force,
Atoms that flash the wink of the lightning-fire.
The sound then follows, which only strikes the ear
After the things that reach the light of vision.
This, you should know, happens in dense and high
Heaped-up clouds, heaped one on another, a fabulous bulwark,
And don't be fooled by the fact that from below
Their width looks greater than their massive height.
Watch and consider, when the crosswinds blow 190
Clouds in the shape of mountains through the air,
Or you see clouds banked up over mountain peaks
Pile one upon the other and crowding down,
Docked in one station while all the winds are buried,
Then you can recognize their massiveness
And see that they're built like grottoes hung with stone,
Which in the rising storm are filled by winds
That grumble and roar, disdaining to be shut
In the clouds, like beasts that bluster from their cages.
Now here, now there, through the clouds they vent their fury, 200
Circling and prowling for the way out, rolling
Fire-atoms together from the clouds and driving
And forcing and spinning the flame in the hollow oven
Till they tear the cloud and glitter and shake with light.

The following too can cause that swift gold blaze
Of liquid fire to fly to the earth: those clouds

Have to possess a multitude of seeds
Of fire. For if the clouds are free of moisture
They'll be the color of resplendent flame.
210   From the sunlight they must catch so many seeds
That naturally they'll blush and brim with fire.
When the driving wind has thrust such clouds together
And cramped them up in one place, the fire-atoms
Will spurt out, spouting the color of light and flame.
And it lightens also when the clouds are thinned.
For when a soft wind separates the clouds
And melts them away, those seeds that make the lightning
Fall, counter to their will. Then the sky gleams
Without the tumult and the thundering terror.

220   As for the lightning bolt and what it's made of,
The strokes themselves declare, and the branded signs
Of heat, and the traces smoking with foul sulfur.
These are the signs of fire—not wind, not rain.
Besides, they'll often set the roofs ablaze
And lord it over the houses with quick flames.
Nature, you see, has fashioned the bolt the subtlest
Fire of all fires, with atoms tiny and readily
Moving, which nothing can resist at all.
For the powerful bolt will pass through the walls of a house,
230   As will shouting, or talk; passes through stones, through bronze,
And in an instant fuses copper and gold.
It takes care too that wine from a solid flask
Steams off, for the bolt can readily loosen up
And rarefy the clay sides, and no wonder,
What with the heat it brings, and slip inside
And swiftly unbind and scatter the atoms of wine.
A thing which the warmth of the sun can't in a lifetime
Cause, with its shimmering heat so powerful;
So much the swifter and stronger the force of lightning.

240   How these are begotten, now, and with such headlong
Thrust, that the stroke can split a tower open,

Leave homes in rubble and rip out planks and joists,
Tumble and demolish monuments of heroes,
Tear a man's soul out, strew to the earth dead cattle,
What force enables it to do such things,
I shall make plain—and I won't keep you waiting.

One must suppose that dense and high-heaped clouds
Make thunderbolts. There are none when the sky is clear,
And none are ever shot from wisps of cloud.
This truth the plain facts show abundantly,   250
For when clouds mass together and cover the air
And we'd think all the gloom of Hell was gushing out
And flooding the vast caverns of the sky,
When everywhere we look specters of Fear
Have surged in the grim cloud-night to hang above us,
Then the storm brandishes its bolts of lightning.
And often over the sea a black cloud-pillar,
Like a river of pitch from the sky, falls packed with darkness
Into the waves, and sweeps from afar off
Black weather in heavy labor of storm and lightning,   260
Itself so full of wind, so full of fire
That even on land men shudder and look for cover.
So we conclude that tempests rise up high
Above our heads. For they would never bury
The earth with such dark mist, unless the clouds
Heaped up, and blotted out the light of the sun;
And they wouldn't be able to batter the earth with rain,
Fill the brooks to flooding and turn the fields to lakes,
If the sky were not buttressed high with clouds.
Up there, then, all is full of wind and fire;   270
That makes for the random roar and the bolt of lightning.
In fact, I've shown above that the clouds, hollow,
Hold multitudes of seeds of heat—they must
Catch many from the rays and the fire of the sun.
Now when a wind by chance drives all of these
Into one place, it flints out many seeds
Of heat, at the same time mingling with that fire;

Thrust into those straits it twists and swirls in an eddy
And whets the lightning in the white-hot foundry
280   (For it's kindled in two ways: its own swift motion
Makes it grow warm, or it catches the touch of the fire);
Hence when the wind is good and hot and the fire
Has lunged to attack, the bolt then, ripe and ready,
Slashes the cloud in an instant and all the world
Is lit up by a torch of glittering fire.
Then follows the deep bass roar and it sounds like heaven's
Temples have suddenly burst to fall upon us.
Then a deep tremor shakes the earth, and a growl
Sweeps through the sky, for the storm's front is all
290   Throttled, and trembles, and rouses the roar of thunder.
Skies quake—and then there comes the heavy downpour,
So that all heaven seems to have turned to rain,
The violent ruin calling to mind the Flood:
So much do the bursting cloud and the tempest winds
Let loose, when the thunder flies with the stroke of lightning.

And a wind whipped up from the outside may attack
A cloud already armed with ready lightning.
As soon as the cloud is torn that swirl of fire
Falls, which our language names the "lightning bolt."
300   So it is, no matter where the cloud is struck.
Or it can happen too that a strong cold wind
Can catch fire in its long and speedy flight,
Losing along its way the larger atoms
That cannot penetrate the air so well,
While shaving that air and sweeping away some atoms,
Some tiny ones that mix with the wind in flight
And set it afire, as when a ball of lead
Seethes in its flight as it loses the many atoms
Of the stiff cold, and kindles in the air.
310   Or it may be that the force of the blow itself
From a cold and fireless wind can rouse the fire.
That's not so strange. When the violent wind strikes home
From that same wind heat-atoms can converge

Along with atoms from the object struck,
As, when we hack a stone with a sword, sparks fly,
And though the iron is cold, no slower for that
Do the bright atoms of fire meet at its stroke.
That's the way lightning too sets things on fire,
If they're ready and waiting and combustible.
Impossible that the cold winds above   320
Should blow with such great force yet never be
Kindled by fire somewhere along the way,
Or made lukewarm at least, with a dash of heat.

But the strike of the lightning bolt is hard and quick,
Racing and falling instantaneously,
Since first the spurred-on force in the clouds builds up
And gathers such momentum to escape
That when the clouds can't hold back the big rush
The bolt breaks through and flies with incredible power,
Like a missile shot from a catapult cranked tight.   330
Add that it's made of smooth and tiny atoms
Whose nature is not easy to withstand,
For it penetrates (and flashes between) the pores.
Despite the many obstructions it does not
Clog, stick; so its swath is quick and smooth in flight.
Since all weight presses down, if you propel
An object with another thrust besides,
It doubles its speed and leans the harder and heavier,
And all the more quickly and violently it blasts
And scatters whatever blocks it on its way.   340
Also because its flight is long, the bolt
Picks up more speed and more and more as it goes,
Growing in power and packing more strength in the punch.
That makes it so that all the lightning's atoms
Are concentrated in one single place,
Hurling them all along its streaking track.
In its journey it may pick up, by chance, some atoms
Of air, whose batterings fire its speed and motion.
It passes through many things and leaves them whole,

350 For the fire, like liquid, streams straight through the pores.
Many it shatters, when the lightning strikes
Just at the junctures of the woven atoms.
Copper, moreover, it readily dissolves
And melts gold instantly, for out of smooth
And tiny atoms is the lightning formed,
Which easily steal inside and, having entered,
Relax the bonds and loosen all the knots.

More often in autumn is the spangled sky
Shaken, the starry dome and all the earth,
360 And more when the flowering time of spring unfolds.
There's not enough fire in winter or wind in summer,
And the clouds' substance is not dense enough.
But when the seasons lie in the between-times
All causes of the lightning bolt concur.
That seasonal crisscross mingles cold with tides
Of heat—and the lightning factory needs both,
Needs discord, so that the raging air will splash
In a great riot of tossing winds and fire.
There is the first of warmth and the end of cold—
370 That season is spring. These unlike things must fight
Against each other, and rumble and mix it up.
And when the utmost warmth with the first cold
Mixes and rolls, that season we call the "autumn";
Here too keen winter dashes against the summer.
We really ought to name these seasons "straits,"
And it's no wonder if at those times more lightning
Strikes, and the sky is dark and wild with storms,
Wild and dark with a dubious, two-flanked war,
On this side flames, on that side wind and rain.

380 That's how to look into the nature of lightning,
Fire-bringer, and see by just what force it acts,
Not to unscroll Etruscan spells in vain,
Snooping for hints of the hidden will of the gods,
Asking what zone of the sky the fire's been shot from,

If it forks left or right, what wall it enters
To lord it in the building and then pass through,
What harm the lightning-stricken spot can cause.
Now if Jupiter and the other big gods shake
The brilliant fields of the sky with terrible thunder
And fling their fire at whomever wherever they will,   390
Why can't they rig it that reckless doers of evil,
The filthiest sinners, be struck, and steam forth flames
From chests impaled by lightning—a sharp lesson,
When instead a man whose mind is pure and free,
An innocent man, writhes in a tangle of flame,
Snatched by the sudden whirl of fire from heaven?
Why do they aim for the deserts, and sweat for nothing?
To toughen their muscles, to get their arms in shape?
Why do they let their daddy's spears get blunted
In the dirt? Why does he allow it? Why doesn't he stockpile   400
Spears for his foes? When the sky's clear, why does Jove
Never hurl his bolt to the earth and vent his roaring?
When a cloud passes below, does he all at once
Jump down to it to fix a closer aim?
In the sea—what's the use of that? Got a grudge against
The waves and the mounds of water and fields of ocean?
If he wants us, besides, to beware the stroke of lightning,
Why hesitate to let us see it coming?
But if he wants to torch us by surprise,
Why does it thunder there so we can shun it?   410
Why all the blustery roaring and rumbling and darkness?
How can you think he strikes in many directions
At once? Or do you have the nerve to insist
That many blows don't fall in a single instant?
But this happens all the time, as it really must:
It rains in many places and showers fall,
So there are many simultaneous lightnings.
Finally, why does he rattle holy shrines
And his own eminent throne with enemy lightning,
Splitting the elegant statues of the gods,   420
Marring with gashes the glory of his own?

And why does he aim for the heights? Why do we find
So many marks of his fire on mountaintops?

Next, from these things it's easy to see how
Cyclones (which the Greeks call "presters," that is, "burners")
Are shot into the ocean from above.
For at times a kind of column drops from heaven
Into the sea, round which the channel currents
Bubble and seethe, whipped up by the blasts that hiss,
430   And whatever ships in such a donnybrook
Are caught unawares, fall into the gravest danger.
These cyclones strike whenever a stirred-up wind
Can't manage to break the cloud, but pushes it down
Into a kind of column dropped from heaven,
Gradually, as if some fist or arm above
Pushed, punched it down and stretched it to the waves.
This splits, and the high wind bursts over the sea,
Bringing about strange boiling in the waves,
For a whirlwind spun like a top descends and carries
440   The pliant substance of the cloud along
And thrusts that swollen mass into the sea,
Then suddenly plunges itself into the water,
Churning the sea to a roaring and frothing boil.
And at times that very whirlwind becomes snagged
Inside the clouds, and shaves away cloud-atoms,
And imitates the "burner" shot from heaven.
When this touches down on the earth and flies apart
It vomits up a hurricane or cyclone.
As these are very rare, and as the mountains
450   Block them on land, more commonly we see them
On the sea's vista and under the open sky.

Clouds clump together and form when many atoms
Flying above in the sky have suddenly joined,
Atoms a little bit rough, that still will clasp
And hold together in their slight attachment.
First these make little clouds that stand entire,

Then those too cluster up and flock (and in
Their clustering, grow) together and carry along
Winds, till at last a savage storm is born.
And it happens that mountain peaks, the higher they are   460
And the nearer they rise to the sky, the more they mist
With a thick constant fog of dust-red cloud.
This is the reason: when the clouds first form,
So slight, before the eye can pick them out,
The winds whisk them away to the mountain peaks.
Finally, in a heavier brew, they thicken
And become visible and all at once
Seem to surge from the summit to the sky.
High places stand more open to the wind—
Our senses prove it when we climb tall mountains.   470
Besides, Nature can filch a wealth of atoms
From the vast sea; clothes hung along a shore
Make this fact clear, when they catch the cling of dampness;
So the clouds can be thickened too by matter
Surging out of the salty whelm of the sea,
For water of ocean and water of cloud are kin.
Moreover, from every stream, and likewise from
The earth itself, we see clouds rise, and mists,
Pressed like an exhalation from below,
Slowly arising to supply the clouds,   480
Mantling the sky, suffusing it with smoke,
And the tides of the spangled fire above press down,
Condensing them, draping with clouds the deep blue sky.
Or it can happen that atoms from beyond
Come to this sky and make the sailing clouds.
Numberless atoms and unfathomable space—
I've proven these, and with what blazing speed
The bodies fly while in a flash they cross
Vast gulfs of space beyond remembering.
Small wonder if often, in a moment, storms   490
Heaped up with mountainous clouds and darkness should
Loom from above, and cover land and sea,
Since from all sides through every pore of the sky,

Through the blowholes, so to speak, of this great world,
The elements have their entrances and exits.

Listen: how it is that water coalesces
In the clouds high up and falls to the earth as showers,
I shall make clear. First point to win is this:
Many seeds of water rise up to those clouds
500 From all things here, so the two of them grow together—
Both the clouds and any water in the clouds—
As in us the body grows up with the blood,
And same for the sweat and for any bodily fluid.
Besides, clouds often soak up lots of water
From the sea—like woolen skins hung at the shore—
When the wind carries them over the great ocean.
Similarly from every stream the water
Is raised to the clouds. When all these water-atoms
From everywhere come together and swell the ranks,
510 The clouds brim full and struggle to let loose
That water—first, the wind may jam them thick,
And the mob of clouds themselves in great confusion
Crowd and press down and cause the showers to fall.
And when the wind attenuates the clouds
Or when they melt away in the warmth of the sun,
They let the raindrops fall, like a wax candle
Dripping and dwindling freely beneath the flame.
Now a violent storm occurs when the violent crush
Of clouds heaped high collide with the rush of the wind.
520 But the rains persist and linger a long time
When many seeds of water are stirred loose,
And dripping mists and clouds are blown above
Still other clouds, on all sides, everywhere,
And all the earth breathes back its watery mist.
Here, when the weather is gloomiest, rays of sunlight
Will gleam across the storm spray; then against
The dark clouds shine the colors of the rainbow.

The rest that are formed on high, that grow on high,
And coalesce in the clouds, all, absolutely

All—snow and wind and hail and the chilling frost 530
And the tough ice, great hardener of the waters,
The delayer, that reins back rivers eager to go—
Are all great things, but easy to examine
And to grasp how and why they come to be,
Once you have understood their elements.

Listen now, learn the explanation for
Earthquakes. And first of all, suppose the earth
Is below the same as it is above, all full
Of windy caves, with plenty of lakes and pools
Cradled in its lap, and boulders, and sheer cliffs. 540
And many rivers under the shell of the earth
Are rolling and billowing on, with sunken stones,
For Nature is the selfsame everywhere.
So with such things embedded from beneath
The earth above will tremble and fall to ruin
When long time undermines the caves below.
Whole mountains in fact will topple, and sudden tremors
Slither their way abroad with a violent shudder—
And rightly so, for houses near the road
Shake when a cart, just a light cart, jolts by, 550
Rocks all as much when some rough patch of the road
Bumps both your iron wheel-rims from the bottom.
Or maybe into a vast subterranean lake
The worn old hills will tumble in a landslide,
And the toss of the flood below makes everything totter,
As vessels sometimes can't stand right—the swish
And splash of the water inside must settle down.

Moreover, within the hollows of the earth,
When from one quarter the wind builds up, lunges,
Muscles the deep caves with its headstrong power, 560
The earth leans hard where the force of the wind has pressed it;
Then above ground, the higher the house is built,
The nearer it rises to the sky, the worse
Will it lean that way and jut out perilously,
The beams wrenched loose and hanging ready to fall.

And to think, men can't believe that for this world
Some time of death and ruin lies in wait,
Yet they see so great a mass of earth collapse!
And the winds pause for breath—that's lucky, for else
570 No force could rein things galloping to destruction.
But since they pause for breath, to rally their force,
Come building up and then fall driven back,
More often the earth will threaten the ruin than
Perform it. The earth will lean and then sway back,
Its wavering mass restored to the right poise.
That explains why all houses reel, top floor
Most, then the middle, and ground floor hardly at all.

The following also causes those great tremors:
When the wind or when some sudden force of air,
580 Arisen from the earth or from without,
Hurls itself into the hollows underground
And growls among the deep caves, sweeping and spinning
In agitation—then, its forces roused,
Immediately it bursts out into riot,
Splits the earth open into a yawning chasm.
Such happened at Syrian Sidon, and at Aegium
On the Peloponnesus: this sort of blast escaping
Rocked both those cities with the ensuing quake.
And many another city wall has fallen
590 In quakes, and many coastal towns with all
Their citizens have sunk into the sea.
Suppose the wind can't blast through? Still its thrust
And fierceness will, through the millions of pores in the earth,
Spread like the shivers—then comes the shudder of horror,
As when a chill strikes straight down to the bones,
Rattles them, making them shake against their will.
Two terrors then cause the city folk to tremble:
The roofs above they fear, and they fear that Nature
May suddenly let the ground cave in below,
600 Wrenching her jaws wide open to swallow them up,
Wishing to cram the gulf with their destruction.

Well, they can say, if they like, that heaven and earth
Are ordered to remain intact forever.
For all their talk those dangers will loom close
And set the spurs or the whip's lash to fear,
As the solid ground might fail beneath our feet,
Withdraw to the pit, and the world from its foundations
Collapse in universal anarchy.

. . . To start with, they're amazed that Nature makes
The sea no bigger, such a tumble of waters   610
Flows into it, all rivers everywhere.
Include the passing squalls and the driven storms
That drizzle or pour over land and sea; include
The ocean springs; all these would hardly add
One drop into the total of the sea.
It's no surprise, then, that the sea won't grow.
And the heat of the sun draws much of it away.
We see, for example, clothes hung dripping wet
Dried through and through by the warm rays of the sun—
And seas are spread out broad beneath the sky.   620
And so no matter how little the moisture is
That's sipped by the sun from one part of the sea,
From the vast stretch of the waves the drink is deep;
What's more, the winds that sweep the ocean plain
Can skim away a good deal, for we'll see
Roads swept dry by the wind in a single night,
And the soft ooze of the mud grown thick and crusty.
Moreover, I've shown that clouds can also lift
A lot of water from the level sea,
Then drizzle it here and there over the world,   630
When the wind carries the weather and it rains.
Finally, since the earth is thin and porous,
And its shores are linked like a belt round all the oceans,
As water flows from the earth into the sea,
So should it seep from the salt sea into the earth.
There its brine is filtered out and the sweet water
Seeps upward and at the source of every stream

Collects—then it's fresh assailing over the land,
Feet cutting a watery way for the waves to follow.

640   The explanation for that fiery whirl
Exhaled at times out of the jaws of Aetna
I'll now make clear. It was no middling slaughter
When the flame-storm rose and swept like a lord through the fields
Of Sicily; neighboring peoples turned their eyes
And saw the smoking temples of the sky
Glitter with sparks; they trembled, for they feared
What revolution Nature had in store.

You must look deeply into these affairs,
Long ponder every part, keep your scope wide,
650   Remembering the vastness of the All,
To see what a tiny portion of the whole
Is this one sky, what a trivial thing it is,
Less to the All than one man is to the earth.
Lay that on the table, look it over closely,
And you will leave off wondering at so much.
For which of us would find it strange if someone
Should catch a good hot fever in the joints
Or any sickness with its aches and pains?
For the foot swells big with the gout, or a sharp throb
660   Catches the teeth, or invades the very eyes;
Or the "holy fire," erysipelas, erupts
Burning and slithering snakelike over the body;
Not strange—for there are seeds of many things.
Earth bears diseases enough, and the sky bears evils,
To breed the power of endless pestilence.
And so from the wide heaven and all the earth
Infinite space supplies the seeds for illness,
And from their force the earth suddenly rocks
Or a whirlwind races over the land and sea,
670   Or Aetna gushes fire, and the skies blaze.
And they will blaze, the fields of the sky will burn,
And heavier thunderstorms will surge and rain

Wherever the water-atoms have been borne.
"But that's too huge a storm to set afire!"
Right—and a river seems the biggest ever
To a man who hasn't seen one bigger; a tree
Or a man or anything of any sort,
The biggest you've ever seen, you think it's huge,
When in fact all this sky and sea and earth
Are as nothing to the All, the universe.   680

Anyway, how that fire, stoked up to a rage,
Explodes out of the vast ovens of Aetna,
I'll now make clear. First, underneath the mountain
It's all a hollow, buttressed by vaults of flint.
Now then, in every cave there's wind and air.
(Wind is just air that's driven or roused up.)
When the wind grows hot and rages and broils the stones
Wherever it happens to touch them, and heats the earth,
It fires from them all the white-hot shooting flames,
And surges straight through the jaws and high in the air.   690
Far off it carries the fire, and far off scatters
Hot ash, and rolls its smoke as thick as night,
Disgorging stones of the most stupendous weight—
Don't doubt then—all this chaos is the wind's!
Moreover, against the deep roots of the mountain
The breakers wash and hiss as they withdraw.
They hollow out caves in the volcano's gullet
From the sea to the top of the mountain. Entering here . . .

And makes them penetrate from the open sea
And be blown out of the mountain, slinging fire   700
Upward, and stones from below, and clouds of sand.
For at the peak are "craters," as they're called,
"Punch bowls," for us the "jaws" or the "mouth" of the mountain.

There are some things for which it's not sufficient
To ascribe one cause—it's better to give many
And have one be right; as when you see far off

A corpse stretched on the ground, you guess each cause
Of death, so that you'll hit upon the truth.
For you can't prove that he died by cold, or the sword,
710   Or by disease or poison even—still
That he was caught by something of this sort
We know. The rule applies to many things.

Unique in the world, the Nile brims full in the summer
And floods the plains, the river of all Egypt.
It waters Egypt when the days are hottest
Maybe because in the summer north winds blow,
In the season when so-called "etesians" rush
South, gusting against the current, slowing it, forcing
The waves to well upstream, to stand and flood.
720   Don't doubt, these storm winds sweep against the current,
Roused by the icy stars of the North Pole,
While the Nile comes from the sweltering lands, the South,
Arising among the black and sun-baked men,
Deep in the region of the equal days.
Or it may be that a great clogging of sand
In the crosscurrents chokes the mouth of the river,
Sand that the wind-whipped ocean washes against it,
Making the outlet of the river less
Free, less of a ready downward glide for the water.
730   Or maybe too much rain at the headwaters
Falls in the summer, as the northern winds
Hurl all the clouds together to those parts.
Sure: when at the land of noon these far-hurled clouds
Arrive, they are pushed and packed together against
The mountain peaks, where they're wrung out by force.
Or in the heart of the Ethiopian mountains
Nile swells, where snow in the warmth of the gliding sun
Dissolves and runs cascading to the plains.

Now listen, and I'll explain the nature of
740   Avernian regions and the lakes nearby.
First, these are called "Avernian," that is, "birdless,"

Because they're fatal to all kinds of birds,
For whenever the birds fly out over those places
They forget their feathered oars, let their sails go slack,
And gently fall like raindrops to the earth
If the place is ground beneath, or into the water
If an Avernian lake awaits below.
There's one near Cumae, where sulfur-stinking mountains
Smoke, and bubble up with hot springs everywhere.
And on the Athenian ramparts, at the very   750
Top of the citadel, at the temple of Pallas
Protectress, is a place where the raucous crows
Never dare fly, no, not when the altar is smoking
With gifts—so much they flee not the keen anger
Of Pallas for their spying, as Greek poets
Sing, but the nature of the place itself.
In Syria too they say you'll find a place
Where horses also cannot go; one step
In, and they're felled by the potency alone,
As if suddenly slaughtered to the gods below.   760
These all can be explained quite naturally,
Their origins apparent, and the causes—
And let's not be so credulous as to think
These are the doors to Hell, where hell-gods, maybe,
Drag the deceased to the shores of Acheron,
As some folks think the snort of a wing-foot stag
Can draw the snakes up wriggling from their holes.
How false this is, how far to be rejected,
Now see—for I will try to give the facts.

First—and I've said this many times before—   770
In the earth are seeds for every kind of thing:
Many give food and life; many inflict
Diseases, to accelerate your death.
And I've shown above that some things for some creatures
Are fitter for the purposes of life—
Natures of things being all dissimilar,
Dissimilar too the weavings of the atoms.

Many invade the ears, many slip in,
Noxious and harsh of texture, through the nostrils,
780   Nor are there few things for the touch to shun
Or the sight to flee, or nauseous to the taste.

See then how many things can injure us,
Things violent to the senses, noisome, nasty:
First off, they say the shade of certain trees
Is so unwholesome that it gives the headache
To anyone stretched beneath them in the grass.
Then there's a tree on high Mount Helicon
Whose flower smells so abhorrent it will kill.
Of course—for out of the soil these things all rise;
790   Many atoms of many things in many ways
Are mixed in the earth, then separated out.
Snuff out the night lamp with its acrid smell;
Instantly it will put to sleep a man
Afflicted with the falling-and-frothing sickness.
A woman will swoon away from the heavy aroma
Of beaver musk (and the bright embroidery slips
From her gentle hands) if it's her menstrual time.
And many other things relax the joints,
Let the limbs hang limp, and shake the soul within.
800   Yes, if you're overfull and you lounge too long
In a hot bathtub full of scalding water,
How easy it is for you to faint right there!
How easily too the unwholesome smoke of charcoal
Invades the brain—better take water first!
And when a fever has mastered all the members
Then a whiff of wine's a slaughter-blow to the head.
And don't you see, besides, that the earth itself
Produces sulfur and the stink of asphalt?
And when those who search for veins of gold and silver
810   Probe with their iron picks the earth's deep secrets,
What odors does Scaptensula Mine exhale!
What evils breathe out of those lodes of gold!
How they do drain all color from the face!

Don't you see, haven't you heard how men will die
In a moment, all their store of life run out,
If they're compelled by force to do such work?
All of these tides of death the earth steams forth,
Breathing them out beneath the open sky.

So the "Avernian" spots must send a power
Deadly to birds, that rises out of the ground   820
Into the air and poisons those parts of the sky;
And there, as soon as the bird has winged his way,
He stalls, seized by the unseen poison, falling
Straight to the place from which the fumes have risen.
And as he plummets, the strength of these same vapors
Saps all his limbs of the last trace of life.
First, if you will, it stirs up dizziness,
Then, when the birds have tumbled into those
Poisonous springs, they vomit up their lives,
For there's a wealth of evil all around.   830
Or maybe the strong vapors from Avernus
Dissipate all the air between the ground
And the birds, leaving a nearly empty pocket.
When birds come flying straight into this zone
Their fluttering hobbles, their feathers are suddenly useless,
And all the effort of their wings betrays them.
Unable to lean or ride upon their wings
They are thus forced to plummet to the earth
By Nature, and as they lie in the emptiness
They lose their souls through every pore of the body . . .   840

Well water, to continue, is colder in summer
Because heat rarefies the earth; what warmth
Earth has of its own it loses to the wind.
So, since the earth is drained of heat, the water
Hidden inside it must be colder too.
But of course when the earth instead is squeezed
With cold, when it shrinks, contracts, in coalescing
It presses all its warmth into the wells.

By the temple of Ammon, they say, there is a fountain
850   That in the day is cold, but hot at night.
Men gape too much at this odd fountain, thinking
Its secret depths seethe from the sun below
When the world is cloaked in the fearful shroud of night.
Now this is a long way from truth and reason.
Look, when the water is bare to the touch of the sun
And the sun can't make that surface warm despite
Its shining with such fervor straight above,
How can this same sun under ground so thick
Boil up the water and glut the place with steam,
860   When its tide of heat can hardly infiltrate
The walls of a house, for all its fiery rays?
What then is the reason? Well, it's surely that
By the spring the ground's more porous than elsewhere,
And many atoms of fire are near the water.
Now, when night covers the earth with its wash of dew,
The earth grows suddenly cold to the core, contracts.
That explains why it squirts its seeds of fire
Into the fountain—as if squeezed out of a fist—
Which makes the water steam up warm to touch.
870   At dawn, when the sun's rays loosen the earth again,
Embroil it, open its pores with steaming heat,
The seeds of fire return to their old places
And the water's warmth retreats into the ground.
That makes the fountain cold when the sun is shining.
Besides, the water is roiled by the rays of the sun,
Rarefied in the shimmering wave of light.
So whatever fire the pool contains, it loses,
Just as it often releases all its cold,
Relaxing and undoing the knots of ice.

880   There's even a cold fountain over which
A flaxen wick will shoot out into flames,
And a torch, lit up in the same manner, will
Shine on the waves as it floats and drifts along;
Not strange, for in the water are multitudes

Of seeds of fire, and from deep underground
Those fiery atoms must surge up with the spring
And rise like breath from the pool into the air—
Yet not so many that the spring grows hot.
Those fiery atoms scattered in the water,
Forced into the air, will suddenly merge together.   890
After all, in the sea the Aradian spring
Gushes fresh water and clears away the salt,
And the sea provides, in many other regions,
What's useful and opportune for thirsty sailors,
Heaving sweet water up amidst the brine.
So too then can the seeds of heat escape
This spring, and splash onto the flax. And when
They've come together, sticking to the torch,
They kindle right away, for the flax and torches
Have many fire-seeds hidden in them too.   900
Haven't you noticed how a lantern's wick,
Just now snuffed out, will flare up if you move it
Close to—not touching—the fire, and the same for torches?
Many other things, before the touch of heat,
Will flare at a distance, before they're steeped in fire.
This is what happens in that spring. Believe it.

Next topic: I shall undertake to show
What natural law draws iron to that stone
Which the Greeks call "magnet" in their native tongue
From the Magenetes' country, where it's found.   910
This stone men gape in wonder at, because
You can link rings in a chain suspended from it,
And sometimes you'll see five or even more
Dangle in order and sway in the light breeze,
One ring depending on the next, as each
Communicates the magnet's binding force
And clings—such potency seeps through them all.

There's much to firm up in this case before
You can provide a cause for magnetism,

920   And we must travel long and roundabout.
I ask then, hear me out, keep your mind open.
To start, from everything we ever see
There must flow forever, be given off, be scattered,
Bodies that strike the eyes and stir the vision;
From certain things there are odors always streaming,
As chill from brooks, or warmth from the sun, or spray
From the surf at the shore, that eater-away of stone;
Sounds never cease to trickle through the air;
And, last, our tongues are touched by the salt taste

930   When we take a turn by the sea, and when we watch
The watering-down of wormwood, we're touched by the bitters.
To that extent do such things stream away
From other things and scatter everywhere.
They're never given a pause or a rest from flowing,
For our sensation is continual—
All may be seen, smelled, heard at any time.
I'd like, now, to remind you again how porous
Things are—as I made clear in my first book.
Indeed, although this knowledge appertains

940   To many things, to the matter I attack
Here, it's essential: thus I must confirm
That all we sense is a blend of body and void.
First off, the stones that hang from the roof of a cave
Sweat, and let trickle down their seeping droplets;
Likewise all over the body the sweat oozes;
Beards grow; hair grows on every limb and member;
Food spreads through the veins and nourishes and swells
The utmost parts of the body, even the nails.
Cold also passes through copper, as will heat;

950   We feel it, as we feel it pass through gold
Or silver, when we're holding a full goblet.
And through the stone partitions of a house
Voices will fly; smells seep through, and cold, and the heat
Of fire, that penetrates the strongest iron.
Then, where the buckler of the sky encloses . . .

Likewise diseases steal in from beyond,
And tempests risen from earth or sky withdraw
Far into the sky or the earth, and justly so,
Since things are stitched with space between the threads.

Now it so happens that not everything   960
That casts its atoms forth can stir the same
Sensation, or in the same way suit all things.
First, the sun cooks the earth to a dry hard crisp,
But melts the ice and makes the heaped white snow
On the high mountains dwindle in its rays.
Yet then its heat will make wax liquefy.
Fire too melts gold, turns copper into liquid,
But flesh and pelts it shrivels together and tightens,
While water tempers steel hot out of the fire,
But flesh and pelts—fire-tempered too!—it softens.   970
And the beardy goats like the wild olive so well
You'd think it really dripped ambrosia or nectar.
No bitterer bait for man, though, spreads its leaves.
A sow will scamper away from marjoram,
And fears perfume—for the bristly swine it's poison
But it refreshes and enlivens us.
By contrast, although stinking mud to us
Seems nasty, for the swine it's a delight
To wallow deep in it, insatiably.

There's one more thing I need to talk about   980
Before I can attack the basic question.
Since there are many pores in various things,
These pores must also differ amongst themselves,
Each with its proper traits and passageways.
In animals, after all, are various senses,
Seizing their proper objects of perception.
Sounds pierce through one, the flavor of juice through another,
Through another we sense the smell of something roasting.
Along with that, one thing will seep through stone,

990 Another through wood, and another will pass through gold,
Another will wind its way through silver or glass.
Through glass an image will flow; through silver, heat;
And down one track *this* pulls ahead of *that*.
See, it's the nature of the pores, which vary
In many ways, as I've just shown above—
Dissimilarities in the weave of things.

Therefore, now all these matters are confirmed,
The groundwork laid and well prepared for us,
What's left is easy: to give the reason, reveal
1000 All causes, for the iron to be lured.
First, by necessity from this stone there flows
An immense swirl of atoms that scatter aside
All air between the magnet and the iron.
Then, when the space is emptied and all's clear
Between, immediately the iron-atoms
Fall headlong into the void, still joined; and thus
The ring, entire, will go and follow too.
Nor is there anything more tangled up
In its own first-elements, tightly woven and bonded,
1010 Than strong-arm iron and its cold ruggedness.
What's said of its atoms then is not so strange—
That not enough can lift free of the iron
To fall to the void and leave the ring behind.
But the ring does follow until it strikes that stone,
Binding itself to it with unseen bonds.
That, too, from any direction. Whatever place
Is empty, whether above or to the side,
Atoms nearby will jump into the vacuum.
Really, they're bumped by blows from the other directions,
1020 And can't leap in the air spontaneously.
Here we can add—this gives a further boost,
This helps make possible the iron's movement—
That once the air's thinned out in front of the ring,
The area made a little emptier,
Right off whatever air's behind the ring

Will push it from the back and drive it forward.
Constant billows of air surround all things,
But now propel the iron, since the space
Is empty in one direction to receive it.
Through the many pores of the iron this air I've mentioned,   1030
Slipping itself into the tiniest holds,
Pushes, propels—like a breeze in the sails of a ship.
And last, all things contain some air in them
Because all things are of a porous structure
And air surrounds them or banks up against them.
This air, then, which is hidden deep in the iron,
Tosses in constant restlessness, so that
It gives the ring a knock from the inside
And gets it going, tumbling to where it had first
Flung itself out into the empty space.   1040

And iron sometimes retreats from magnets too,
Accustomed both to follow and run away.
For I've seen iron rings of Samothrace
Leap, and iron filings in bronze drinking bowls
Go wild inside, when the magnet's placed beneath them:
So anxious they appear to flee that stone.
Now, you see, all this discord in the bronze
Is caused when a first wave of the bronze-atoms
Seizes and occupies the open highways
In the iron, but then a troop comes from the magnet,   1050
Finds all the ways full, finds nowhere to wade, as before.
Then it's forced to give that iron mesh a knocking
And pound it away with its tides. So, through the bronze,
It spits back what it would suck in without it.

Along these lines, leave off your wondering that
Magnet-tides can't push other things the same.
Some things stand still, relying on their weight,
Like gold; and some, so rarefied that streams
Flow through intact, can't ever be impelled,
And it seems wooden things are of this sort.   1060

Between these two, then, iron lies, so when
It has absorbed some particles of bronze
The lodestone's stream of atoms will repel it.

These traits are not so foreign to other things—
Many examples of things suited for
Each other only, I might mention here.
First of all, stones cement together only
With mortar, and only bull's glue will bond wood,
So a flaw in the grain of a board more often gapes
1070   Than will the bull's glue's bonds relax their grip;
The juice of the vine is bold to mingle with water,
When tar is too heavy to do so, and olive oil
Too light; the purple of shellfish dye unites
With wool alone and can never be rent asunder—
Not if you tried to wash it new again
In the ocean stream, in all the waves of the sea.
Gold things need gold-glue (borax) to be coupled,
Bronze welds to bronze only by white-bronze (tin).
Other examples—how many there are! What then?
1080   No need to keep you wandering roundabout,
Nor should I use up so much labor here:
Better to grasp a lot in a few short words.
Take textures settled against each other: where
The gaps in A are filled by the solid in B
And likewise in reverse—they're joined the best.
Yet some things can be held coupled together
By a kind of chain made up of hooks and ringlets.
That's probably so with iron and the magnet.

Now for disease, and how to explain the sudden
1090   Slaughter fanned high by the rising force of the plague,
Against mankind and against the herds of cattle;
I'll make all clear. First, as I've shown above,
There are seeds, in many things, that give us life,
And so by contrast many too that bring

Disease and death. When it chances that these have risen
To thicken the sky, then the air is pestilent.

This power of disease and pestilence
Comes either from without, from the sky above
Through mists and clouds; or from the earth itself
It surges, whenever the earth is moist with rot   1100
And stricken with unseasonable rains and heat.
You see how a man who's traveled far from home
Is roughed up by the strangeness of the weather
And water—so far discrepant are these things.
Think how far the weather in Britain must differ
From that in Egypt, where the earth's axis stoops,
Or the Black Sea from the climate at Cadiz
And far beyond in the land of the sun-burnt blacks?
Not only do we see the four directions
And the four winds produce four separate climates,   1110
But the people differ widely in color and features,
And various diseases grip their races.
There's the elephant sickness, bred by the waters of
The middle Nile, in Egypt, and nowhere else.
Attica vexes the footsteps; Achaia, the eyes;
Each part of the world's an enemy to certain
Parts of the body. That's caused by the various climates.
When weather which we're unaccustomed to
Stirs, and the enemy air begins to drift
Like the slow snaking of a mist or fog,   1120
Wherever it goes, it alters and disturbs,
And when this weather reaches our air too
It spoils it, makes it alien, like itself.
Then this quick killing, this strange new pestilence
Settles into the wells, or lives in the very grain
Or in other human food, or cattle fodder,
Or it hangs mingling with the air, and when
We draw a breath we thereby draw disease
Into our bodies, by necessity.

1130 In the same way sometimes comes the hoof-and-mouth
For cows, and distemper for the lazy sheep.
It's all the same—we travel to lands averse
To us, and swap the tunic of our skies,
Or a corrupting air is brought from beyond
By Nature, or something else that we're not used to
Which can attack us with its sudden coming.

That's how, one time, in the land of Greece, a wave
Of deadly plague turned fields to burial grounds,
Left the streets desolate, drained the city of people.
1140 For rising deep in Egypt, and measuring miles
And miles through the air and over the plains of the sea,
It bedded down at last in Attica.
Then they fell ill by armies, and so died.
First they would have a head flushed hot with fever,
And both eyes red with a sort of bleary light,
Then in the throat an ooze of bitter black
Blood, and the ulcerous sores would choke the voice,
And the tongue, interpreter of thoughts, dripped gore,
Made feeble by pain, of speech sluggish, rough to touch.
1150 Then down the throat the plague filled up the chest
Finally pooling up in the sad heart;
Then all the battlements of life gave way.
The breath through the mouth gave off a sour, bad smell,
Like the rank stench of a corpse tossed out to rot.
Then all the strength of the mind and all the body
Lay limp, now at the very brink of Death.
With the unbearable pain walked tight-grip Fear
Tirelessly mingling groans of body and soul.
And constant retching and choking day and night
1160 Doubled them up, cramping the muscles, till
They would dissolve in utter weariness.
You couldn't sense, on the surface of anyone's body,
So high a fever; rather, against the hand
It felt lukewarm, and the body all flushed red
As if inflamed with sores, as when the limbs

Flare up with erysipelas, "holy fire."
Men burned inside down to the very bones.
The stomach was a furnace blaze of flames.
Not the sheerest, lightest clothing could you use
To comfort them—only a cool breeze helped.   1170
Burning up with the plague, some threw their bodies
Into cold streams, and lay in the water, naked.
Many, so thirsty, dove headfirst into
Deep wells, their mouths wide open as they plunged.
A flood was but a drop for their dry bodies
Drowning in thirst that was unquenchable.
No respite for the sickness. Bodies lay
Weary; physicians muttered their hushed fear
When the victims rolled their bright and suffering eyes,
The eyes deprived of sleep, the heralds of death.   1180
Then they gave many other signs of death:
A mind deranged, troubled with fear and sadness,
A furrowed brow, the countenance crazed and fierce,
Ears tickled and tormented with constant noise,
Thick breathing, or long and rare, from deep in the chest,
Or a neck glistening with the drip of sweat,
Thin, scanty spittle, flecked with yellow, and salty,
Hardly hacked up through the throat by a raw cough.
Tics in the tendons of the hands, the shakes,
Chills creeping in their slow pace from the feet,   1190
No lull with these. Then at the latest moment:
The nostrils pinched, the tip of the nose filed down
To a point, hollow eyes, hollow temples, the skin cold
And rough; on the mouth a taut grin, the face swollen.
Not long then till their limbs lay stiff in death.
Around the eighth day with its shining light,
Or the ninth, they passed along the torch of life.
If any managed to avoid death's gloom,
With festering ulcers and black diarrhea
The rot of death awaited them anyway,   1200
Or often, as their heads throbbed, pus-filled blood
Gushed through the nose and gorged them; from this blood

Flowed all the person's substance and his strength.
And if a man survived this foul discharge
Of blood, well, the plague passed into his joints and muscles
And even settled in the genitals.
Some, grievously frightened by the brink of Death,
Survived by cutting off what made them men,
And many without hands or without feet

1210   Still stayed alive, and many lost their eyes:
So fierce and violent was their fear of death.
Sometimes obliviousness of everything
Seized them; they couldn't tell you who they were.
And bodies lay over bodies, heaped on the ground,
Unburied, yet the birds and the wild beasts
Would shy far off to get away from the stink,
Or, if they nibbled, would drop half-dead on the spot.
Yet in those days hardly any birds appeared,
And none of the sullen beasts would leave the forest,

1220   For many lay ill likewise with the plague
And so would die. Even the faithful dogs
Stretched flat in the street and laid down their sick souls,
For the plague wrung all the life out of their limbs.
Men found no certain, common remedy.
What allowed some to draw into their mouths
The breath of life, and look up at the sky,
That same for others brought destruction, death.
What was the most pathetic thing of all,
Worst wretchedness: when someone saw himself

1230   Snared by the sickness and so sentenced to die,
He lay undone, dispirited, sad at heart,
And gazing upon death he lost all life.
To say the truth, they never ceased to catch
The ravenous epidemic from one to the next,
Rather like herds of cattle or wool-clad sheep.
That above all would pile up death on death.
For a man who feared to visit his own sick friends,
Grasping too hard for life, afraid of death,
Paid for it soon with a shameful and bad end,

Abandoned, helpless, victim of indifference.   1240
Those who nursed the sick, though, died from handling them,
Or from the works shame made them undergo,
With the pleading of the weary, and their complaining.
The noblest people therefore suffered death.
They tried to hurry their unmourned funerals . . .

. . . in any old grave, fighting to bury their crowd
Of kindred. Then they went home, weary with tears.
A good many of them took to their beds in sadness.
You couldn't find one person at that time
Unbruised by sickness, death, or misery.   1250

Worse still, the shepherds and the cattle drovers
And even the ruddy farmer who steered the plow
Fell faint; deep in their huts the bodies stacked,
Consigned by plague and poverty to die.
Lifeless bodies of parents heaped atop
Lifeless bodies of children—such you'd see,
Or children dying upon their mothers and fathers.
No small part of the plague flowed from the farms
Into the city, brought by the crowds of sick
Farmers, who gathered from every pestilent quarter.   1260
They filled the homes, the squares. So tightly packed
Were these human swarms; Death piled them all the higher.
Many lay flat in the street for thirst, lay prostrate
Before the fountain-statues of Silenus,
Breath choked by the great desire for that sweet water.
And strewn about in the roads and parks you'd see
Legs and arms, nerveless, attached to half-dead bodies,
Ragged and dirty, clothes caked with excrement,
Dying, with only bare skin left to the bone,
Nearly buried already in pus and sores and filth.   1270
Yes, all those holy temples of the gods—
Death stuffed 'em with corpses, and the shrines of heaven
Were charnel houses, burdened by cadavers,
Places the priests had filled with worshipers.

Now their religion, now the will of the gods
Meant nothing: present pain was conqueror.
Nor did the city observe the burial rites—
Its people had always buried their dead before.
For all was chaos, fear, and every man
1280   Had his own buried as his means allowed.
The suddenness and poverty incited
Horrors. On funeral pyres heaped up for others
People would lay their own kin down, and wail,
And set their torches underneath, and sometimes
Brawl and shed blood, rather than leave their dead.

NOTES

These notes, I hope, will aid students unfamiliar with ancient history and lore; they suggest a few of the main sources for Lucretius's ideas. Students who require exhaustive notes will find them in the editions of Bailey (1947), Leonard and Smith (1942), Merrill (1907), and Munro (1900). All citations of Epicurus are from Bailey's edition (1926). Ancient and modern allusions to Lucretius are so numerous that their recording would fill volumes. I have noted a few of the most remarkable ones.

The line numbers for Lucretius are keyed to this translation. Because the Latin contains some lines universally regarded as spurious or corrupt beyond recognition, these numbers may not correspond precisely with the appropriate lines in the editions above.

Book One

In his first book Lucretius establishes the fundamental laws of the world, that nothing comes from nothing and that things cannot be reduced to nothing. These laws, which affirm the conservation of matter, require the existence of material which is indissoluble—namely, the atoms, whose mobility requires in turn the existence of empty space, or "void." The doctrines of atoms and void can, according to Lucretius, be inferred from the growth and decay of all we see. They arm us against the threats of Religion and against the near-mystical fancies of such philosophers as Heraclitus and Anaxagoras.

Epicurean physics dictates that this topic be treated first, since if all things rise from invisible and indivisible atoms, then one should begin the study of nature by considering those fundamental particles. This is the bedrock upon which Lucretius builds his epistemology, psychology, morality, and cosmology. Yet before he can discuss the atoms he must capture the reader's good will, or at least soothe his ill will, by meeting the main objection to investigating the atoms, that such prying into unseen things is blasphemy. Thus, Lucretius begins his poem with a spirited hymn to Venus, who for him is far more than a literary convention and far other than a divine personage: she is the force of life itself, the ceaselessly creative (and, we shall see, destructive) activity of the atoms.

If an Epicurean can worship ardently, Lucretius does so here. Yet he follows his prayer to Venus with praise of the master Epicurus, whose fearless discoveries help us lift our heads to the heavens and tread hateful Religion underfoot. That is no impiety, says Lucretius, for Religion herself has been the mother of wickedness. As an example he recounts the tale of Iphigenia, led to the altar by her father Agamemnon's henchmen not to be given away in marriage but by her sacrificial death to appease Artemis, goddess of chastity, and enable Agamemnon and his troops to sail to Troy. In Lucretius's source, Euripides' *Iphigenia at Aulis,* the girl is at last rescued by Artemis. But no goddess of virginity intervenes here, since the gods can neither touch, nor be touched by, anything in this world. And so Iphigenia dies, by her own father's hand. That she is of marrying age makes the sin all the fouler; it is a sin against life itself, against the procreation that Lucretius has just celebrated so passionately.

This sin is prologue to the greater sin of the ten years' war against Troy, a leitmotif for this book. Since Venus is the mother of Trojan Aeneas, whom Romans regarded as their patriarch, any criticism of Greek vice could don the garb of patriotism. Further, Lucretius wants to adapt for his own purposes the poetry of his two great predecessors in epic, Homer and Ennius. He thus reduces the subject of Homer's *Iliad* to an "accident" of the place where it occurred and the people involved, and Ennius's claim to be Homer reincarnate he dismisses, insisting that though the poetry of Homer and Ennius will never die, their souls surely have. Nature, not war, Venus, not Mars, is the deity he contemplates.

The last line of the Iphigenia scene, "Such wickedness Religion can incite," completes the link between religion and war. It is Lucretius's version of lines 1335–36 of *Iphigenia*—but for Euripides the culprit is Helen of Troy. Helen gives birth to the slaughter of a city, just as Lucretius's Trojan horse "gave birth in the dead of night / To Greeks who burnt the city to the ground" (476–77). Religion, like Helen, brings unbridled passion, brings war, is the "mother" of death. The study of the atom will, the poet hopes, carry the reader away from those forces that lay waste to our lives.

For a summary of the physics presented in book 1, see Epicurus, *To Herodotus* 35–42, 56–60 (Bailey 1926). Epicurus's letters, his *Principal Doctrines,* and his biography can also be found in any edition of Diogenes

Laertius, *Lives of Eminent Philosophers,* referred to as *Life* in the Notes. The book can be divided thus:

1. Proem (1–145)
   A. Invocation of Venus—proem to the entire work (1–49)
   B. Address to Memmius (50–61)
   C. Praise of Epicurus and criticism of Religion (62–145)

2. The Fundamental Laws of Atomism (146–918)
   A. No creation *ex nihilo* (146–214)
   B. No destruction *ad nihilum* (215–64)
   C. Existence of unseen particles (265–328)
      1. Wind (271–97)
      2. Scents, heat, cold, and sounds (298–304)
      3. Evaporation and humidity (305–10)
      4. Attrition (311–28)
   D. Existence of empty space, or the "void" (329–417)
      1. Motion (334–45)
      2. Porosity (346–57)
      3. Differences in density (358–69)
      4. Objections to the notion of a plenum (370–97)
      5. Encouragement of Memmius's powers of induction (398–417)
   E. Fundamentality of atoms and void (418–634)
      1. No third component (418–48)
      2. Accidents and properties (449–82)
      3. Atomic solidity (483–550)
      4. Atomic indivisibility (551–98)
      5. Atomic parts (599–634)
   F. Refutation of philosophical opponents (635–918)
      1. Heraclitus (635–704)
      2. Empedocles (705–80)
      3. Stoic objectors (781–828)
      4. Anaxagoras (829–918)

3. The Infinity of the Universe (919–1102)
   A. Epicureanism as medicine for the soul (919–48)
   B. Limitlessness of the universe (949–98)
      1. Nothing beyond the All (956–65)
      2. The spear flung from the universe's edge (966–81)

    3. Infinite space for infinite numbers of atoms (982–98)
  c. Characteristics of a boundless universe (999–1102)
      1. Infinite matter and infinite void (999–1010)
      2. Creation by atomic collision (1011–48)
      3. Centerlessness (1049–90)
      4. Ubiquity of atoms (1091–1102)

4. Coda (1103–6)

1   *Mother of Romans*] see introduction above. Venus is called *alma,* not simply "sweet" but "nourishing, giving increase." The phrase, notes Munro, passed into common parlance. She personifies the natural cycle of birth, growth, and maturity, and with gusto Lucretius celebrates her spring awakening and her bringing to all creatures the delights of love.

25   *On the Nature of Things*] Lucretius translates the titles of works by both Epicurus and Empedocles. The name *Natura* retains much of its verbal sense, denoting "those things which are to be born."

26   *my friend Memmius*] a dissolute young aristocrat, Memmius is ripe for Lucretius's gospel. It seems to have done him little good. The character given him by Catullus, poems 10 and 28, is uninspiring. Kelsey (1884) surmises that Memmius was "one who would gladly welcome the doctrine of eternal death and a world without a deity," so that he might enjoy his selfishness the more. Cicero, *Epistulae ad familiares* 13.1, pleads with him not to tear down the ruins of Epicurus's house at Mytilene—but this was after the poet who had tried to reform his friend had died.

32   *Mars*] god of war, said to have fathered Romulus and Remus, founders of Rome. His affair with Venus is related by Ovid, *Metamorphoses* 4.169–89.

41   *while my country suffers*] see general introduction. Kelsey thinks that Lucretius may have written these lines in 58 during the consulship of Caesar, whom Cicero and then-praetor Memmius fiercely opposed. Later Memmius shamelessly joined Caesar's party but betrayed him too and was finally impeached for election fraud. On Epicurus's patriotism, see Diogenes Laertius, *Life* 9–10.

44–49   ] repeated at 2.646–51.

55   *atoms*] Lucretius's epithets for the atoms reveal how these bits of indivisible matter underlie a living world. They are "seeds," "engendering bodies,"

both temporally and ontologically our first principles. Note here and at 168 a pun on *materies,* matter, and *mater,* mother.

66   *one man*] Epicurus, the hero who conquered superstition (*religio,* with its etymological sense of shackling) by discovering Nature's laws.

76–77   *boundary stone*] Romans used these to mark off cities and plots of land. Their festival in honor of the god Terminus testifies to their deep conservatism and desire for order, which Lucretius applies here to Epicurean physics. Lines are repeated at 5.89–90, 6.66–67.

84   *At Aulis*] see discussion above. Iphigenia is just old enough to be a bride, but instead of wedding braids she wears the fillets of a sacrificial beast. Gale (1994, 96) remarks that for orators she was an exemplum of heroic self-sacrifice; but Lucretius does not salve over the offense done her.

117   *our Ennius*] Quintus Ennius (239–169), first great Roman poet, whose epic *Annales* chronicles the second and most famous war between Rome and Carthage. Ennius used the Pythagorean doctrine of the soul's transmigration to establish himself as a Latin avatar of Homer. Mount Helicon, near Thebes, was the haunt of the Muses, goddesses of the arts.

132–34   ] nearly repeated at 4.33–35.

141   *friendship*] Lucretius invites Memmius into his circle of Epicurean friends. For Epicurus on friendship, see *Principal Doctrines* 27; Fragments 23–28, 39, 52, 66, 78, *Life* 120b–21a.

146–48   ] a powerful refrain, repeated at 2.60–62, 3.91–93, and 6.39–41. Our minds are opened by observing Nature and deriving from our observation her inner laws.

153–54   ] repeated at 6.57–58, 91–92.

182   *no atoms to be blocked*] obscure. Atoms do not share the same shape and so cannot combine in just any fashion. Here, the characteristics of seeds (or of the atoms that constitute them) prevent them from combining during the wrong seasons.

211–12   *we stir these seeds to life*] not literally. The seeds are dormant, too deep in the earth to combine with others to produce life. Tilling brings them closer to the surface, increasing their chances for combination. Lines nearly repeated at 5.210–11.

250–51 *Father Sky, Mother Earth*] a commonplace. *Father Sky* is Deus-piter, Jupiter (Greek Zeus, Vedic Dyaushpita, Germanic Tiw), an ancient Indo-European god of the bright heavens.

264] the converse is false, since in book 5 Lucretius discusses the annihilation of our particular cosmos.

316 *bronze guardians of the gates*] Romans touched or kissed the statues of gods whose favor they sought. Cicero, *Verres* 4.94, describes the attrition of a statue of Hercules in Agrigentum.

354–55] see 6.952–53.

371 *what some pretend*] Plato and Aristotle argued that motion could be explained by a simultaneous shifting, one object displacing another.

418] nearly repeated at 6.42.

450 *property, accident*] Epicurus, *To Herod.* 70–72. Lucretius shows that everything is either an accidental combination of matter or an essential quality of such combinations. Heat is a property of fire because cold fire would cease to be fire. But "burning Troy to the ground" is only an accident of that fateful fire. Even time, despite what the Stoics say, is an accident of material things and not an immaterial entity. "Div-" here translates a tmesis, the splitting of a word by insertion of another word or particle. Lucretius highlights his point by dividing the word that denotes division. The reader will note some half-dozen of these scattered throughout the translation.

473–74 *Helen, Phrygian Paris*] Paris, a prince of Troy, kidnapped the lovely Helen from his host (and her husband) Menelaus, who with his brother Agamemnon raised an army to recapture her. The ten years' war ended when, its belly full of Greek warriors, the gigantic Trojan Horse was brought into the city. See discussion above.

489–90] see 6.229–30.

494–95] see 6.949–50.

600 *vertices*] limits, literally "peaks," whose arrangement gives each type of atom its peculiar traits. Epicurus, *To Herod.* 56–59, is no clearer.

617 *infinitely many tiny parts*] the ancients could not imagine infinite series leading to finite sums. Newton's calculus resolved the issue. Munro cites Newton's second letter to the Lucretian editor Richard Bentley on the inequality of infinities.

633–34] see 2.725–27.

638 *Heraclitus*] Lucretius attacks philosophers who think the world is made up of some few elements. Foremost is Heraclitus, who reduced the world's volatile change to the operation of one fire. Known for an obscure style that invited the excesses of allegorical interpretation, Heraclitus was revered by the Stoics, who took his fire to symbolize the light of a providential Mind governing all.

670–73] refrain nearly repeated at 1.789–92; 2.751–54; 3.517–18.

693 *he battles the senses*] Heraclitus's fascination with the world's fickleness led him to disparage the senses, which he thought unreliable. Lucretius's objection is a bit unfair. If all things are made up of fire, and if fire is the only element the senses can perceive, then they can perceive everything.

716 *Empedocles*] Greek-Sicilian poet and philosopher; his epic *On Nature* asserts that the four elements and the forces of Love and Strife create the world. A self-styled prophet whose mysticism attracted many disciples, Empedocles pretended to deity, and to fulfill his union with the divine fire he leapt into the crater of Mount Aetna. Despite these quirks Lucretius admired him for advancing the materialist cause and looked to his work as a model for didactic poetry.

738–39 *the laurel-toking Priestess*] of Apollo at Delphi. She chewed laurel leaves—a hallucinogen—and sat upon a tripod perched above a crevice in the rock, inhaling fumes from below. Epicurus believed that even if prophecy were true it would be of no concern to us, *Life* 135. For Epicurus as oracle, see Fragments 66. Lines are repeated at 5.111–12.

789–92] nearly repeated from above, 670–73; see also 2.751–54, 3.517–18.

816–18] nearly repeated at 906–8; 2.760–62, 883–85, 894–96, 1007–9.

819–20] repeated at 2.1015–16.

822–25] see 2.688–90, 1013–14.

829 *Anaxagoras*] Greek philosopher, 5th c. B.C., friend of the Athenian statesman Pericles. His theory of "likepartedness" argues that elements share the qualities of the compounds they create. Since the ancients had no notion of chemical change, it was hard for them to see how, for example, grain could be transmuted into flesh and blood. Anaxagoras denied the transmutation by supposing that there were tiny bits of flesh and blood hidden in the grain.

Anaxagoras's insight should not be lost on us: food is food largely because it is made of the same carbon, water, and other materials of which we too are made. Taken literally the theory is nonsense. Little sparks, says Lucretius, cannot be seen hiding away in wood; change is caused by rearrangement of atoms.

859   *blood and bones*] a line or so is lost. Its sense might have been "And muscles are all made up of foreign parts."

887   *tiny portions*] Munro observes that Anaxagoras's particles "were infinite in number and in smallness; from the necessity of the case everything was mixed with everything." Lucretius has denied that atoms can be infinitely small; but even so, his insistence upon invisible particles should have led him to be fairer to Anaxagoras.

906–9   ] see 816–18; 2.760–62, 883–85, 894–96, 1007–9.

912   *"flame"* and *"elm"*] pun on *ignis*, "fire," and *lignum*, "wood," whose spelling exemplifies the three possible operations upon atomic compounds: subtraction, addition, and rearrangement. See Epicurus, *To Herod.* 54.

921–22   ] Lucretius is stung by the *thyrsis*, the wand carried by the wine god Dionysus and his worshipers during their orgiastic rites. The Pierides are the Muses, daughters of Pierus. Lines 924–48 are largely repeated as the proem to book 4, 1–25.

934–48   ] this sugar-coated pill theory of poetry became a commonplace in the Renaissance; see Sidney's *Defense of Poesie* and Tasso's *Gerusalemme Liberata* 1.3.

968   *fling a spear*] the traditional Roman mode of declaring war was to cast a spear over the boundary into the enemy's territory (West 1969, 48).

1001   ] repeated at 5.1213.

1010   ] the lost line may have suggested what would happen if the infinite void were not balanced by an infinite supply of atoms.

1021–25   ] see 5.187–94.

1026   *Great Year*] the time it takes all the heavenly bodies to return to their original positions relative to each other. Munro notes that it was a Stoic idea, and so Lucretius's reference to it here is probably tinct with irony.

1040 *the ones still free*] atoms which have not yet combined with any others to produce things. The "world," or cosmos, is made up of those atoms that have fallen into combinations. The "free" atoms might temporarily supply the lack of combinatory atoms, but even at that their blows from outside might instead weaken the fabric of the world. Yet even to have enough of these loose atoms we must have a limitless stock of atoms everywhere.

1049 *this belief*] the Stoic idea that matter tends toward the center of the universe. An infinite universe, Lucretius argues, has no center. Unfortunately, he did not distinguish between the center of the universe and the center of the earth, and that failure leads to his derision for "stoneheads" (*sto-lidi,* a pun on *Stoici*) who think that creatures in the Southern Hemisphere can stand upright. He will later contradict himself, arguing in book 2 that all matter tends to fall (but what can "downward" mean in an infinite universe?) and in book 5 that the heaviest matter sank to the bottom of the universe and formed the earth.

1091] the missing passage probably completed the theory of the preceding lines, that fire can rise naturally just as water rises through the trunk of a tree.

BOOK TWO

Lucretius describes how the properties of atoms (size, shape, weight, motion) can explain the properties of things — can show us why water is fluid and honey sticky, why light is quicker than sound, or how the earth can produce so many forms of life. And life is the focus, finally, life and decay, since the ceaseless activity of the atoms implies the instability of everything they create.

Though the subject of this book is not grand, the poetry is. Nowhere else does Lucretius sustain for so long such a high level of artfulness and play. The sorts of poetry he entertains us with reflect the creative variety of the atoms: we have the proem's oratory, the mock-epic of the Mater Magna, the lyric of the cow seeking her lost calf, the satire of sensate atoms investigating their own composition, and the superb final elegy on the ravages of time.

We open with a view of a ship struggling at sea, emblem of man tossed by fear and passion, contrasted with the easy meal of friends by the riverside, content with their simple fare and the fine weather. This tension between frenzy and peace continues throughout the book. Its site is the earth, our mother, whose nurturing powers are violated by men on the battlefield and priests at the altar. We need food, and the earth gives enough to sustain us for a while; it is fitting that Lucretius discusses, among other things, the atomic structure of honey, pickling spice, myrrh, olive oil, saffron, salt, and water. But Earth cannot give us enough to live forever, since she obeys the same laws of life and death as we. She too needs to be shored up with food, but as with us her shoring up can be but temporary. Like an old woman she no longer bears what she used to. Despite our sweat and labor, all things end in the imperturbable peace of death.

For Epicurus's views on atomic motion, see *To Herod.* 42–45, 60–62, 68–69, 73–77; *To Pythocles* 88–90; on frugality and contentment, see *To Menoeceus* 127–32; *Prin. Doc.* and Fragments passim; *Life* 10–12.

1. Proem (1–62)

2. Atomic Motion (63–333)
    A. Its ceaselessness (68–142)
        1. The growth and decay of all things (68–80)
        2. Atomic unstoppability (81–89)
        3. Atomic ricochets (90–112)
        4. Motes in the sunbeam (113–42)
    B. Atomic velocity (143–67)
    C. Lack of divine control (168–84)
    D. Nothing spontaneously born (185–216)
    E. Atomic swerve, and free will (217–94)
    F. Uniform distribution of atoms (295–308)
    G. The appearance of stability (309–33)

3. Atomic Forms (334–729)
    A. Variety of shapes (334–81)
    B. Atomic shapes and the properties of objects (382–478)
        1. Light and lightning (382–91)
        2. Viscosity (392–98)
        3. Taste (399–408)
        4. Texture; primacy of touch (409–44)
        5. Hardness, fluidity, sharpness, saltiness (445–78)
    C. Finite number of atomic shapes (479–522)
    D. Infinitude of atoms of each atomic shape (523–69)
    E. Life-giving and lethal atomic collisions (570–81)
    F. Atomic compounds (582–699)

1. Earth and the Mater Magna (590–660)
2. The many properties each object possesses (661–99)
G. Impossible linkages (700–729)

4. What Atoms Lack (730–1021)
   A. Atomic colorlessness (730–841)
   B. No perishable qualities in the atom (842–64)
   C. Lack of sensation (865–990)
      1. Universal need for food (865–85)
      2. Sensation and atomic arrangement (886–901)
      3. Sensation and perishability (902–30)
      4. Atomic arrangement and birth (931–43)
      5. Pain and atomic dislocation (944–72)
      6. Satire against sentient atoms (973–90)
   D. Summation (991–1021)

5. The Growth and Decay of Our World (1022–1173)
   A. Novelty no reason to reject an idea (1022–46)
   B. The plurality of worlds (1047–75)
   C. No uniqueness (1076–88)
   D. No divine providence (1089–1103)
   E. Universal birth, growth, decay, and death (1104–42)
   F. The barrenness of our old earth (1143–73)

1. *How sweet*] the pleasure is not malicious. Lucretius wishes no one ill, yet men insist upon imperiling their lives and the lives of others for the sake of money or a scrap of land. It's sweet to consider one's narrow escape from these plights. The wise Epicurean from his fastness "looks down upon" the benighted, with pity, for so much of our suffering is unnecessary. Gale (124–26) argues that the poem is an Epicurean Odyssey toward our only home, the *templa serena* of wisdom. We should be satisfied with limits (*Prin. Doc.* 19, 20); ambition is useless (*Prin. Doc.* 7, 21; Fragments 58, 63; *Life* 120a–21b); freedom from pain is all. The thought is summed up in an aphorism that Cicero, good Roman that he was, found scandalous: "Live unknown" (Fragments 86).

29–33] repeated at 5.1387–91.

40 *perhaps*] mocking. Lucretius dares to suggest that war does nothing to fortify a man's courage.

56–59] repeated at 3.87–90, 6.35–38.

60–62] repeated at 1.146–48, 3.91–93, 6.39–41.

101 *tiny spaces*] Epicureans taught that atoms moved continually, including such apparently still atoms as those of stone or iron.

145 *new light*] perhaps quite literally new; see the discussion of dawn, 5.658–63.

158 *solid, single-natured*] "in solid simplicity." Single atoms traveling through a void must move at incomprehensible speed.

165] a lacuna follows. The missing lines probably described how the atoms travel so fast that their precise motions can never be discerned.

168 *some say*] Stoics, whose world was a cosmos providentially designed to meet men's needs. See Cicero, *De natura deorum* 2.127–68.

182 *too much wrong with it*] repeated at 5.199, where Lucretius discusses the origin of this imperfect world.

188 *fire*] another attack on the Stoics, who believed that fire—divine in substance—naturally rises. For the Epicureans, as we see below, fire still occupies the "highest" position in the universe, if "highest" measures altitude and not worth. Fire atoms are lighter than those that make earth and water, so the latter push them aside. The attack is motivated not so much by a disagreement about the physics of fire as by a desire to deny any divine principle in matter.

217 *Another fact*] the notorious Epicurean "swerve," an infinitesimal jolt in motion from the vertical. Atoms plunging at equal speeds along parallel paths would never create anything because they would never strike each other. Moreover, since Epicurean ethics stresses our decision to embrace pleasure and friendship, Epicurean physics must allow for that decision. Epicurus tartly rejects determinism as worse than superstition, "for indeed it were better to follow the myths about the gods than to become a slave to the destiny of the natural philosophers" (*To Men.* 134). The "swerve" is thus necessary for both creation and freedom. Since atoms veer, they can strike each other and begin the pinball game of creation. But since they are not quite predictable, they introduce into our behavior enough uncertainty to allow for free will; see Cicero, *De fato* 22–25. One is tempted to call the swerve a

deus ex machina, and in fact the Epicureans were derided for the doctrine; see Cicero, *De finibus* 1.19.

286   *beyond collision*] if we think that atoms move only on account of weight (which makes them hurtle down) or collision (which makes them ricochet), then the world is a billiard game, determined by fixed physical laws. So if we are to have free will, some third cause of motion must exist. And just as weight prevents the external force of collision from making anything at all—a heavy atom may free itself from a light atom that strikes it, frustrating the collision—so too the interior motions of atoms which would determine our thoughts are counteracted by that little swerve.

297   *no matter dies*] Epicurean conservation of matter also conserves its density in the universe. Such conservation ensures that the laws of nature remain uniform through time.

304   *no force*] the universe, being all there is and infinite, can never be altered fundamentally, though whole worlds in it come and go.

334   *what atom-fabrics*] for Epicureans there was no quasi-divine element that founded the world. Nor did they follow Anaxagoras and posit a variety of elements corresponding to the variety of objects. Thus the types of atoms must be many but not innumerable, and the number of atoms of any one type, in order to give that type any role in an infinite universe, must in turn be infinite.

382–478   ] Lucretius shows how atomic shapes account for the properties of objects we sense. The reasoning may be naive, but the insight is valid: diamond is hard precisely because of its utterly interlocked structure.

423–24   ] cf. Anaxagoras's idea, 1.829–40. Smoothness must come from somewhere, since nothing comes from nothing. Lucretius and Anaxagoras differ over the sort of smoothness they attribute to the atoms. For Lucretius, atoms themselves are not really smooth but are shaped so as to produce our sensation of smoothness. Munro wonders how Lucretius would have explained a lovely but malodorous plant.

435   *touch*] Since Epicureans posit only space and impinging bodies, all sensation, including our mental images, is really a form of touch.

466   ] a short lacuna follows, but the sense of the sentence seems clear.

501–12   ] endless types of atoms would produce an endless range of things bright and beautiful or nasty and foul. But since the range of such qualities is limited, the types of atoms too must be limited.

536   *thousands*] Lucretius assumes that if there were a finite number of any sort of atom, those atoms would fail to merge in the infinite sea of atoms, or they would create one-of-a-kind wonders like the phoenix. The logic is shaky. First, in an unbounded universe an infinite number of atoms of type A can still be far more thinly spread than the infinite number of atoms of type B. Second, the atoms whose number is limited need not connect with each other to create objects; they might connect with atoms of a different sort. Third, if these atoms do *not* produce anything, how can we be sure that they don't exist? Last, unless Lucretius wants to posit an *infinite* number of elephants, it is hard to see what difference there is between the world's producing a thousand elephants and its producing twenty or even one. The real gulfs are those separating zero from any finite number, and any finite number from infinity. But, as Merrill notes, Epicurus was fixed upon the idea of *isonomia,* a general uniformity in the number of things. See Cicero, *Nat. deor.* 1.50, 109.

574   *deadlocked*] Munro comments: "He elsewhere teaches, as his system required him to do, that our world came into being only yesterday, and sooner or later must be destroyed in an instant with all that is in it. What becomes then of this balance as far as we are concerned?"

594   *Aetna*] active volcano in Sicily. For the origin of volcanoes, see 6.640–703 and note.

599   *Great Mother*] earth, the *mater magna,* identified by the Romans with the eastern fertility goddess Cybele. Lucretius gives rationalized explanations for the details of Cybele's iconography, sometimes poking fun at them by showing them to be based upon absurd puns. The reasons for worshiping Cybele—she bestows health, family harmony, good harvests, and social order—are valid enough, unless one remembers that the earth is no goddess and so can grant no favors. (The priests, however, run a fine racket in the alms trade.) Cybele is usually pictured seated in a chariot led by two lions whose rage is restrained by harness and bit. The lions were once lovers whom Cybele caught having sex in her temple (Ovid, *Fasti* 4.215–18). She is crowned with towers; Munro notes that such a "mural" crown was given to the first soldier to scale an enemy's walls. She wields the caduceus, a snake-wreathed wand that induced tranquillity and sleep. Paradoxically, Cybele is a goddess of concord and civilization who inspires frenzy in her worshipers.

Her priests receive their holy orders in an orgiastic ritual that climaxes in their self-castration.

612 *Mother Ida*] Mount Ida, near Troy in Phrygia (northwest Asia Minor). The cult of Cybele was thought to have originated in Phrygia.

614 *"phruited"*] the joke is that the myth turns on a chance resemblance between the words *Phrygia* and *fruges* (grain).

615 *Capon-priests*] probably another joke. The Romans called these eunuchs *galli*, a word that also means "cocks." Chickens, after all, do not bear live offspring!

621 *Phrygian tempo*] the ancients thought this measure ideal for setting emotions ablaze—and the would-be priests might need all the help they could get. See Catullus 63.9, 64.262; Ovid, *Met.* 4.30, *Fasti* 4.183.

633 *Curetes*] Lucretius identifies the Corybantes, Cybele's attendants, with the Curetes, who sang and danced so loud that Saturn could not hear his baby son Jupiter wailing on Mount Dicte. Saturn had planned to eat the boy, but his mother used this ruse to hide him. Lucretius's grossly comical "send him down the gullet" reduces the whole matter to nonsense.

646–51] see 1.44–49 and note.

655–57 *Neptune, Bacchus, Ceres*] gods of the sea, of wine, and of grain. Munro thinks this is another attack on the Stoics, who so abused allegorical interpretation of the gods that they nearly ended up divinizing everything in the world.

688–90] repeated from 1.822–24.

694] repeats 338.

706 *Chimera*] beast with the head of a lion, the trunk of a goat, and the tail of a dragon. See 5.898–903.

714 *the foreign stuff*] i.e., by excretion.

723–24] see 337–38, 692–94.

725–26] cf. 1.633–34.

738 *not colored*] the primacy of touch assures that sharp things can be made of needle-like atoms. Whiteness, however, must be produced by an atomic network resulting in the visual-tactile sensation of "white." Clay (1983, 166)

observes that the atoms are "widowed" and "orphaned" of all human qualities, as is fitting in a world indifferent to human concerns.

748   ] a lacuna; the point was probably that atoms are colorless.

751–54   ] see 1.670–73 and 789–93.

760–62   ] see 1.816–18.

763   ] optical illusions were, as Merrill notes, frequent topics of discussion between the Skeptics and their opponents. Lucretius treats illusions in
greater depth at 4.377–519.

801   *plumes of doves*] example used by Skeptics to deny the reliability of
the senses. How could one object be blue and red at the same time? Actually, these colors are caused by light refracted through the prisms of a dove's
plumage. See Cicero, *Academics* 2.19, 79.

830   *Tyrian scarlet*] see 35. The Phoenicians of Tyre crushed the shell of the
murex to make valuable red-purple dye.

848   *balm*] the ancients used oil as a base for distilling perfume. Lucretius's
analogy, though exquisite, is loose, since the atoms form not the base for fragrances but the fragrances themselves.

860   *the pliable soften*] severely compressed line. Atoms can possess no qualities that would make them perishable. They must be perfectly solid, indivisible. These other qualities belong only to atomic combinations—like ours.

870   *animal life*] "animal" preserves its sense of "possessing the breath of
life." Epicureans do not distinguish between body and soul. Since all is body,
atoms that create stones can also create life. The point prepares for the subject of the third book, the nature of the soul.

872   *raw manure*] belief in spontaneous generation lasted into the eighteenth
century. In particular, worms were thought to be spawned by sunlight im-
pregnating the deposited mud of the Nile.

883–85, 894–96   ] see 1.817–18, 906–9; 2.1007–9.

903   ] in the missing lines Lucretius evidently argued that if atoms could
sense, they would have to be "soft," divisible, and thus not atoms at all.

931   ] Stoics, says Merrill, thought that an animal was really an animal only
after it had taken its first breath.

950   *knots of soul*] as we learn in book 3, the soul is made of very subtle atoms that at death slip through the "pores" or interstices between the flesh's atoms.

973–90   ] as often, Lucretius ends his argument by reducing the opposing view to silliness. Cf. his dismissal of Anaxagoras, 1.913–18.

991   *sky-born seed*] our father and mother are not deities of sky and earth but are the sky and earth themselves, since they provide the atoms we need for birth. See also 1.250–64, 5.792–93, 5.818.

1007–9   ] see 1.905–8, 2.883–85.

1013–14   ] see 1.822–25, 2.884.

1015–16   ] see 1.819–20.

1020   ] see 1.686.

1035   ] for the observation, but used to argue for providence, see Cicero, *Nat. deor.* 2.94–96.

1049   ] cf. 1.956–1004.

1086   ] for the image see 1.77 and note.

1149   *so crippled is our age*] the contradiction between this passage and 570–581 is more apparent than real. The universe is deadlocked between "life-giving" and "lethal" atomic motions, but any one of its parts will have its day of birth and death. Although our experience is of a balance between life and death, that balance is unsteady, and our world is slowly wearing out and growing old.

1152   *golden cord*] Lucretius laughs at the idea of a "chain of being" stretching from heaven to earth and linking creatures of descending degrees of divinity. His trick is to shift from ontology to material causality. We are not "heaven-born" because we are, physically, creatures of earth. No long rope was needed.

BOOK THREE

Lucretius applies his atomic theory to the nature of the mind or soul, proving that it is material and subject to death. Central to his argument is the close connection between mind and body: when the body falls ill, the mind is discomposed too. It takes the right twinings of body- and spirit-atoms to stitch our subtle weave of consciousness and life. The book ends with a famous "hymn to death," as Lucretius scoffs at those who make their lives miserable by fearing what cannot possibly happen to them after they die.

This book is a minor or anticipatory climax to the whole work. The atom's existence has been shown, as has the atomic structure of objects; now we build to the atomic structure of the soul. The lesson that the soul is corporeal and mortal concludes the first great movement of the poem. The implications of that lesson will be taken up in the next book, where Lucretius shows how far we are deceived by our ignorance of the nature of sensation and thought.

There is little sweetness here. Lucretius attacks his opponents, and at his most sympathetic he can but shake his head at the folly of a man whose fear of death gives him no peace. His examples of the linking of body and soul are disturbing—the epileptic, the decapitated soldier, the hacked snake, the dodderer—and his tone is brusque. No quarter is left for those who hope for immortality, not when the master himself, Epicurus, has died. Who do we think we are, huffs Lucretius, to be reluctant about going?

For the soul's composition, see Epicurus, *To Herod.* 63–68; for the fear of death, see *To Men.* 124–33, *Prin. Doc.* 19, 20, 28.

1. Proem
   A. Praise of Epicurus as father (1–30)
   B. The misery of men who fear death (31–93)

2. The Nature of the Soul and Spirit (94–416)
   A. A body part, not some harmonious state (95–135)
   B. Unity of animus and anima (136–60)
   C. The soul's corporeality (161–76)
   D. Subtlety of the soul's atoms (177–230)
   E. The soul's composition (231–322)
      1. Air, breath, and warmth (231–40)
      2. The nameless fourth element (241–57)
      3. How these unite in motion (258–87)
      4. How they produce various characters of men (288–322)
   F. The unity of soul and body (323–49)
   G. The soul's dependence on the body for sensation (350–69)
   H. Sparseness of soul-atoms (370–95)
   I. Dominance of the animus over the anima (396–416)

3. Mortality of the Soul (417–826)
   A. Tininess and mobility of soul-atoms (425–44)
   B. Mutual growth and decay of body and soul (445–58)
   C. Physical and mental disorders (459–523)
   D. Loss of sensation in the dying (524–45)
   E. The soul as body part (546–55)
   F. Inability of body and soul to endure separation (556–612)
   G. Proper dwellings required for all things (613–21)
   H. No sensation without body parts (622–31)
   I. Dismemberment (632–67)
   J. No memory of events before birth (668–76)
   K. Souls not infused at birth (677–710)
   L. Residual soul-atoms in a corpse (711–38)
   M. Heredity and the soul's death (739–72)
   N. No infusion of souls during coitus (773–80)
   O. The body as the soul's jar (781–802)
   P. Sicknesses of the soul (803–26)

4. The Hymn to Death (827–1091)
   A. "Death is nothing to us" (827–927)
      1. Past and future alike irrelevant (827–66)
      2. No sensation in corpses (867–90)
      3. Death, the end of desires (891–900)
      4. Death not to be mourned (901–8)
      5. Death as sleep (909–27)
   B. The rebuke by *Natura rerum* (928–74)
   C. Hell within us (975–1020)
   D. Universality of death (1021–49)
   E. Life spoiled by fear of death (1050–83)
   F. Death everlasting (1084–91)

1 *you*] Epicurus, both intellectual leader and *paterfamilias,* the Roman head of household whose fatherly precepts a child was duty-bound to honor. Merrill notes that Epicurus's disciples regarded him as divine even during his lifetime.

14 *sprung from a godlike mind*] Kenney (1971) argues that Lucretius alludes to the birth of Athena, goddess of wisdom, from the head of Zeus.

18 *The quiet dwellings of the gods*] cf. Epicurus, *To Herod.* 77, *To Men.* 123, *Prin. Doc.* 1; these lines adapt Homer's description of divine existence, *Od.* 6.42–46. In this book, devoted to the materiality and mortality of the soul, Lucretius must show that the gods can neither reward their followers nor punish their foes. Epicurus's trumpet call to arms, ironically, is the announcement of divine peace, blissful carelessness of human sin or virtue. Epicurus strips the veil from heaven and hell to show us that they exist only in the unenlightened mind.

36 *mind and soul*] *animus,* or mind, is the rational principle; the *anima,* life-spirit or breath of life, the principle of internal motion. The controlling animus is located in the breast, while the anima is spread throughout the body. Together they constitute the soul. For the distinction see Augustine, *Civitate Dei* 7.23. Poetic exigencies lead Lucretius to use either term to refer to the pair in concord. I have been free with my use of "mind," "soul," and "spirit," as the context demands.

37 *that fear*] Cicero rejoins, "What terror? What fear? What old woman is so senile as to fear what you [Epicureans] would have feared?" (*Tusculanarum disputationum* 1.48).

42 *infamous*] unmentionable, as determined by a court of law. Aulus Gellius, 6.18.11, describes the suicide of men so declared.

48 *men driven out of their country*] for the ancients, whose identity and survival depended upon associations with fellow citizens, exile was a dire punishment. Kenney (1971) adds that during Lucretius's time "freebooting political ambition was bringing the Roman commonwealth to its knees, and exile, disgrace and death were part of the common experience of the upper classes of Rome." Lucretius cleverly links treason with backsliding into one's native religion. The true patriot does not have to be driven away for crimes and does not take the state cult seriously. For Epicurus's own love of his country, see *Life* 9–10.

53 *the gods of the dead*] Romans slaughtered black victims and offered them to the *Manes,* the protective spirits of their ancestors, particularly during the feast of Parentalia. Lucretius's braggart turns to the old hexes when times are bad; he has not learned to revere Epicurus as his spiritual ancestor.

62] see 2.12. Sallust, *Catiline* 10–11, describes the eruption of wickedness and ambition during the ascendancy of Caesar.

70 *forge*] *rem conflant;* they literally "blow" their wealth up, as a fire is stoked by a bellows.

75 *envy*] the pun is invisible in English. Latin *invidia* suggests a looking askance or squinting, contrasting with everyone else's gaze upon the latest idol.

79] Epicurus argued that some people actually killed themselves because they were afraid to die. See Seneca, *Epistulae* 24.22–23.

84 *piety*] implies not only religious devotion but duties that bind parent and child, friend and friend, citizen and country. Epicureans, who eschewed war and politics, were accused of impiety, but here Lucretius turns the accusation against the accusers.

87–93] see 1.146–48, 2.56–62, 6.35–41.

98 *the mind's sense*] a missing line precedes this clause, the sense of which may have been "There are some who foolishly insist that." The theory attacked is that the soul is some ordering of parts, a symmetry or mathematical harmony. See Plato, *Phaedo* 86.

121 *tiny atoms of heat*] in a way the anima really is a breath, which by nature requires warmth and moisture.

132 *Helicon*] mountain haunt of the Muses; see 1.119.

137 *common nature*] animus and anima are inseparable, although only the animus thinks, decides, and feels emotion.

215 *save life-giving sense*] the point, which almost proves rather the *incorporeality* of the soul, is that after death we can see no difference in the body besides its lack of warmth, breath, and sensation. The soul's matter is so subtle as to be hardly detectable.

240 *sense-bearing motion*] not surprisingly, Epicureans believe that sensation is produced by atomic motions.

241 *a fourth element*] if atomic rearrangement can produce any object, why cannot rearrangement of the three elements above produce sensation? This fourth element is a hypothesis smuggled in to make the materiality of the soul more plausible; see Plutarch, *Adversus Coloten* 20. But then, as Lactantius replied (*Opificio Dei* 17), why not just posit an immaterial soul?

255 *torn up*] shredded, as through a strainer.

288 *that warmth*] if the soul consists of three elements, then a preponderance of one will produce a corresponding sort of personality. Yet Lucretius insists that these elements do not fully determine our behavior. The good Epicurean can overcome any character flaw.

323 *And so the soul*] here begins this book's main concern, to free us from the fear of death by proving that the soul will die too. Lucretius shows that the soul needs the body as much as the body needs the soul.

350 *someone*] Stoics. See Cicero, *Tusc.* 1.46.

360 *open doors*] cf. Plato, *Theaetetus* 184. Sextus, *Mathematicos* 7.350, attributes it to Heraclitus.

378 *intervals*] what we cannot sense must be smaller than the spaces between the soul-atoms in our flesh. These atoms are diffused throughout the body, but there are gaps between them nonetheless.

396 *the soul*] animus, so translated throughout this passage.

416 *such bonds*] one can lose a lot of anima, just as one can lose a part of the eyeball. But one cannot lose the whole anima, just as an eye cannot see if the eyeball is wholly cut away. Nor can one lose the animus, no matter how compact it is. A man without animus is dead, even if he has all his limbs, as an eye without a pupil is blind, even if the eyeball is intact.

424 *conjoint*] Latin suggests wedlock, more than mere physical welding.

430 *shadows of cloud*] dreams of clouds are more tenuous even than clouds, yet the atoms that make these dreams can still stir the soul. The topic is treated at length at 4.26–519, 720–853.

481 *in the body*] argument *a fortiori*. If the soul can be so discomposed while in its bodily fortress, what will happen to it when it is released into the air? See Cicero, *Tusc.* 1.79.

487 *He crumples*] Lucretius's description of an epileptic fit is purely physicalistic—the atoms run wild in the body. When they settle down, proper consciousness returns.

494 *vocal-atoms*] Lucretius will show at 4.533–46 that sounds are made up of atoms.

517–18] see 1.670–71, 791–92; 2.753–54.

640   *sickle-wheeled chariots*] cf. Xenophon, *Anabasis* 1.7. Some eastern armies used chariots with blades protruding from the wheel hubs.

671   *preserve the traces of our former lives*] as Pythagoras claimed to do, in recognizing the shield he carried in the Trojan War. Lucretius may be attacking Plato's theory in *Meno* that all knowledge is recollection.

700   *It would be strained*] a soul instilled in us at birth would have to be strained through atomic interstices, just as food is broken down in our bodies. It would die in the process, and the new soul it produced would likewise have its day of birth and death.

718   *worms*] for spontaneous generation, see 2.872 and note; see also Vergil, *Georgics* 4.554–58; Ovid, *Met.* 15.361–78.

748   *Hyrcanian hounds*] from the savage Caucasus regions. Kenney (1971) notes that they were thought to have been bred with tigers.

752   *they say*] Pythagoreans, believers in the transmigration of souls.

781–94   ] nearly repeated at 5.128–41.

783   *no sap in stone*] cf. Lucretius's rejection of Anaxagoras's *homoeomerian*, 1.873–918.

803–15   ] repeated at 5.351–63.

820   ] short lacuna follows. Missing is some assertion that the soul is disturbed by influences from outside the body.

827   *Death*] having shown that the soul will die, Lucretius argues that death therefore cannot concern us. Not death but fear of death, with all the immoderate desires that attend that fear, plunges us into a living hell. For the line see Epicurus, *To Men.* 124, which as Kenney notes became a popular inscription on tombstones.

830   *Carthaginians*] in the Second Punic War (219–202) between Rome and Carthage, the one made famous by the brilliant generals Hannibal and Scipio. Hannibal's guerrilla tactics devastated the Italian peninsula for years and nearly destroyed the Roman republic. Imagine the effect of an American poet's saying that the Revolutionary War is of no concern to us. What a deflation of the patriotic and the epic—but that is little compared with the audacity of the carelessness expressed in 839. Let the universe be destroyed; after we die that will mean nothing to us. Sextus Empiricus, *Outlines of Pyrrhonism* 3.229, discusses the sentiment.

854   *the same order*] since the ancients had no conception of different orders of infinity, it seemed reasonable to suppose that an infinite span of time would guarantee *palingenesis,* the exact re-creation of the world. See Epicurus, Fragments 55; Augustine, *Civ. Dei* 22.28.

885–90   ] as Kenney notes, many writers belittle popular worries about the proper disposal of the dead. See Cicero, *Tusc.* 1.102–8.

895   *poor boy, poor boy*] a maudlin line. In Lucretius's phrase *misero misere,* the first word is an ablative referring to the dead man, "from you O pitiable one," and the second an adverb of manner, "in this most pitiable way." Merrill says that Lucretius is imitating obituaries and standard condolences. Kenney cites Gray's "Elegy written in a country Church yard," 21–24.

904   *Insatiably lamenting*] only three-word hexameter in Latin epic (*insatiabiliter defleuimus, aeternumque*). Its rhetorical pitch is absurdly high; Lucretius smiles at the inordinate outburst of grief.

909   *When men lie back*] the barflies of Rome bemoan their lost youth, addled both by wine and by their fear of death. "*Breuis hic est fructus homullis,*" hiccoughs one, complaining that the life we "poor little men" enjoy is short. Cf. Petronius, *Satyricon* 34.10.

924   *sleep*] death is a sort of sleep and thus not to be feared. The idea was a commonplace; see Cicero, *Tusc.* 1.92.

928   *Nature herself*] *rerum natura,* the nature of things, personified. Lucretius has shown the foolishness of fearing death; now he attacks that fear for its selfishness and ingratitude.

929   *one of us*] Leonard and Smith refer the reader to the self-pitying partygoers above, but that is a long reach backward. I think Lucretius refers to himself and his reader, especially his reader Memmius, whose life has not been very smooth.

933   *leaky pot*] see 1005 and note.

975   ] hell is what we make in ourselves out of irrational fear and unbounded desire. What follows is a euhemeristic interpretation of the myths of several notable sinners. None of these myths was taken very seriously as literal truth; see Seneca, *Consolatio ad Marciam* 19.4.

977   *Tantalus*] one of the two "tantalizing" punishments of this ancient sinner is the threat of the impending rock; see Cicero, *Tusc.* 4.35. The other is

better known. Tantalus stands in a lake beneath the laden boughs of fruit trees. When he tries to sip the water, it recedes; when he makes for the fruit, the wind blows the branches out of reach (for Tantalus and other stock sinners see Homer, *Od.* 11.582–92). He is an apt sinner to begin the list, since he was punished for a very Epicurean "sin"—revealing the secrets of the gods. But according to another legend, he is punished for his desire to sample ambrosia.

981   *Tityus*] when Leto, mother of Apollo and Athena, came to Delphi, Tityus tried to rape her but was slain by the arrows of her marksmen children. For punishment he was splayed out in hell, where vultures tore at his liver. West (1969, 99) hears a vicious pun in Lucretius's account: Tityus, mad with lust, is just the sinner to be pricked and pecked apart by his desires. Servius, commenting on *Aen.* 6.596, says that Tityus is lust—an urge that doctors believed originated in the liver. His liver grows back after the vultures have eaten it, just as desire returns soon after the deed is done.

992   *Sisyphus*] the conniver has to roll a boulder up a hill, but whenever he reaches the top the boulder rolls all the way back down; see Homer, *Od.* 11.593–600. The comparison with political ambition is shrewd. The politician sets his heart on reaching the top of the heap; the voters always send him home disappointed. Epicurus disdained politics; see *Life* 120a–21b.

1005   *ripe young virgins*] all but one of the fifty Danaids, forced to marry their cousins, murdered them on their wedding night. There is gruesome humor in Lucretius's calling them virgins, since, as Leonard and Smith point out, they never did consummate those marriages. For the story see Horace, *Odes* 3.11, Ovid, *Heroides* 14; for the leaky pot as image of insatiability see Plato, *Gorgias* 493–94.

1008   *Cerberus and the Furies*] Cerberus is the three-headed hellhound; the Furies are the infernal goddesses of vengeance who pursue sinners. But Seneca says, "No one is such a child as to be afraid of Cerberus" (*Epist.* 24.18).

1009   *Tartarus*] Hades, that is.

1013   *the frightful Rock*] The Tarpeian, overlooking the Tiber outside of Rome. From its peak notorious criminals were flung to their deaths.

1014   *tarring, torching*] prisoners were smeared with inflammable pitch; had red-hot plates or *lammina* applied to their bellies; were tied to huge torches and set afire. For the lamination see Horace, *Epistulae* 1.15.36.

1022   *good King Ancus*] for the line see Ennius, *Annales* 149. Ancus Marcius was the legendary fourth king of Rome. The sentiment, used in stock consolations, is that at least one is not the only person dying. See Cicero, *Tusc.* 3.79.

1026   *that ruler*] Xerxes, leader of the Persians in their great war against the Greeks. Attacking them in 480 B.C., Xerxes marched his men over the Hellespont, building a bridge of ships and gangways. He lost the war and was murdered in 465 by one of his royal guards. Xerxes became a byword for arrogance; see Catullus 66.45.

1031   *Scipio*] Publius Cornelius Scipio, surnamed Africanus for his glorious defeat of the Carthaginians in 202 B.C.

1036   *Democritus*] said to have committed suicide some time after his ninetieth year.

1039   *Epicurus*] the only time Lucretius uses the master's name. Even the wisest of all men must obey the laws of life and death.

1056   ] change of scenery brings no change of heart. Cf. Horace, *Epist.* 1.11.27.

BOOK FOUR

Having settled that the world is made of atoms and space, described the properties and motions of atoms, and argued that the soul is made of atoms and so is mortal, Lucretius now shows how atoms can produce images that the soul apprehends. The argument relies upon a similarity between imagination and vision. Since all events occur because of unseen atoms, vision must involve the impinging of unseen atoms upon the eye. Atomists resolve the conundrum—that invisible atoms produce vision—by maintaining that objects shed "simulacra," films or peels or ghosts. These films are too slight to be seen one by one, but when they assault the eye in force they cause it to see the object of their origin. This explanation, though crudely physical, distantly anticipates the truth. Our eyes are struck, if not by slices of boulder-atoms, by waves of light reflected from the boulder.

But the shift from physical vision to thought is not easy. Vision, say the atomists, is passive: the eye registers whatever films impinge upon it. Our eyes never deceive us, because they never really *do* anything at all. We are deceived, rather, by misinterpretations. This is to defer, not solve, the problem. For the atomists conceive of thought as a subtle sort of vision:

we see films thick enough for the eye, but we "think" films so thin that only the soul can notice them. Then is the inner eye of the mind deceived? Or is reasoning independent of the thoughts that strike our minds? If the former, then it is hard to see why the physical eye cannot also be deceived. If the latter, then one may ask what reasoning consists of and whether it really arises from the senses, as the atomists hold. In any case, thought is passive. We imagine a Centaur because we happen upon a horse-film and a man-film stuck together in the air. The mind produces nothing of its own; hard thinking is like straining the eyes to see what is there. Needless to say, this theory ignores our experience of thought, which feels active, willed, creative. It does not distinguish between sense impressions and knowledge. It evades the question of memory and ignores logic. It fails to account for imaginations that are *not* visual. Boulder-films can explain why we see boulders, but can they explain how we imagine their hardness?

Like all Epicurean tenets, that of the simulacra is put to moral use. People do not know how easily they can be fooled by these films, and so they give themselves up to mere dreams and specters, of woodland gods that are no more than echoes, of the dead that are no more than residual images, of a heaven whose glory can be reduced to its reflection in a puddle in the street. As Wormell suggests (Dudley 1965, 57), they are like the little boys afraid of the dark: they worry about "ghosts." Most notably, they pursue the phantasms of *amor,* a malady to which Lucretius devotes the famous satire that ends the book.

For the theory see Epicurus, *To Herod.* 46–53.

1. Proem (1–25)

2. The Senses and the Simulacra (26–719)
   A. What simulacra are (26–107)
   B. Their thinness (108–26)
   C. Their mutability (127–40)
   D. Their speed (141–227)
   E. How they cause vision (228–384)
      1. Vision and touch (228–36)
      2. How we judge distance (237–53)
      3. The invisibility of a single simulacrum (254–66)
      4. Peculiarities of vision (267–384)
   F. Optical illusions and the mind (385–466)
   G. Refutation of skepticism (467–519)

I. Sound (520–612)
  1. Atomic composition (520–46)
  2. Voice and garble (547–69)
  3. Echoes; Pan (570–92)
  4. Why sound can penetrate walls (593–612)
J. Taste (613–70)
K. Smell (671–703)
L. Why certain sensations agree with certain creatures (704–19)

3. Inner Senses (720–1028)
  A. Invisible films and the cause of thought (720–46)
  B. Similarity between vision and thought (747–54)
  C. The cause of dreams (755–74)
  D. Thought and the mind's preparation to see (775–819)
  E. Against teleology (820–53)
  F. Hunger and thirst (854–72)
  G. The will to act (873–902)
  H. Fatigue, sleep, and dreams (903–1028)
    1. Discomposing of spirit-atoms during sleep (912–24)
    2. Air lashing against the body (925–57)
    3. Dreams of daytime activity (958–1002)
    4. Dreams of what we desire and fear (1003–28)

4. Sexual Desire and Procreation (1029–1278)
  A. Libido and the simulacra of lovely bodies (1029–48)
  B. The disease of love (1049–1111)
  C. Lovers' misery (1112–31)
  D. The illusion-inducing effect of love (1132–82)
  E. Female libido (1183–99)
  F. Heredity (1200–1223)
  G. Natural causes of infertility (1224–68)
    1. Quality of the semen (1231–53)
    2. Good positions for conception (1254–68)
  H. True love and habit (1269–78)

1–25   nearly repeated from 1.924–48; see notes to these lines.

30   *semblances*] simulacra; see discussion in the synopsis of this book, above. The point is to provide a mechanical theory of perception, so that we will

not be fooled by visions or dreams of the dead or of the afterlife. Godwin (1986) comments: "The images we see are indeed those of the dead, but were emitted from the body *before* death and are still travelling abroad." We are to be dis-illusioned by this book, made to see the trivial causes of our fear and devotion.

33–35] see 1.132–34.

45–53 *Since I've taught*] an unrevised doublet of 26–44.

68 *tiny bodies*] according to Godwin, Epicurus's opponents scoffed at the notion that an elephant's "peel" could squeeze itself into the eye.

76 *theaters*] Godwin (note on ll. 969–79) comments that this is the first of several images of the theater in book 4. The image is apt, since for Epicureans all sensation is, as it were, staged: we see what we are presented with, and we see only the surface. Epicureanism teaches us how to see the hidden causes of things, how to avoid the superficial interpretation that leads, among other things, to religion.

124 *so lightly*] a lacuna follows; the sense must have been that substances like absinthe give off the strongest odors at the slightest touch; perhaps Lucretius also discussed brightly colored things.

126 *impotent, insensible*] i.e., singly. When the images assail in force they cause perception.

142] a short lacuna follows.

145 *veil*] most editors emend *vestem* to *vitrum,* "glass," but the original reading is more interesting. We can, after all, see through a thin veil, and any image of anything we see must first pass through the air and whatever floats in it.

168–71] repeated at 6.252–55; cf. Vergil, *Georg.* 1.322–24, *Aen.* 12.335.

178–80] repeated at 905–7.

216–27] nearly repeated at 6.925–36.

227] anything may be sensed if we are in the right state to sense it.

245 *all the air*] we judge distance by the blurring caused when an image has to drive before it a long stream of air. Epicureans do not explain why we never sense so much air passing through our eyes, nor why the image enters both eyes at once.

288] perhaps, as Leonard and Smith suggest, the missing lines compared the image in a mirror with the image of an object equidistant with us from the door through which we see it.

309] a mirror concave enough to preserve left and right. The first hypothesis is correct; such images are reflected twice by the concavity.

330 *a jaundiced man*] in this piece of classical nonsense, Bailey (1947) detects a trace of Plato's theory of vision, according to which sight is produced by emanations from the eyes. But atoms, as Lucretius showed in book 2, are not supposed to be yellow.

351] for other classical discussions of optical illusions and the philosophical problems they pose, see Cicero, *Acad.* 2.81–82, *De divinatione* 2.120; Seneca, *De beneficiis* 7.15, *Naturales questiones* 1.3.9–11; Plutarch, *Adv. Col.* 25; Macrobius, 7.14; Sextus Empiricus, *Pyrrh.* 1.118–23.

384 *Pin the blame*] according to Epicurus, our senses are never deceived (*Prin. Doc.* 22–24, *Life* 31–34). The eyes see what is there, but the mind draws false conclusions.

467 *whoever*] a Skeptic. Lucretius ridicules the idea that we can know nothing, since anyone who says so pretends to know just that. Since, then, we have a notion of truth, we must have some criterion for judging truth. That criterion, for Lucretius, is the evidence of our senses. As Godwin notes, the Skeptics were "no slight opponents to face," as the Academy had for two centuries stressed the skepticism of Socrates (cf. *Apology* 23), and even atomism had its strain of skepticism; see Cicero, *Acad.* 2.73.

545 *Helicon*] mountain haunt of the Muses; cf. 1.119.

578–80 *Nymphs*] goddesses of streams, pools, springs, trees; often followers of Diana, chaste goddess of the hunt.
   Goat-foot Satyrs] impish semi-savage gods of sylvan revelry, known for their sensual appetites and their remarkably large means of satisfying them.
   Fauns] manifestations of the rural god Faunus, whom the Romans identified with Pan, Greek god of music and shepherding. Faunus was considered one of the ancestors of the Roman race; Ovid tells of his role in founding the merry feast of Lupercal, *Fasti* 2.303–58.

586] see 5.1402. Bailey notes that Lucretius makes double use of his theory of sound, explaining why echoes occur and then suggesting that these

echoes gave rise to the superstitions here described, as people are "all ears" for the bizarre.

638 *Hellebore*] the herb, mentioned again at 5.896–97, may be lethal in large doses, but it was widely used by the ancients to cure insanity. The ancients disagreed on what to make of such paradoxes. Sextus, *Pyrrh.* 1.57, uses the example of hemlock to show that the senses are unreliable. Why should what kills a man nourish a beast? See also Pliny, *Naturalis historiae* 7.15, 10.69.

660 *rough and hooked atoms*] the palate's pores sift from the food those atoms whose shapes match theirs. For us honey is sweet because its round atoms are ideally shaped to pass through the round pores in our palates, leaving honey's "bitter" atoms stranded above. But if our pores are altered by illness, then the angular, "bitter" atoms may be ideally shaped to pass through, leaving the easy "sweet" atoms unsensed. Thus, says Bailey, taste depends upon the taster far more than color depends upon the observer.

680 *the white goose*] legend had it that white geese sacred to Jove alerted the Romans to an attack by the Gauls, 387 B.C. See Livy, 5.47.

704 *this property*] of agreement between certain creatures and certain sensations. See 675–84.

710 *The savage lions*] the belief that lions can't abide a crowing cock was common; see Pliny, *Nat. hist.* 10.47. The naturalist Cuvier, notes Merrill, placed a cock in a lion's cage, and the lion ate it.

720 *what moves the soul*] the most important point. Thoughts (and thus love, dreams, visions) are explainable in material terms.

726 *more subtly woven*] how can this be, asks Bailey, if the films that stir vision are already the thinnest peels of things?

730–31 *Centaurs*] creatures with heads and chests of men and bodies of horses.
Scylla] sea monster, woman to the waist, fish below, belted around with barking hounds. She dwelt in a cave off the Italian shore in the Strait of Messina. Ships had to thread the needle between Scylla and Charybdis—on one side a ravenous whirlpool, on the other a menacing rock; see Homer, *Od.* 12. *Cerberus:* Three-headed watchdog of Hades. See also 127–40; 2.700–717; 5.875–921. Munro notes that Cicero, *Nat. deor.* 1.108, uses these very examples to disprove the theory in question.

769] the semblances are like snapshots in a strip of film. They arrive so fast that the images they present seem to move.

796 *All the shadows are ready*] to keep the mind from having any part in creating sensation, Lucretius posits a wealth of images of everything everywhere. Munro suggests that the poet was embarrassed by the difficulties of his system.

798–99] see 769–70 and note.

821 *a vicious flaw*] the error of teleology. We are not endowed with faculties *in order* that we might use them—no ends are promoted by our being so formed (Epicurus, *To Herod.* 76–77), as Aristotle (*De partibus animalium* 4.10) and the Stoics said (Cicero, *Nat. deor.* 2.133–68). Lactantius countered that since eyes can do nothing but see, seeing must be what they were made for (*Op. Dei* 6.7). Lucretius anticipates Darwin's theory of natural selection. If we had not had such useful arms and legs, we would not now be here to worry about it.

886 *its whole bulk*] despite the will, Lucretius's presentation of locomotion is deterministic and mechanical. An image moves the mind, which moves the will and the spirit, which jerks the body into a hulking, robotic motion.

905–7] repeated from 178–80.

941] Lucretius does not say how the ejected atoms enter the body again.

962–66] the Epicurean enjoys peace in his dreams too.

1039 *The body seeks*] the torments of love are a war to be shunned by the serene Epicurean. For the master's attitude toward sex, see *Life* 118, *Fragments* 18, 51.

1044 *young boy*] cf. Martial, 4.7. Unwomanly hairiness was a sign that the beloved was no longer a proper object of homosexual love. Godwin notes that while romantic love between men was rare in Rome, casual pederasty was not.

1049 *"amor" and "umor"*] love and juice. The words are mine, to suggest the poet's fanciful etymology linking love with the fluids of intercourse.

1088 *thirsty*] Godwin notes that Lucretius is still thinking of coital fluids; the illogical lover trusts that his thirst will be quenched by ejaculation.

1116   *Sicyonian slippers*] dainty footwear made near Corinth. Young lovers running through their fathers' estates are standard heroes of Roman comedy.

1151   *black as soot*] Lucretius satirizes how we allow love to cloud the testimony of our senses. Sextus Empiricus, *Pyrrh.* 1.108, uses the same facts to show that the senses are unreliable. Most of the euphemisms are Greek, which served for Latin the same role French serves for English, as the language of the pretentious and super-sophisticated. For imitations, Munro cites Ovid, *Ars amatoria* 2.657–62, and Moliere, *Le Misanthrope* 2.5.

1177   *the secrets of the hoary deep*] literally, of the room backstage. Ovid, *Ars* 3.229, quips that there are some things a man is better off not knowing. Brown (1987, 296) says that the "douche" used by the lady is a "medical fumigation" for typical gynecological problems.

1200   ] for the following ancient discussion of heredity, see Aristotle, *De generatione* 4.1–3.

1268   ] whether this line expresses admiration or contempt for Roman matrons, the reader must decide.

BOOK FIVE

Lucretius now discusses ultimate questions that trouble us. How was the world made? What are the heavens? How did the earth first produce life? How did civilization develop? Whence do we derive our ideas of the gods?

This longest of Lucretius's books is also his most humane, for here he is most ardently concerned with how we ought to live. From the first line of the proem to the celebration of human achievement at the end, Lucretius shows us the emptiness of what we fear above, and the delights of friendship and simple pleasure. He does not sentimentalize primitive life—his accounts of early tussles with wild beasts, and of early combat, are gruesome. But for all that, his heart goes out to the savages, who are never, as are the Romans of his day, objects of his scorn. Poor man, born into a world where only the fit survive, discovers not only fire and language but the social contract itself. It is telling that Lucretius combines his best description of Epicurean life with an account of the discovery of music. Those "soil-bred dwellers of the woods" danced so clumsily they had to laugh at themselves, only adding to the inexpressible sweetness of their games.

But we are not to gather acorns forever. As Nichols argues (1976, 22),

Lucretius believes in progress, so long as it helps give us pleasure and free us from pain. Since the gods are remote, and since the lovely and awful lights in the sky are mortal just as we, the responsibility for making a decent life rests with us alone. The rejection of teleology, of a divine purpose in things, is also a celebration of human ingenuity and art. That such ingenuity should be used both for music and for battle cries, for medicine and for poison, is man's glory and his shame.

For Epicurus's views on the social contract, see *Prin. Doc.* 31–40; on human inventions and divine negligence, see *To Herod.* 75–77; on heavenly phenomena, see *To Herod* 81–82; *to Pyth.* 88–98; *Prin. Doc.* 11–13.

1. Proem and Plan (1–234)
  A. Proem: Epicurus, our Hercules, greatest of gods (1–54)
  B. Announcement of the book's controversies (55–109)
  C. No blasphemy in broaching these subjects (110–234)
    1. Heavenly bodies inanimate (110–45)
    2. No gods in our world (146–55)
    3. No motive for the gods to create (156–94)
    4. Earth not perfectly suited for our existence (195–234)

2. Celestial Phenomena (235–779)
  A. Mutability and mortality of the world (235–415)
    1. World composed of mortal parts (235–305)
    2. Universal decay (306–17)
    3. Birth and death (318–23)
    4. Recent inception of history (324–37)
    5. Natural disasters (338–50)
    6. Perpetuity of atoms, void, and the All (351–79)
    7. Destruction caused by the elements (380–415)
  B. Cosmos risen from the random collisions of atoms (416–508)
  C. Why stars move (509–33)
  D. Earth's union with air (534–63)
  E. Tininess of the sun, moon, and stars (564–90)
  F. How a tiny sun could fill the world with light (591–611)
  G. Reasons for the apparent speeds of heavenly bodies (612–47)
    1. Relative distances from the earth (619–34)
    2. Different gusts of wind in the heavens (635–47)
  H. Causes of sunrise and sunset (648–77)
  I. Lengthening and shortening of days (678–702)

    J. Moonlight (703–48)
    K. Eclipses (749–68)

3. Early Life on Earth (780–1452)
    A. Earth as origin of plant and animal life (780–817)
    B. Earth's present barrenness (818–33)
    C. Freaks and abortions (834–74)
    D. The impossibility of such hybrids as centaurs (875–921)
    E. The life of early man, a selfish fight for survival (922–84)
    F. Causes of death for early and modern man (985–1007)
    G. Civilization (1008–1452)
        1. Marriage and the social contract (1008–24)
        2. The natural origin of language (1025–87)
        3. Fire and cooking (1088–1101)
        4. The rise of kings and social classes (1102–32)
        5. Law (1133–57)
        6. Religion (1158–1237)
        7. Metallurgy (1238–77)
        8. Metal weapons (1278–1304)
        9. Wild beasts used in warfare (1305–46)
      10. Weaving (1347–57)
      11. Agriculture (1358–75)
      12. Music (1376–1406)
      13. Desire for newer and newer trifles (1407–30)
      14. Astronomy (1431–34)
      15. All the arts and sciences of civilized life (1435–52)

5   *prize*] *praemia vitae*, the best of life; Epicurean peace.

8   *a god*] Cicero scoffs at the insolence of those who revere philosophers as gods; see *Tusc.* 1.48. But Gale (1994, 80) notes the irony that "Epicurus was worthy to be called a god" because he denied "the possibility that man can undergo apotheosis or that the gods have any concern with mankind."

14   *Ceres, Bacchus*] goddess of the harvest, god of wine. Even supposing they exist, these benefactors do not compare with Epicurus, whose gifts enable us not just to live but to live well.

20   *worldwide*] Epicureanism had spread from Greece to Rome in the west, and to Asia Minor and Syria in the east.

22–38 *Hercules*] hero of the Stoics, Hercules was thought a benefactor of mankind for his slaying of various monsters; for the tale see Apollodorus, 2.4–5. For Hercules as father and protector of the Arcadians, ancestors of the Romans, see Vergil, *Aen.* 8.185–279.

31 *Mount Ismarus*] on the coast of Bistonia or Thrace, the northern arm of Greece. No one would travel that far anyway, so what difference did Hercules' victory make?

62 *semblances*] for the topic see 4.755–59.

76 *helmsman Nature*] Lucretius's personification of Nature does not imply teleology or providence.

82–90] repeated at 6.59–67; for 89–90 see 1.76–77. Horace, *Odes* 1.34, celebrates just such backsliding.

98 *heaven and earth*] our part of the All which has fallen into order. The All can never die, since atoms are indestructible.

111–12] repeated from 1.738–39.

117 *Giants*] offspring of Earth and Sky who fought with Chronos (for Romans, Saturn) to regain the throne seized from him by his son Zeus (Jupiter). The Giants lost, and for their pains Zeus transfixed them with thunderbolts and plunged them beneath the earth (cf. Apollodorus, 1.6). They exemplify the sin of presumption. Lucretius's opponent believes that to talk about the mortality of heaven would be as blasphemous as the rebellion of the Giants. The Stoics imbued the celestial bodies with divine will; see Cicero, *Nat. deor.* 2.43.

128–41] repeated from 3.781–94.

146 *the gods*] they exist but affect nothing on earth. Made of the subtlest atoms, their specters strike our minds and give us a notion of what they are like. We do them pious duty when we imitate their peace. They dwell in the *intermundia,* the spaces between ordered worlds like ours. For much of the following discussion, see Cicero, *Nat. deor.* 1.18–22.

155 *later*] implied by the mortality of the earth and heaven, proved at 235–432, is the total separation of the gods from us.

183] cf. 4.880–81; 5.1044–46. Lucretius's objection is valid only if one assumes that all thought is a product of sensory information.

186 *no peek*] Latin *specimen,* an example to look at.

187–94] see 1.1021–25, 5.422–26.

195–99] repeated from 2.178–82.

210–11] see 1.211–12.

218] if the world is made by design, why is so much of it lethal? See Cicero, *Acad.* 2.120; Lactantius quips that the earth is not our mother but our stepmother, *Op. Dei* 3.

237 *the four*] Costa (1984) notes that although the atomists rejected the notion of the four elements, "they seem to have regarded them at least as basic observable components whose atomic composition could be distinguished."

259] Milton quotes this superb line in *Paradise Lost,* 2.911. Lucretius may be alluding to Aeschylus, *Choephori* 127.

269–72] repeated at 6.636–39.

283] see 4.187.

319 *some*] Stoics, especially Chrysippus. See Cicero, *Nat. deor.* 1.39–41.

327 *Theban war*] Oedipus's sons Polynices and Eteocles fought for control over Thebes after the exile of their father. The argument became a commonplace; see Horace, *Odes* 4.9.

339–41] in *Critias* 110–13, Plato muses that civilizations like that of the fabled Atlantis may have been destroyed by natural catastrophes. Lucretius may be alluding to the fire that singed the earth when Phaethon lost control of the sun god's horses (see 396–405), and to the story of Deucalion and Pyrrha, the husband and wife who were the only survivors when Zeus, in a fit of pique, flooded the world. See Ovid, *Met.* 2.1–400; 1.274–415.

351–63] repeated from 3.803–15.

379] nearly repeated at 1214.

381 *unholy war*] Lucretius may refer to the Empedoclean Strife which, along with Love, governs the world. More likely, he is thinking of the internecine strife that tore the Rome of his day.

388–89] see above, 266–67.

416–31] a web of repetitions. See 5.67–68, 5.76, 1.1018–20, 5.187 and 1.1021, 5.188–91, 1.1023, and 2.1059–62. For the cosmogony, see Aetius [Plutarch], *De placitis philosophorum* 1.4.

438–39] aee 2.725–26.

458 *ether*] this most rarefied of substances makes up the heavens. Since it is so light, its atoms are the first to be squirted out by the pressure of the heavier atoms of earth.

509 *now let us sing*] Epicurus was not interested in what really makes the stars move, since the causes cannot be determined. Rather he wished to show that heavenly phenomena could be explained without bringing the gods into it. The more explanations possible, the better. See *To Herod.* 78–80, *To Pyth.* 85–88. Some of the explanations are on target; others are nonsense which could hardly square with observation. But all are designed to quiet our fear of gods.

512 *axis*] i.e., of the cosmos, denoted in this passage by the capitalized "World."

538 *one with the air*] Lucretius betrays uncertainty over whether the earth rests in the center of the cosmos (see 1.1049–79 for his assertion that it does not). If the earth is surrounded by a boundless universe, how does it stay in place? Something must be grafted onto the earth to keep it from falling, and that something is air. Aetius, 3.15, attributes the theory to Anaximenes; see also Pliny, *Nat. hist.* 2.10.

554] repeated from 3.325.

564 *can't be much bigger*] Epicurus was no geometrician. Democritus, who was, believed the sun was enormous (see Cicero, *De fin.* 1.20, *Acad.* 2.82). The Epicurean assertion is motivated by an insistence on the validity of the senses and by a depreciation of things heavenly. See also below, 574–83, on the moon's size. Epicurus was not alone in his view. Aetius, 2.21, reports that Heraclitus thought the sun was a foot broad.

598 *mingle*] perhaps like the soaking up of a sponge or a pumice stone, an opinion Aetius, 2.20, attributes to Epicurus.

614–15 *Capricorn, Cancer*] zodiacal signs that the sun occupies at the winter and summer solstices. Lucretius refers to the ecliptic, the path the sun traces across the sky through the year.

661   *Mount Ida*] on Crete. Lucretius reports a legend that seemed credible enough to many. He tries to counter the charge of exceptionalism by alluding to other events that occur, suddenly but regularly, at the proper times. Aristotle attributes this opinion about the dawn to Heraclitus, *Meterologica* 2.355a.

685   *node of the year*] the equinox. Because of the earth's tilt, the sun's path describes unequal arcs in the northern and southern hemispheres, except at equinox.

689   *wheel of signs*] zodiac.

702   ] the lacuna makes it hard to tell who "they" are. Perhaps Lucretius refers to those who say that a new sun is born every morning from a gathering of flames. If so, "they" may be Xenophanes and Heraclitus.

725–26   *Chaldeans*] the Chaldean Berosus, an account of whose theory is given by Vitruvius, 9.2.4.

735   *Spring comes*] cf. 667–75. Although the explanation is wrong, Lucretius bases it upon faith in the uniformity of physical law. The "herald of Love" is Venus's mischievous son Cupid; Flora is the lusty goddess of springtime blossoming; Ceres is goddess of the harvest; the Wine-god is Bacchus; Volturnus is the winter wind from the east, Auster a wind from the south.

790–91   ] see 2.1152–53.

824   ] thereafter sexual intercourse had to do the job.

875–921   ] for the origin of our notions of such hybrids as Centaurs, Scyllas, and Chimeras, see 4.730–46.

922   *the human race*] the final portion of the book, containing some of the most splendid poetry in Latin, shows us the aim of Epicurean cosmology. Men are products of the chance collision of atoms that gave birth to the world, and just as the blind atoms hurtle against each other and "try" all combinations, of which only the fit survive, so too men begin, by trial and error, a long step-by-step advance toward civilization. This notion of progress had become common in philosophy of the fifth century B.C. and later; see Plato, *Protagoras* 320–22. Lucretius's love for human beings, despite his disappointment in their folly, is nowhere clearer. Unlike Hobbes, his admirer of very different temperament, Lucretius forgives the savages, who only try to attain what we all want: a happy and peaceful life. And of all the inventions that

make Epicureanism possible, the two most prominent have nothing to do with tools, and were discovered long before civilization with its ships and towers and roads. They are the family, that great heart of the social contract, and music. For the traditional account of the Golden Age, see Hesiod, *Works and Days* 109–201.

945 *sacred groves*] religion begins with a naive awe for natural phenomena. The savages discover the streams upon which their lives depend, and attribute divinity to them.

955 *the common good*] under such harsh conditions, the social imagination does not thrive. The savages are, here at least, soldiers in the Hobbesian war of all against all. Compare with Vergil's very different view, *Aen.* 7.203–4.

962] she holds out for the best pears she can get.

970] Lucretius avoids attributing inanity to the savages merely because they lived a few years ago. If anything, they were less liable to superstition than we, since their lives were full of events that called for immediate attention. It is hard to theologize when a lion is prowling outside your cave.

987 *more often it happened then*] the savages lacked the knowledge and tools to prevent the calamity described. As for us, we use our expertise to make ourselves miserable. Their problems were largely technological, ours moral.

996 *thousands of men*] direct attack on Roman militarism. The poor man devoured by the lion is pitiable, but he is still shown as a man; these thousands are foolish and command no pity.

1009 *wedlock*] Epicurus warned against marriage, but his Garden admitted both women and men, and in his will he made generous provision for the children of his dearest friends (*Life* 19–22). The emphasis on the family and the love of children is typically Roman (and our poet was fond of children and animals, as his many genial references to them attest). The rise of the family is related to the social contract: people who want to raise families need to protect them, and there is no better protection than the mutual agreement to live in peace. See the more pessimistic version in Plato, *Republic* 2.358–59. A short lacuna follows this line.

1025 *language*] no gift of the gods or invention of some one human genius, language develops because our vocal organs allow for it, and because in trying to fashion a society we find it indispensable. It thus rises gradually and naturally from the conditions of human life. The opposing view of language as Promethean invention or law linking things with their true names is treated at length in Plato's *Cratylus*. Lucretius's understanding of language is modern in one respect: language is a system of signs, verbal or otherwise, whose link with what they signify is mainly conventional.

1060 *Molossian bloodhound*] raised on the east coast of the Adriatic. Lucretius's alliteration mimics the growling.

1089 *lightning*] men happened upon fire produced by natural causes and learned to use it. No Prometheus was necessary.

1115] also a Stoic doctrine; cf. Seneca, *Epist.* 4.10.

1130 *what others tell them*] Epicureans do not fret about who is to be consul or general. They believe that all knowledge comes from the senses. These political and epistemological tenets seem unrelated, yet anyone who violates the first must violate the second. That is because *ambitio* (literally, making the rounds) fools the politician into identifying himself with the reports he receives from others. He can never subject things to the calm scrutiny of his own senses.

1133 *When the kings were slain*] according to Roman legend, the last king of Rome, the tyrant Tarquinius Superbus, was overthrown in 509 B.C. by a republican conspiracy. Shortly afterwards the Roman plebeians—unfairly called the "dregs" here—forced the aristocrats to codify the laws so that everyone could be sure what they were. The results were the famous Twelve Tables (444–443 B.C.).

1143 *lack of friendship*] literally, enmity. But the Latin word for enmity, as Farrington notes (Dudley 1965, 26), is *inimicitia*, the negative of *amicitia*, friendship. Before there was law, men suffered not just from strife but from the impossibility of making friends.

1148 *fear of punishment*] cf. *Prin. Doc.* 34–35. That fear would have to be based on punishments actually witnessed. Epicureans never figured out how to treat malefactors who can rely on escaping punishment.

1158 *the idea of gods*] cf. 146 and note. Since the gods are made of the finest, first-rate atoms, their images can be sensed only by our subtlest faculty, the soul. Thus we see the gods mainly in dreams. But why, if the gods are made of atoms, will they not also suffer atomic dissolution? Or why are not these god-images like the delusive images of Centaurs and Scyllas? Indeed, according to Sextus (*Math.* 9.25), Epicurus believed that our notion of the gods derived from dreams of gigantic *human* forms.

1180   *systems of the sky*] above, religion is shown to spring from our misinterpretation of images. Here it springs from ignorance. Lucretius feels the grandeur of the heavens, but believes that men should learn the very ordinary causes at work there, and not render to gods what can be rendered to random collisions of atoms.

1201   *piety*] it is not one's duty to wash altars with the blood of poor, dumb animals while making of oneself a thrall. One is pious when one can contemplate the heavens and not fear eternal retribution.

1214   ] see 379.

1215   *contract in fear*] in foxholes there are no atheists. For the same idea applied to death, see 3.41–58. But Seneca ridicules the idea that men are actually afraid of these things, *Nat. quest.* 6.2.

1226   *Peace of the Gods*] Costa (1984) notes, " 'The peace of the gods' was an immemorial phrase of Roman religious ritual, the prayer invoking in a wide sense divine blessing and approval for the worshiper."

1238   *bronze and gold and iron*] the hardship that leads men to abase themselves before gods is eased by the discovery of metalworking, which leads to agriculture. Unfortunately, men turn their plowshares into swords, as ingenuity can discover a brutal use for anything. Yet even here there is a touch of pathos in the primitives' childlike curiosity as they stoop to pick up the shiny nuggets. See Seneca, *Epist.* 90.11–13.

1298   *sickle-spokes*] cf. 3.640.

1302   *Discord*] our own incorrigibility. Men devise weapons and methods of warfare which result in a self-destruction that should have been evident to anyone from the beginning. Tools of peace, of farming, are corrupted; but nature takes her revenge. Men try to channel the ferocity of lions and boars and bulls gainst the enemy, but the beasts resist being used as tools and simply slaughter everyone in sight. No one knows whether the following astonishing passage refers to any historical or legendary event. Lines 1338–46 should be read as mock-disbelief—how could men be so stupid as to do what they must have known would destroy them? And yet, says Lucretius, these early warriors were morally superior to us, since their motive was defense and not conquest.

1312] see 2.632.

1376 *liquid warble of birds*] haunting vision, not of a lost Golden Age, but of the joy and friendship possible when men are content with having enough to satisfy the mind and body.

1382] repeated from 4.583.

1387–91] nearly repeated from 2.29–33.

BOOK SIX

In this final book Lucretius tries to expunge from his readers' minds any lingering trace of belief in divine intervention. In book 5 he discussed the origins and mortality of heaven and earth; now he clinches their mortality by discussing the irruptions and maladies they suffer. The celestial and infernal realms are no different from ours, indeed no different from our own bodies. Just as bad air brings us pestilence, so a strong wind can destroy a cloud or blow the top off a volcano. Far from signs of divine power, thunder and lightning, cyclones, earthquakes, and volcanoes are signs of vulnerability. To attribute divinity to them would be madness. One does not prevent harm by worshiping it.

Lucretius closes with a horrific account of the plague at Athens in 430, a counterpoint to the paean to Venus which began the work. The poem's form is a lesson in Epicureanism: Nature allows "no birth, without a corresponding death." There is no consolation for the Athenians, only death and miserable survival, since they pathetically fail to grasp that there are limits to both pleasure and pain.

For Epicurus's discussion of meteorology and of natural wonders, see *Pyth.* 99–110. Other discussions of natural wonders can be found in Aristotle, *Meteorologica;* Diogenes Laertius 7.151–56.

The book is organized as follows:

1. Proem (1–96)
   A. Epicurus, greatest Athenian and benefactor of mankind (1–42)
   B. Introduction of the main topic: thunder and lightning (43–92)
   C. Invocation of the Muse Calliope (93–96)

2. Meteorology (97–535)
   A. Thunder and its causes (97–160)
   B. Lightning and lightning bolts (161–423)
      1. Sparks from cloud collisions (161–64)
      2. Why thunder is slower than lightning (165–73)
      3. Lightning caused by wind trapped in a cloud (174–204)
      4. Or by fire-seeds from the sun (205–19)
      5. The incredible force of lightning bolts (220–46)
      6. Bolts fired by wind in a mass of clouds (247–95)
      7. Or produced by various causes (296–323)
      8. What makes lightning so violent (324–57)
      9. Why lightning strikes oftenest in spring and fall (358–79)
     10. Lightning no weapon of the gods (380–423)
   C. Waterspouts and cyclones (424–51)
   D. Clouds (452–95)
   E. Precipitation (496–535)

3. Terrestrial Wonders (536–1088)
   A. Earthquakes (536–608)
      1. Caused by subterranean landslides (536–57)
      2. Or by subterranean wind (558–608)
   B. The constant volume of the sea (609–39)
   C. Volcanoes (640–703)
      1. Like diseases of the earth (648–80)
      2. Caused by underground explosions of hot air (681–703)
   D. The flooding of the Nile (704–38)
      1. The doctrine of multiple explanations (704–12)
      2. Possible causes of its floods (713–38)
   E. "Avernian" regions (739–840)
      1. What these are and where (739–69)
      2. Plenitude of atoms noxious to life (770–818)
      3. Poisonous fumes from the Avernian regions (819–30)
      4. Vacuums above the Avernian regions (831–40)
   F. Strange fountains (841–906)
   G. Magnets (907–1088)
      1. Emission of atoms from all things (922–36)
      2. Porosity of all things (937–59)
      3. Variable effects of atoms on things (960–79)
      4. Variable porosity (980–96)

5. Vacuums created by magnet emanations (997–1040)
6. Magnetic repulsion (1041–54)
7. Why magnets attract only iron (1055–88)

4. Pestilence (1089–1285)
   A. Why weather alien to us causes disease (1089–1136)
   B. The plague at Athens (1137–1285)

2   *Athens*] Lucretius began with bitter satire against the Greeks who sacrificed the girl Iphigenia so as to make their way to Troy and a long and senseless war. He has attacked the Greek cult of Cybele, and centuries of Greek philosophy. Now he pays tribute to the cultural gifts Athens has bestowed upon the world, the greatest of which is Epicurus. Others establish civil laws; Epicurus engraves his on the heart. The proem looks forward to the plague that ends the book, a critical event in Athenian history, since its toll included the statesman Pericles and his dream of Athenian domination over the Greek world. Zeno the Stoic said that the god of the heavens is also called "Athena" because his empire stretches throughout the *aether* or heavens (Diogenes Laertius, 7.147). The Athenian plague is thus a fit end for both the book and the poem. Nations and epics, like men, like the flowers of spring, like the very stars, come to dust.

35–41] see 1.146–48, 2.56–62, 3.87–93. This incantatory refrain now gains a powerful irony: the plague was no bogeyman to be laughed at in the light of day. Yet even that plague, worst of miseries, can be understood and sadly accepted if one heeds the wisdom of Epicurus.

42] see 1.418.

48] a lacuna follows of most uncertain length. Possibly Lucretius discusses the inefficacy of prayer in times of trouble.

57–58] repeated at 91–92; see also 1.153–54.

59–67] see 5.82–90; for 66–67 see also 1.76–77 and note.

76 *a calm heart*] true worship of the gods is calm worship of their calm lives. But it is impious to suppose that the gods punish impiety. The supposition is its own punishment, since it sullies the worshiper's peace of mind.

85 *thunder*] book 6 discusses those curiosities that might lead the weak-minded to slide into superstition. To examine the cause of thunder is to strip

it of divinity. Jove is called the Thunderer, but what if thunder is caused by the bumping of a couple of big clouds? Compare with Cicero, *De div.* 2.42.

91–92] repeated from 55–56 above; see also 1.153–54.

93–96] terse, triumphant invocation of the Muse, balancing the long hymn to Venus that begins the poem. Calliope is the Muse of history.

100 *when the sky is calm*] mocking. Does Jove have to check the weather before he can express his pique? Bailey notes that popular superstition held that thunder could sound from a clear sky. See Vergil, *Aen.* 9.630–31.

125 *surf of a strong wind*] first of many fanciful hypotheses in this book. Wind in the cloud acts with the centrifugal force of a potter's wheel, throwing the mass of the cloud to the outside where it forms a sort of shell.

154 *laurel*] sacred to Apollo and his oracle at Delphi; here reduced to tinder.

180 *liquefy*] popular misconception. Yet if the pellet attains speeds that no ancient could have imagined, it will heat up and melt, and for the very reason that Seneca gives (*Nat. quest.* 2.57): friction with the air.

205–9] the ancients did not link the breaking of light through a prism with the color of clouds on the horizon, here supposed to be caused by fireseeds caught from the sun. See Seneca, *Nat. quest.* 2.12.

229–30] see 1.489–90.

252–55] repeated from 4.168–71.

272] for the reference see 207–11.

307 *ball of lead*] see 180.

357 *the bonds*] those holding the gold or copper atoms together.

380 *That's how*] scientifically, not superstitiously. The Romans adopted from the Etruscans the art of observing lightning bolts to tell the future. In the Roman cult, a spot struck by lightning had to be purified by the sacrifice of sheep. See Seneca, *Nat. quest.* 2.32; Cicero, *De div.* 2.42–45. For 384–86, see 88–90.

388 *Jupiter*] Roman sky-father, Deus-pater, an old Indo-European god of the heavens (Vedic *Dyaushpita*, Greek *Zeus*, Germanic *Tiw*). What follows is masterly derision of Roman superstitions concerning Jove. The underlying

theology, however, is deadly serious. If a just God rules the world, why will lightning—or the plague—strike an innocent man, while a killer walks off hale and hearty? Lucretius takes his cue from Aristophanes, *Clouds* 395–402.

425   *cyclones*] perhaps also hurricanes; the Greek *prester* means "burner." For discussions see Pliny, *Nat. hist.* 2.133; Seneca, *Nat. quest.* 5.13.

559   *the wind*] according to Seneca, *Nat. quest.* 6.20, Democritus believed that earthquakes were caused by wind or water. Seneca's sixth book is devoted to seismology.

609   *To start with*] a lacuna precedes this line. Missing, perhaps, is an argument by believers in providence that the earth is designed to last forever, evidence of which is the wonderful stability of the seas.

636–39   ] repeated from 5.269–72.

641   *Aetna*] the great volcano of Sicily erupted in 123 B.C. The anonymous epic *Aetna* discusses the characteristics of this mountain.

650   *the vastness of the All*] prodigies seem less prodigious when one remembers that the universe they occur in is infinite.

657   *fever*] Lucretius cannily introduces the subject of the end of his poem as an offhand argument here. Volcanoes astonish us, but they are only, as it were, fevers of the earth.

661   *erysipelas*] nerve disease, called "holy fire"—ironically, as no one ever thought there was anything holy about it. The epithet is the more fitting for Lucretius' debunking of religion.

698   ] a lacuna follows. Aetna, near the coast of Sicily, may be hollowed out from under by retreating tides. Presumably this gives the wind a chance to enter the mountain and do its incendiary job.

704   *there are some things*] for the motive behind presenting several plausible explanations, see 5.509–30 and note.

717   *etesians*] winds whipping south across the Aegean Sea, against the mouth of the Nile.

740   *Avernian*] thought to derive from the Greek *aornos*, "birdless." One Avernian region at Cumae near Naples was supposed to be the entrance to the underworld. See Vergil, *Aen.* 6.237–42. Sulfurous effluvia from a large bog may have kept the birds away.

750   *Athenian ramparts*] Acropolis, citadel dedicated to Pallas Athena, patron goddess of Athens. Legend had it that crows could not perch above her temple, as punishment for the officious spying of one of their breed; see Ovid, *Met.* 2.529–72.

766–67   ] cf. Pliny, *Nat. hist.* 28.149.

770   ] for the reference see 1.808–28, 2.399–478, 4.631–70.

782   *injure us*] note Lucretius's shift from the supposedly unique and fantastic to the everyday reality of illness and death. Some of the following bits of "evidence" are just old wives' tales. Yet others may have some truth to them—as, perhaps, the headache tree, the hot bathwater that causes fainting, the noxious charcoal smoke.

811   *Scaptensula*] Thracian mine (Herodotus, 6.46.3). The men in this passage are literally being killed for gold.

841   ] the illusory "warmth" of wells in the winter was much pondered in the days before thermometers. Bailey notes that Cicero, *Nat. deor.* 2.25–28, linked it with the Stoic doctrine of the world's internal fire.

849   *Ammon*] cf. Herodotus, 4.181. This temple to Ammonian Jupiter is in Libya, about 150 miles from the Mediterranean. It is not actually colder during the day; it is only cooler than the surrounding air.

854   ] see 2.177.

880   *a cold fountain*] according to Pliny, *Nat. hist.* 2.228, the fountain was near Dodona in Greece.

891   *Aradian spring*] supposed freshwater spring in the sea south of Spain; see Pliny, *Nat. hist.* 2.227.

909   *magnet*] no mere curiosity for the ancients. Thales attributed a soul to the magnet, and its mysterious power of attraction has proved a useful vehicle for theologians trying to explain the relationship between the earthly and the divine. Augustine remarks on the awe with which one regards the first magnet one has seen, *Civ. Dei* 21.4. Munro thinks that Lucretius's discussion owes much to Plato's *Ion*.

925–36   ] see 4.216–28.

938   ] for the reference see 1.329–69.

949–50] see 1.494–45.

952–53] see 1.354–55.

955] a lacuna follows. The sense must be that just as fire can penetrate iron, so disease can pierce the buckler of the sky.

1007 *the ring entire*] a film of iron atoms drawn to the magnet draws the rest of the ring along.

1044 *bronze drinking bowls*] Lucretius is under the odd impression that bronze has something to do with magnetic repulsion.

1057 *stand still*] they are too heavy to be attracted by the magnet. Other substances, like wood, are so porous that the magnet stream flows right through.

1089 *disease*] finally to the natural eruptions that destroy the body. They are not marvels; they warrant no fear of punitive gods.

1092] for the reference see 770–81.

1100–1101] repeated from 2.872–73.

1106 *where the earth's axis stoops*] as one approaches the equator the North Star appears to approach the horizon.

1113 *elephant sickness*] elephantiasis, insect-carried disease that causes great swelling and coarsening of the skin.

1138 *plague*] cf. Pallas's anger (749–55); in neither case is there really any divine intervention. Lucretius now shows the futility of religion and the pitiable state of man unenlightened by the Epicurean gospel. The plague-stricken people are led by fear, ignorance, and immoderate desires to aggravate their misery. The temples become morgues. All piety is overthrown. Parents neglect their children, friend forgets friend, citizens brawl over burial plots, long-cherished customs for the dead fall into disuse, and men even castrate themselves in a desperate attempt to halt the infection. Lucretius's source is Thucydides, 2.47–52.

1166] see 661.

1245] a short lacuna follows; the sense is clear even so.

1264 *Silenus*] old boozy woodland god associated with the worship of Dionysus.

1275–76] in bad times men turn to religion; but *these* times were so bad that men could think only of their pain.

1285] far from the lack of concern with which we are to regard death. So the poem ends, with the poignant lesson of men who do not understand how and why they, like all things, must end.

WORKS CITED

Bailey, Cyril. 1926. *Epicurus: The Extant Remains.* Oxford: Clarendon Press.

————. 1947. *De Rerum Natura of Lucretius.* 3 vols. Oxford: Clarendon Press.

Brown, Robert D. 1987. *Lucretius on Love and Sex: A Commentary on De Rerum Natura IV, 1030–1287.* Leyden: E. J. Brill.

Clay, Diskin. 1983. *Lucretius and Epicurus.* Ithaca, N.Y.: Cornell University Press.

Costa, C. D. N. 1984. *Lucretius: De Rerum Natura V.* Oxford University Press.

Dudley, Donald R. 1965. *Lucretius.* New York: Basic Books.

Farrington, Benjamin. "Form and Purpose in the *De Rerum Natura.*" In *Lucretius. See* Dudley 1965.

Gale, Monica. 1994. *The Myth and Poetry of Lucretius.* Cambridge: Cambridge University Press.

Godwin, John. 1986. *De Rerum Natura IV.* Warminster, Eng.: Aris and Phillips.

Kelsey, Francis W. 1884. *T. Lucreti Cari Libri Sex.* Boston: Allyn and Bacon.

Kenney, E. J. 1971. *De Rerum Natura Book III.* Cambridge: Cambridge University Press.

Leonard, William Ellery, and Stanley Barney Smith, eds. 1942. *T. Lvcreti Cari De Rervm Natvra Libri Sex.* Madison: University of Wisconsin Press.

Merrill, William Augustus. 1907. *T. Lucreti Cari de rerum natura libri sex.* New York: American Book Co.

Munro, H. A. J. 1900. *T. Lucreti Cari de rerum natura libri sex.* 4th ed. 2 vols. London: George Bell.

Nichols, James H., Jr. 1976. *Epicurean Political Philosophy: The De Rerum Natura of Lucretius.* Ithaca, N.Y.: Cornell University Press.

Panichas, George A. 1967. *Epicurus.* New York: Twayne.

West, David A. 1969. *The Imagery and Poetry of Lucretius.* Edinburgh: Edinburgh University Press.

Wormell, D. E. W. 1965. "The Personal World of Lucretius." In *Lucretius. See* Dudley 1965.

INDEX

accidents, 37–38, 242
Achaia, 231
Acheron, 221
Aegium, 216
Aeneas, 15–17, 238
Aeschylus, *Choephori,* 273
Aetius [Plutarch], *De placitis philosophorum,* 274
Aetna, Mount, 45, 74, 218–19, 243, 283
afterlife. *See* underworld
Agamemnon, 27, 238
aging, 34, 59, 88–90, 103–4, 167–68, 253
agriculture, 31, 90, 164–65, 241; origin of, 197
Agrigentum, 45, 242
air: linked with earth, 174–75, 274; location in cosmos, 172–73; mutability of, 166–67
Alexander, 2
Anaxagoras, 48–50, 237, 239, 243–44, 249, 253
Anaximenes, 274
Ancus Marcius, 120, 262
Apollo, 170, 204, 243, 261, 282
Apollodorus, 272
Aristophanes, *Clouds,* 283
Aristotle, 3; *De generatione,* 269; *De partibus animalium,* 268; *Meteorologica,* 275, 279
Arnobius, 18
ataraxia, 2–3, 10
Athena (Pallas), 154, 221, 255, 261, 281, 284, 285
Athens, 2, 4, 200, 281, 284; plague at, 232–36, 281, 285–86

Atlantis, 273
Attica, 231, 232
atomism: axioms of, 29–32, 237, 239; Epicurus and, 3; poetry and, 6–8
atoms (first-beginnings, seeds; *see also* matter): as alphabet, 48, 50, 76–77, 85–86, 244; and attrition, 33–34; and Avernian regions, 220–23; beyond the world, 54, 86–88, 245; in clouds, 212–15; and color, 78–81, 251–52; compounds of, 73–77; death and, 8, 31–32, 85, 89–90, 94; disease and, 218, 227, 230–32; as dust motes, 60–61; existence of, 32–34, 237; falling of, 62–63, 245; and fluidity, 70; free will and, 64–65, 248–49; as fundamental material, 6–8, 40–42, 240–41; of gods, 272, 277–78; and hardness, 41, 60, 69–70, 249; indestructibility of, 38–44, 46–49, 114, 169; infinitude of, 51, 53–56, 72–74, 249–50; injury and, 83–84; insensate, 81–85; lacking qualities, 47–50; of light, 131–32; of lightning, 205–10; and magnetism, 228–30, 285; necessary for orderly world, 29–32, 41–42; not anthropomorphic, 7, 13–14, 50, 84–85; nourishment from, 47–50, 88–90, 139–40, 146, 243–44; origin of the world and, 53–54, 88, 171–73; pain and, 83–84; parts of, 42–43, 46, 71, 242; and perception, 6–7, 68–72, 76, 78–81, 101–2, 227–28, 262–63; perpetual motion of, 13–14, 52–53, 58–66, 245; porosity and, 227–28; shapes of, 66–73, 249; shuffling

atoms (*continued*)
of, 44, 47–48, 50, 53–54, 71, 76–79, 85–86, 164, 171, 244, 257; simulacra and, 262–63; size of, 60–61, 66, 70–71; and smell, 141; of the soul, 96–99, 101–2, 257, 258; and sound, 136–38, 264; swerve of, 3, 63–65, 248–49; and taste, 139–40, 267; and temperature, 223–25; terms for, 26; velocity of, 61, 248

attrition, 33–34

Augustine, Saint, *De civitate Dei,* 256, 260, 284

Augustus, 17

Aulis, 27, 241

Aulus Gellius, 256

Avernus, 220–23, 283

Bacchus (Dionysus), 75, 159, 180, 244, 251, 271, 275, 285

Bacon, Sir Francis, 19

Bailey, Cyril, 266

Berosus, 275

Black Sea, 173, 231

Brown, Robert D., 269

Byron, George Gordon, Lord, 19

Caesar, Gaius Julius, 1, 256

Calliope, 202, 282

Carthage, 114, 120, 241, 259

Catiline, 1

Catullus, Valerianus, 240, 251, 262

centaurs, 8, 77, 142, 183, 267, 275, 278

centerlessness, 54–55, 245

Cerberus, 119, 142, 261, 267

Ceres, 75, 159, 180, 251, 271, 275

Charybdis, 45, 267

chimeras, 8, 77, 184, 251, 275

Chrysippus, 273

Cicero, 1, 4, 17–19, 247; *Academici,* 252, 266, 273, 274; *De divinatione,* 266, 282; *De fato,* 248; *De finibus,* 274; *De natura deorum,* 248, 250, 267, 268, 272, 284; *Epistulae,* 240; *Tusculanarum disputationum,* 18, 256, 258, 260, 262, 271; *Verres,* 242

civilization. *See* man, primitive life of

Clay, Diskin, 251–52

Clodius, 1

clouds, 127–28; explanation of, 212–14; lightning and, 205–10; rain from, 214–15; thunder and, 202–5, 282

color, 78–81, 251–52

Corybantes, 251

cosmos. *See* universe; world

Costa, C. D. N., 273, 278

Cumae, 221

Cupid, 179, 275

Curetes, 75, 251

Cybele. *See* Mater Magna

cyclones, 212, 283

Danaids, 119, 261

Darwin, Charles, 268

death: atoms and, 8, 31–32, 85, 89–90, 94; everlasting, 121; fear of, 5, 9–15, 28, 92–93, 114–21, 193, 234–36, 253–54, 256, 257, 259, 278, 285–86; funerary superstitions and, 115–16, 235–36, 260, 285; "nothing to us," 114–15, 259; plague at Athens, 232–36, 279, 281, 285–86; as sleep, 116–17, 260; of the soul with the body, 97, 100–101, 103–14, 162–63, 253–54, 258, 259; warring with life, 73

Delphic oracle, 45, 162, 204, 243, 282

Democritus, 3, 18, 101, 120, 176, 262, 274, 283

De rerum natura (*see also* Lucretius), 25; Cicero as editor of, 1; meter of, 19–20; title, 240

design, lack of: in atomic motion, 53–54; in the body, 145–46, 268; in the world, 61–62, 164–65, 270, 273

Deucalion, 273

Diana (Artemis), 27, 238

Dicte, Mount, 75, 251

Diogenes Laertius, *Life of Epicurus,* 3–4, 238–39, 240, 241, 243, 246, 247, 256, 261, 266, 276, 279, 281

Diomedes, 160

Dionysus. *See* Bacchus

disease, 83–84, 95, 98, 104–6, 107–8, 218, 221–23, 227, 258, 279, 283; plague, 230–36, 279, 281, 285–86
Divine Comedy, The, 12
Dodona, 284
dreams, 103, 123, 134–35, 143–45, 149–51, 264–65, 268, 277–78; of gods, 191–92, 277–78
Dryden, John, 19
Du Bartas, Guillaume Salluste, *Divine Weeks,* 19

earth: air and, 174–75, 274; barrenness of, 88–90, 182, 246; diseased, 218, 283; as dregs, 171–73, 274; fertility of, 181–83; hollow below, 215–16, 219; as mother, 32, 74–76, 85, 182, 245–46, 250, 253, 273; mutability of, 166, 215–17
earthquakes, 215–17
echoes, 138, 266–67
eclipses, 180–81
Egypt, 220, 224, 231, 284
elements (*see also* air; earth; fire; water): composed of atoms, 45–47; strife of, 169–70, 273
elephantiasis, 231, 285
Empedocles, 45–46, 238, 243, 273
Ennius, Quintus, 2, 28, 238, 241, 262
Epicureanism: doctrine of *ataraxia,* 10–12, 57–58, 247; friendship and, 3, 6, 10–11, 241, 277; influence upon Cicero, 17–18; pacifistic, 13–15; piety and, 28, 202, 238, 257; poetry and, 6–8; quietism of, 18, 247, 277; utility of, 92–93, 285
Epicurus (*see also* Diogenes Laertius, Epicureanism): atomism of, 3; belief in *isonomia,* 250; death of, 120, 262; disciples of, 4, 255; discoverer of truth, 26–27, 91–92, 159–60, 200–201, 279; Fragments, 241, 243, 246; Garden of, 4; as Hercules, 159–60, 270, 271; influenced by Pyrrho, 2–3; influenced by Socratic tradition, 3; life of, 2–4; love for the family, 276; as military hero, 14–15, 26–27; as *paterfamilias,* 15,

91–92, 254–55; patriotism of, 4, 240, 256; *Principal Doctrines,* 241, 247, 254, 256, 266, 270, 277; quietism of, 3–4, 261; against superstition, 5, 8–9, 26–27, 238, 241, 277; *To Herodotus,* 238, 242, 244, 246, 254, 256, 263, 268, 270, 274; *To Menoeceus,* 246, 248, 254, 256, 259; *To Pythocles,* 246, 270, 274, 279; works of, 4
epilepsy, 105, 222, 258
erysipelas, 218, 233, 283
eternal life. *See* underworld
ether, 171–72, 274
Euripides, *Iphigenia at Aulis,* 238
extinction, 182–83

family, origin of, 187, 276
Farrington, Benjamin, 277
fauns, 138, 266
fire, discovery of, 189–90; falling of, 62–63, 248; in forests, 50; mutability of, 167; not the only element, 43–45; of Phaethon, 170; of the stars, 172–74; thunderstorms and, 204–12; in wells, 224–25
floods, 33, 170, 273
Flora, 179, 275
food, 30, 47–50, 57–58, 77, 81–82, 85, 88–90, 139–40, 146, 243–44, 246, 267; of primitive man, 185–86
Fortune, 162
free will, 64–65, 248–49
friendship. *See* Epicureanism, friendship and
Furies, 119

Gale, Monica, 241, 247, 271
Gassendi, Pierre, 19
Geryon, 159
ghosts, 28, 142, 143, 263, 264–65
giants, 29–30, 126, 162, 272
gods: atomic tenuousness of, 53, 272, 277–78; origin of belief in, 191–93, 277–78; tranquillity and indifference of, 26, 29, 61–62, 75–76, 88, 91, 100, 161, 162, 163–

gods (*continued*)
  64, 201–2, 210–12, 235–36, 256, 270, 271, 272, 279, 281
Godwin, John, 266, 268
Gray, Thomas, *Elegy Written in a Country Churchyard,* 260

Hannibal, 259
harmony, wrongly identified with the soul, 93–95
Helen of Troy, 38, 238
Helicon, Mount, 28, 94, 137, 222, 241
Hell. *See* underworld
Heraclitus, 237, 258, 274, 275; theory of universal fire, 43–44, 243
Hercules, 159–60, 242, 270, 272
heredity, 41, 76, 112, 155–56
hermaphrodites, 182
Herodotus, *The Persian Wars,* 284
Hesiod, *Works and Days,* 276
Hobbes, Thomas, 11, 19, 275–76
Homer, 28, 120, 241; *Iliad,* 238; *Odyssey,* 256, 261, 267
homoeomeria, 48–50
Horace, 18; *Odes,* 261, 272, 273; *Epistulae,* 261–62
humidity, 33
hurricanes, 212, 283
hydra, 159

Ida, Mount (Asia Minor), 74, 251
Ida, Mount (Crete), 177, 275
images. *See* simulacra
India, 72
infinity. *See* void
Iphigenia, 27, 238, 281

jaundice, 131, 266
Jerome, Saint, 1
Jupiter (Zeus): Ammonian, 284; father of Athena, 255; Father Sky, 32, 85, 242, 253; infancy of, 75, 251; Phaethon and, 170; supposed savior of Rome, 267; Thunderer, 88, 170, 211–12, 281–83; and the Titans, 272

Kelsey, Francis W., 240
Kenney, E. J., 255, 256, 259, 260

Lactantius, 18; *De opificio Dei,* 257, 268, 273
language, development of, 188–89, 276–77
Leonard, William Ellery, 1, 260, 266
Leto, 261
Leucippus, 3
light. *See* sun; sunlight
lightning, 53, 63, 68, 88, 189–90, 202, 211–12, 277, 282; causes of, 204–10
Livy, *Ab urbe condita,* 267
locomotion, 146–47, 268
love. *See* sex
Lucretius: discoverer of truth, 36; on fear of death, 9–10; on friendship, 10–13; friendship with Memmius, 6, 25–26, 29, 36, 240, 241; influence of, 15–19; observer of nature, 4–5, 8; patriotism of, 2; as physician, 51, 122; poetic project of, 5–15; as prophet, 51, 122, 162, 244; Rome and, 1, 10–15, 256, 269, 273, 276; on simplicity of life, 11; against superstition, 8–9, 11–12; on war, 13–15, 276
Lupercal, 266

Macrobius, *Saturnalia,* 266
magnetism, 225–30, 284–85
man, primitive life of, 185–99, 269–70, 275–76; agriculture, 197; art, 199; clothing, 198–99; discovery of fire, 189–90; disease and death, 186–87; government, 190–91; hunting, 186; ignorance of seamanship, 187; language, 188–89, 276–77; marriage, 187, 276; metallurgy, 193–95, 278; music, 197–98; religion, 191–93, 277–78; social contract, 187, 276; war, 195–96, 278–79; weaving, 197
Manes, 256
marriage, 187, 276
Mars (god), 13, 26, 238, 240
Martial, *Epigrammae,* 268
Mater Magna (Cybele, Mother Earth), 32,

74–76, 85, 181–82, 242, 245–46, 250–51, 253

matter (*see also* atoms): made of invisible particles, 32–34; tangibility of, 33, 37–38

Memmius, Quintus: friendship with Lucretius, 6, 25–26, 29, 36, 240, 241; mentioned in text, 25–26, 36, 54, 61, 62, 161, 163, 183, 195

Merrill, William Augustus, 250, 252, 260, 267

metallurgy, origin of, 193–95

Milton, John, *Paradise Lost,* 19, 273

mirrors, 124–25, 126, 129–31, 266

Molière, Jean-Baptiste, 19; *Le Misanthrope,* 269

Montaigne, Michel de, 19

moon, 161; eclipses of, 180–81; motion through zodiac, 176–77; origin of, 172; phases of, 179–80; size of, 175

Mother Earth. *See* Mater Magna

motion: of atoms, 13–14, 52–53, 58–66, 226, 245; requires empty space, 34–36

Munro, H. A. J., 240, 242, 244, 249, 250, 251, 267–68, 269, 284

Muses, 43, 51, 71, 122, 198, 202, 241, 244, 282

music, 68–69, 71, 138; origin of, 197–98

Mytilene, home of Epicurus, 4, 240

Nature, 26, 34, 39, 51, 53, 63, 64, 65, 67, 82, 91, 92, 93, 131, 133, 143, 144, 145, 148, 161, 167, 169, 188, 201, 206, 213, 217, 223, 232; barrenness of, 88–90, 164–65; extinction and, 182–83; free from gods, 88; laws of, 29–32, 47–48, 65, 185, 241; orderliness of, 66–68, 71–72, 77, 80, 178–80, 199; preserving the atoms, 40, 42; rebuking those unwilling to die, 117–18, 260; requiring little for our bodies, 57–58

Neptune (god), 75, 251

Newton, Sir Isaac, 242

Nichols, James H., 269–70

night, cause of, 177–78

Nile River, 231, 252; northerly current of, 220

nourishment. *See* food

Numa Pompilius, 12

nymphs, 138, 185, 266

optical illusions, 133–35, 266

Ovid, 16, 18; *Ars amatoria,* 269; *Fasti,* 251, 266; *Heroides,* 261; *Metamorphoses,* 240, 251

pain, 83–84

palingenesis, 260

Palinurus, 16–17

Pallas. *See* Athena

Pan, 138, 266

Panichas, George, 2, 4

Parentalia, 256

Paris, 38

perception. *See* sensation; senses; simulacra

Pericles, 281

Petronius, 18; *Satyricon,* 260

Phaethon, 170, 273

Philip of Macedon, King, 2

Philodemus, 4

Phrygia, 74–75, 251

plague (*see also* disease), 230–36; at Athens, 232–36, 279, 281, 285–86

Plato, *Cratylus,* 277; *Critias,* 273; *Gorgias,* 261; *Ion,* 284; *Meno,* 259; *Phaedo,* 18, 257; *Phaedrus,* 3; *Protagoras,* 275; *Republic,* 276; *Symposium,* 3; *Theaetetus,* 258; on vision, 266

plenum, nonexistence of, 35–36

Pliny (Gaius Plinius Secundus), *Historia naturalis,* 267, 274, 283, 284

Plutarch, 4; *Adversus Coloten,* 257, 266

porosity, 34–35, 39, 227–29, 253

Porphyry, 4

procreation (*see also* heredity; sex): orderliness of, 29–31, 76–77; prodigies prevented from, 182–83

Prometheus, 277

properties, 37–38, 242

Providence. *See* design

Pyrrho, 2–3

Pythagoras (Pythagoreans), 241, 259

rain, 214–15

reason: as guide for living, 5; less reliable than senses, 135–36, 266

religion: conquered by Epicurus, 26–27, 238, 241; cult of the Mater Magna, 74–76, 251–52; disutility and impiety of, 5, 8–9, 12, 26–29, 58, 161, 191–93, 201–2, 210–12, 235–36, 238, 257, 278, 281; origin of, 185, 191–93, 271, 276, 277–78

Rome, 26, 277; during the life of Lucretius, 1–2, 6, 256, 269, 273; at war with Carthage, 114, 119, 259, 262; at war with the Gauls, 267

Sallust, 1; *Catiline*, 256

saltwater, 70

Samos, birthplace of Epicurus, 2

Samothrace, 229

Saturn (god), 75, 251, 272

satyrs, 138, 266

Scaptensula mine, 222, 284

Scipio, Gaius Aemilianus, 2

Scipio, Gaius Cornelius (Africanus), 18, 120, 262

Scylla, 142, 184, 267, 275, 278

semblances. *See* simulacra

Seneca, *Consolatio ad Marciam*, 260; *De beneficiis*, 266; *Epistulae*, 257, 261, 277, 278; *Naturales questiones*, 266, 278, 282–83

sensation: disruptions of, 83–84; nonexistent before birth, 83; soul and, 101–2

senses (*see also* simulacra, sound, smell, taste, touch, vision): atoms and, 81–85; effect of passion upon, 153–55, 269; reliability of, 37, 44, 135–36, 266, 277

Servius, 261

sex (*see also* procreation): as appetite, 119, 152–53, 268–69; and conception, 155–57; cure for the malady of, 152, 154–55; deceptiveness of, 153–55, 269; heredity and, 155–56; role of simulacra in, 151–55; sterility and, 156–57; true love and, 157–58; women's desire and, 155

Sextus Empiricus, *Mathematicos*, 258, 278; *Outlines of Pyrrhonism*, 259, 266, 267, 269

shadows, 132–33

Sicily, 45, 243, 283

Sidney, Philip, *Defense of Poesie*, 244

Sidon, 216

sight. *See* vision

Silenus, 235, 285

simulacra (images, semblances): causing smell, 141–42; causing sound, 136–39; causing taste, 139–40, 267; causing thought, 142–45, 262–64, 268; and dreams, 123, 143, 147–51; emission of, 123–28; existence of, 123–25, 264–65; of gods, 191–92; invisibility of, 129; in mirrors, 124–25, 126, 129–31; mutability of, 125–26; optical illusions and, 133–35, 266; slenderness of, 125–29; and the soul, 142–47; spontaneous generation of, 125–26; ubiquity of, 128–29, 268; velocity of, 127–28; vision and, 127–36, 262–63

Sisyphus, 119

skepticism (Skeptics), 135–36, 252, 266; influence of, upon Epicurus, 2–3

sleep (*see also* dreams), 94, 95, 116–17, 134–35, 145; cause of, 147–49

smell, 81, 141–42

Smith, Stanley Barney, 260, 266

Socrates, 3, 18, 266

soul (animus, anima, mind, spirit): as body part, 93–96, 106–8, 258; character and, 99–100, 258; components of, 97–100, 257; at conception, 110–13, 259; in corpses, 111; dreams and, 94, 147–51, 263; effects of disease upon, 104–8, 114, 258; fineness of, 97, 103, 257; not a "harmony," 94–95, 257; locomotion and, 146–47; materiality of, 95–96, 253; mobility of, 96–97; mortality of, 84, 103–14, 162–63, 253–54, 258, 259; moved by semblances, 142–47, 262–63; role of, in vision, 101, 127–36; severing of the anima, 109–10; sexual desire and, 151–55; during sleep, 147–48; sparseness of atoms of, 101–2, 258; superiority of

animus, 102–3, 258; union of animus and anima, 95; united with the body, 100–101, 106–15, 162–63, 253–54
sound, 136–39, 266–67
space. See void
Spenser, Edmund, The Faerie Queene, 19
spontaneous generation, 81, 83, 252, 259
stars, 63, 133, 34, 192–93; motions of, 173–74, 274; origin of, 172; in zodiac, 176–77
sterility, sexual, 156–57
Stoicism (Stoics; see also Heraclitus), 43, 242, 243, 244, 245, 248, 251, 252, 258, 272, 273, 277, 281
Suetonius, 1
suicide, 93, 256, 257
sun, 161; at dawn and dusk, 177–78, 275; eclipses of, 180–81; as fountain, 175–76; origin of, 172; size of, 175, 274; yearly path of, 176–80, 274–75
sunlight, 60–61, 63, 79–80, 127–28, 131–32, 133, 167, 172, 175–76
superstition. See religion
Swift, Jonathan, 19
Sybil, 16–17
Syria, 216, 221

Tantalus, 118–19, 260–61
Tasso, Torquato, Jerusalem Delivered, 19, 244
taste, 68, 70, 139–40, 264, 267
teleology. See design, lack of
Tennyson, Alfred, Lord, "Lucretius," 19
Terminus, 241
Thales, 284
theater, 69, 124, 149, 265
Thebes, 168, 273
Thessaly, 71
Thucydides, History of the Peloponnesian War, 285
thunder, 202–4, 281–82
time, as accident, 38
Tityus, 118–19, 261
touch, 68–70, 249; gods and, 163; matter and, 33, 38; vision and, 128, 251–52
Troy, 38, 238, 242, 281
Tyre, 80, 252

underworld, 108–9, 126–27; fear of, 28–29, 91–93; as illusion, 118–19, 128, 221, 260–61
uniqueness, nonexistence of, 72–73, 87–88, 250
universe (the All; see also world): annihilation of, 55–56; boundlessness of, 52–53, 59–60, 86–87, 114; centerlessness of, 54–55, 245; composition of, 37–38; unalterable, 65–66, 169

Venus (goddess of love): euphemism for male genitals, 153, 156; euphemism for sexual desire and intercourse, 113, 151–54, 157, 186; hymn to, 25–26, 238, 240, 279; hymn to, translated by Spenser, 19; and Mars, 13, 26, 238, 240; mother of Romans, 25–26; nickname for the beloved, 154; springtime and, 25–26, 179, 240, 275; symbol for procreative Nature, 31, 62, 156, 179, 238, 240, 275
Vergil, 8; Aeneid, 15, 17–19, 261, 265, 276, 282, 283; Georgics, 15, 16, 259, 265; influence of Lucretius upon, 17–19
Verres, 1
vision, 101; mirrors and, 129–31, 266; observation of distance, 129–30, 265; optical illusions, 132–35, 266; problems of, 131–35; simulacra and, 127–36, 143, 262–63, 265–66
Vitruvius, 275
voice (see also echoes; sound), 136–38
void: boundlessness of, 51–53, 65, 86–87, 169; density of objects and, 34–35; existence of, 6–7, 34–36, 237; gravity and, 54–55; magnetism and, 228–30; motion through, 35–37, 43, 46, 59–60, 63–64; purity of, 39–40
volcanoes, 218–19, 283

war, 12–15, 38, 66, 109, 114, 149, 150, 210, 238, 244, 259, 276, 277; futility of, 57–58; innovations in, 195; between life and death, 73; Second Punic, 114, 120, 241, 259, 262; sexual desire as, 151; wild beasts used in, 195–96, 278–79

water: and cyclones, 212, 283; in floods, 33, 170, 273; mutability of, 166; in the oceans, 70, 217–18, 225, 284; temperature of, 223–25
waterspouts, 212
weaving, development of, 197
weight, 34–35, 63–65, 249
West, David A., 244, 261
wind, materiality of, 32–33
world (*see also* earth; universe): decay of, 89–90; mortality of, 89, 161–70, 279; newness of, 168–69; not created, 164–65; origin of, 53–54, 88, 170–73, 269–70; plurality of worlds, 86–87
Wormell, D. E. W., 11, 263

Xenophanes, 275
Xenophon, *Anabasis,* 259
Xerxes, 120, 262

Zeno, 281

Library of Congress Cataloging-in-Publication Data

Lucretius Carus, Titus.

[De rerum natura. English]

De rerum natura = On the nature of things / Lucretius : edited
and translated by Anthony M. Esolen.

p.   cm.

Includes bibliographical references and index.

ISBN 0-8018-5054-1 (hc : alk. paper). —
ISBN 0-8018-5055-X (pbk. : alk. paper)

1. Didactic poetry, Latin — Translations into English.

2. Philosophy, Ancient — Poetry.   I. Esolen, Anthony M.   II. Title.

III. Title: On the nature of things.

PA6483.E5E83   1995

187 — dc20   94-25165

CIP

Printed in the United States
2756